Musical New York

An Informal Guide to Its History and Legends
and
A Walking Tour of Its Sites and Landmarks

by
Carol J. Binkowski

Camino Books, Inc.
Philadelphia

Manufactured in the United States of America

1 2 3 4 5   01 00 99

Library of Congress Cataloging-in-Publication Data

Binkowski, Carol J.
        Musical New York : an informal guide to its history & legends and
a walking tour of its sites & landmarks / by Carol J. Binkowski.
                p.   cm.
        Includes bibliographical references (p.   ).
        ISBN 0-940159-47-3
        1. Music—New York (State)—New York—History and criticism.
    2. New York (N.Y.)—Guidebooks.   I. Title.
    ML200.8.N5B56   1998
    780'.9747'1—dc21   98-11733

Cover and interior design: Jerilyn Bockorick

For information write:

Camino Books, Inc.
P.O. Box 59026
Philadelphia, PA 19102
http://www.caminobooks.com

For my family

CONTENTS

Preface

New York's musical heritage is a fascinating mixture of cultures, history, performance traditions, and creative spirit. A lifetime and many volumes would certainly be needed to do justice to its music in anything approaching its entirety—not my intention here. *Musical New York* is meant to be a fun glimpse into the history, points of interest, and cultural treasures relating to music. If readers discover some new information or are motivated to explore a topic in more depth, then I will be happy. If they happen upon an institution or a site that gives them lasting enjoyment through concerts, research collections, special events, or educational opportunities, then I will be ecstatic!

Part One is a brief history of the cultural background of each of several broad time categories, providing a frame of reference for what follows.

The entries in Part Two are a potpourri of statues, plaques, concert halls, museum collections, sites, educational/cultural centers, and the like—each with a unique story. They can provide many hours of enjoyable walking, leisurely visiting, or armchair traveling. It would be impossible to include everything, though. I have tried to incorporate as much as possible to illustrate the range of sites and offerings that exist within a given locale. I heartily apologize for omissions as well as for any errors.

Walking around specific areas is relatively feasible in Manhattan where geographical proximity makes visiting multiple sites a bit easier. A car can make touring the boroughs a bit less time-consuming, although a well-organized public transportation plan is good, too. Enjoy.

There is something for everyone here—the mainstream traveler and the more experienced walker included. If you are totally unfamiliar with New York, taking one of the many excellent bus tours available is a good way to get an initial overview for later visits. Since everyone's comfort level is different and circumstances may vary in particular locales, check with the New York Convention & Visitors Bureau, your hotel concierge, or a tour guide if you have any questions pertaining to the timing or feasibility of a visit, particularly if you are new in town. Getting lost or arriving at an inopportune time can be frustrating and may lead to difficulties. Also, it is good to remember that change happens quickly. A plaque or a site that exists today may not be there tomorrow.

My sincere thanks to everyone who offered information, leads, advice, help, and encouragement. The list of individuals and organizations is too long to specify by name—the staffs at historical societies, site locations, museums, archives, libraries, special interest groups, and associations, as well as friends, both old and new. I appreciate each and every one of you.

Thanks, also, to my family—my husband, Richard, for his constant encouragement on this and many other projects; my daughter, Daria, for her enthusiastic help, suggestions, and companionship; and my parents, A. Robert and Dorothy Knobloch, for their support over the years.

Last, but not least, a special thank you to Edward Jutkowitz at Camino Books, Inc., for having faith in this book, to Michelle Scolnick for her infinite patience, and to Brad Fisher for his fine editing.

New York *is* music—from the hum of traffic in the street to the stage of Carnegie Hall. I have enjoyed pursuing its many fascinating paths, and I hope you will, too.

Carol J. Binkowski

The Story

Colonial Times

Early explorers wrote in glowing praise of a fine forested land and a beautiful bay of water. This attractive harbor location with its abundant natural resources and exotic native inhabitants commanded marked interest because of its boundless possibilities for settlement and trade. From the arrival of the first boat of Dutch settlers in 1624 to Peter Minuet's famous "purchase" of Manhattan Island from the Indians in 1626, the fledgling town seemed destined to occupy an important place in the New World. Although the original settlement was a crude trading post that experienced its share of severe problems, New Amsterdam was still an exciting springboard for the city to come.

During the rule of the colorful and infamous Peter Stuyvesant, beginning in 1647, the city quickly grew into a bustling hub of diverse activity. On the positive side, Stuyvesant instituted many reforms such as the development of a hospital, a pier, a Latin school, and a market. Also, a commercial center with an interesting array of shops and businesses quickly grew. Stuyvesant's influence stamped a strong Dutch imprint on the city that remained a tangible part of its culture. On the negative side, Stuyvesant was considered to be a tyrant and was often blamed for the loss of the city to the British. Despite his controversial leadership, though, New Amsterdam did blossom and attracted the interest of a number of foreign countries. Stuyvesant's name still lives on not only in historical tales, but also on modern-day signs for parks, schools, and streets.

The social life of New Amsterdam revolved around its homes, taverns, and streets. The Dutch had a reputation as boisterous revelers. Activities ranged from copious drinking in the town's numerous taverns to indulging in the game of ball and nine pins, introduced to the new city at Bowling Green. (One can certainly assume that some form of song was not unknown during pursuit of the former activity.)

No real record survives of a formal concert life, but there are some informal references to the affection with which music was regarded in New Amsterdam. Historians have mentioned that the beautiful *Mrs.* Stuyvesant loved music. Also, holiday celebrations, reminiscent of Old World traditions, included festive rituals with special times for singing, particularly during the merry Twelfth Night proceedings.[1]

After the British staged a peaceful takeover in 1664, the city—eventually renamed New York—continued to grow. The new governor, Richard Nicolls, was a highly educated, humane, and open-minded man. He kept what was positive from the Dutch system, including its patterns of local government and land grants. However, he curtailed many of the more negative practices such as active forms of religious persecution. Despite the turbulence that followed under successive leaders, Nicolls' regime left a strong British impact. This, coupled with the existing Dutch influence, brought an exciting sense of diversity to the city.

A great deal of money came into New York by the 1690s and the resulting development included the building of new houses, the advancement of trade, the creation of newspapers, and similar signs of civilized progress. A new city hall replaced the old, Trinity Church was built, and Wall Street was honored with the first permanent pavement in the city. Along with this growth and expansion came more complex political, social, and cultural patterns that blended into the fabric of city life.

Some musical references from this time period were surprisingly controversial. Lyrics, published in newspapers or on broadsides, were penned in response to current events and were often intended to be sung to standard, well-known melodies. Evidently, the scandalous "ballads" that were written concerning the 1734 election of new magistrates and published in the *Weekly Journal* were a driving force behind the arrest of its editor, John Peter Zenger, and the ensuing outcry over freedom of the press. (Zenger, incidentally, was reported to have moonlighted as a church organist during his colorful career.[2])

Most of the city's creative life, though, was less flamboyant. As early as 1732, the New Theatre was in business, and there was proof of the existence of another theater within the city's boundaries. New forms of entertainment were well received, and formal events soon followed. Newcomers were obviously familiar with the latest in European musical trends, and they helped to introduce both the music and the instruments to the city. Now it was time for the public to enjoy and actively participate in this art form.

The first documented public concert was held on January 21, 1736. (There is a vague poetic reference to an earlier concert which appears in a 1733 newspaper clipping, and certain historians have speculated that this event may have been held at the New Theatre or Play-House. No real evidence, however, remains.)

William Bradford's paper, *The New-York Gazette*, advertised the 1736 concert with all due ceremony and with a six-day lead over the announcement in Zenger's *New-York Weekly Journal*. The concert, with an admission price of four shillings, was held at the house of Robert Todd, located next to Fraunces Tavern. Both of these dwellings were the focus of much social activity in early city life.

The featured performer at this noteworthy premiere was harpsichordist C.T. (Charles Theodore) Pachelbel, thought to be the son of the famous Johann Pachelbel. Other performers, referred to as "private hands," sang and played the violin and the German flute. The concert was billed as a benefit for Mr. Pachelbel, a common practice during this and subsequent years. Pachelbel was well known through his musical activities in Boston and its environs and was welcomed in New York with the respect due such a distinguished performer.

It was evident that Robert Todd knew how to promote culture while keeping a finger on the pulse of the city. A vintner and prominent citizen, he hosted many events—political, social, and artistic. Committee conferences for the Council and Assembly often met at his house, and he sponsored various entertainments for political guests in addition to his public concert offerings. The indefatigable Todd held a celebration and a ball on January 20th, the day prior to the Pachelbel concert, in honor of the governor's party.

After the Pachelbel event, public concerts rapidly assumed a role in city life, yet we may never know just how many concerts actually took place since popular forms of advertising were still the broadside or the town crier. However, 46 formal concert notices did appear in the newspapers between Pachelbel's debut in 1736 and the year 1775, a greater number than in other American colonial cities. They included benefit concerts to aid various military and charity causes, subscription concerts, and religious concerts, to name a few categories.

(Robert Todd evidently continued in his career as concert host. A frequently mentioned event was his 1745 benefit held for John Rice, the organist at Trinity Church.)

Concerts took place at a variety of sites including the New Exchange Room, Mr. Burn's Assembly Room, and Mr. Hull's Assembly Room, to name a few. Many of these events, featuring gentlemen as the performers, were often followed by "a ball for the ladies."

Open-air concerts, held during summer's mild evenings, came into fashion in the 1760s. Ranelagh Gardens featured a musical bill of fare along with fireworks for patrons, who flocked to its doors to enjoy the rural atmosphere. Vauxhall Gardens also provided frequent programs with both vocal and instrumental performances.

On an amateur level, music was a required social accomplishment for wealthy and educated gentlemen. More than just a pastime for individual amusement, private concerts and musical entertainments were an important part of social life. The arrival of good amateur musicians in the city did not go unnoticed. These newcomers were often immediately requested to participate in some sort of concert or musical event.

Repertoire was rife with the music of Bach, Corelli, Scarlatti, Haydn, and Handel. Instrumental music consisted of works that were composed in a variety of dance forms—gigues, gavottes, bourrees—since the dance was quite popular. Rivington's store kept a supply of music on sale for the harpsichord, violin, flute, and other instruments. Many business and retail establishments also sold music as a sideline. (An account from 1761 speaks of a milliner who offered a choice collection of music for sale by the likes of Handel and Corelli.[3])

Many households were the proud owners of several instruments. The violin, pianoforte, German flute, and fife were among the most popular instruments of the time. They were imported from England, obtained at local estate sales, or purchased at one of the city's multifaceted retail establishments.

Singing was enormously popular. Glee clubs and musical organizations began to spring up, one of the earliest being the Harmonic Society. These groups performed hymns and anthems in public concerts and served as social organizations, as well. They also assisted featured performers at subscription concerts. These types of singing groups were to be popular in the city throughout its musical development.

Of course, the singing of psalms and hymns had always had a place in church services. As early as 1740, private lessons were offered to improve techniques in this pursuit. However, this type of musical literature, intended primarily for the purpose of worship, only began to be considered for more public occasions with the growth of concert venues.

Ballad opera became popular, often hand-in-hand with the flourishing theater trade. As early as the 1750s, audiences could attend performances of *The Beggar's Opera* at the Nassau Street Theatre. Lewis Hallam's theatrical troupe, arriving in 1753, performed operas as well as plays, and his group served as a forerunner for a later and quite popular company run by Lewis Hallam, Jr. Performers and singers from Hallam's were also featured in concerts around town, including those held at the popular outdoor gardens such as Vauxhall.

Although the year 1724 saw the city's first organ installation in the Dutch Reformed Church, church music really became integral to musical life with the addition of the organ at Trinity Church, built by J.G. Klemm, in 1741. John Clemm, purportedly the son of the organ-builder (despite the variation in name), acted as the church's first organist from 1741 to 1744.

Neither the organ nor the liturgical repertoire was solely confined to the church, though. The new organ at City Hall was the occasion for a 1756 benefit concert of miscellaneous instrumental and vocal music as well as an organ concerto. And in 1766, a complete program of church music was offered at Mr. Burn's New Room.

Teachers were in demand, particularly for the violin, and an interesting group of these individuals advertised their services. William Tuckey, the first clerk of Trinity Church (1753), not only enriched the city's musical awareness through his consummate teaching skills, but also through his superb artistic influence. Tuckey quickly formed a vocal music program for the children at the church's Charity School, calling them his "singing scholars," and he served as a strong and innovative leader of the Trinity choir. He introduced the overture to local concert halls and enthusiastically endorsed Handel's compositions. Throughout the 1760s, Tuckey promoted subscription concerts and balls which were well attended. He also managed to find time to appear in the role of Mr. Peachum in a 1762 performance of *The*

Beggar's Opera at the New Theatre[4] and to do some composing, as well. (All this in addition to his teaching schedule!)

William Charles Hulett started a music school that had a marked influence on instrumentalists throughout the city. An apparently versatile man, he also taught dancing. He arrived with Hallam's theater troupe and was among the few musicians who stayed in New York for an extended amount of time.

Meanwhile, change was in the air as the city began moving toward its pivotal role in the quest for independence. As always, music would play its own special part during these turbulent times.

Revolution and Independence

By 1765, New York had developed quite a civilized atmosphere in comparison to former days. Its streets were relatively clean, its population reasonably literate, and its rich fairly visible. Yet political discontent was growing in the colonies as a whole, and rebellious sentiments were being voiced in New York. Political convictions often find artistic expression and, in this case, music helped to transmit information about crucial events, raise patriotic spirit, and express the feelings on both sides of the rising debate.

Britain's imposition of the Stamp Act of 1765 on the colonies was intended to garner revenue, partially to pay the cost of maintaining troops in America. Since stamps were required for most legal transactions, this was no small matter in either financial or political terms. The colonies were not fond of having a standing army on its shores and, more to the point, they did not want to pay for this dubious privilege without a voice in the decision.

New York became a central platform in the debate over this issue. It was here that a collection of delegates met to discuss the Stamp Act and to initiate a petition to be sent to England requesting its repeal.

These initial efforts seemed in vain for, despite the petition, a cargo of stamps arrived in New York Harbor on October 22nd. On October 31st, 200 merchants convened at George Burns' tavern and decided to boycott British goods until the repeal of the Act. Protest was definitely in the air.

Shortly thereafter, the Sons of Liberty led crowds through the streets, inciting boisterous outcries. They were heard not only by their shouts, but also by their songs of defiance as they marched en route to further demonstrations.

The boycotts agreed upon by the merchants held fast until the Stamp Act was finally repealed the following spring. It appeared that a truce was in effect, no matter how tentative.

This time, cheers were heard during a celebration and, later, a vote was taken in favor of erecting a statue of George III on the Commons. The crowd sang "God Save the King" upon this momentous occasion. During the celebration, the Sons of Liberty dedicated a liberty pole on the Commons. It was intended to serve both as a symbol of their cause and as a meeting place for patriots to pledge their allegiance to freedom.

The liberty pole and its subsequent replacements were to figure prominently in the growing schism between loyalists and patriots. The British soldiers hacked the pole to bits on the first anniversary of the Stamp Act repeal and, thereafter, destroyed several of its hardy successors. While thus engaged, the soldiers marked their efforts by singing witty parodies, often to the tune of "Yankee Doodle," ridiculing the growing patriotic activities of the Sons of Liberty. It was increasingly apparent how important music had become in both celebrations and protests during these turbulent times.

Unrest was already arising as a result of other issues. The Quartering Act as well as the often offensive behavior of British soldiers stationed in New York provided additional fuel for the already scorching patriotic fires. Acutely aware of this growing turmoil, George III labeled New York as rebellious and, as a means of punishment, demanded that the Quartering Act (requiring colonial authorities to provide lodging and supplies for British soldiers) be enforced to the letter. Until this was accomplished, no new legislation would be permitted to be passed by the colonial assembly. In addition, he implemented another series of taxes and acts that served as a direct affront to any quest for political freedom and self-determination.

Another boycott was staged, but this time, New Yorkers agreed to it more reluctantly, despite the nobility of its cause. A once prosperous city, the boycott struck at the very root of its mercantile enterprise. The livelihoods of many citizens were beginning to noticeably suffer.

Fighting was breaking out more frequently, too. In 1770, after another attack on the liberty pole, the Battle of Golden Hill erupted on John Street. Although more of a skirmish than a real battle, it was often called the precursor to the Boston Massacre two months later. This was just one of many warnings of events to come.

The Sons of Liberty again bravely raised a new pole to the accompaniment of French horns playing "God Save the

King."[1] In response, loyalists composed a medley to cutting-ly satirize the event. It was called "The Procession, With the Standard of Faction" and was set to the tune of "Yankee Doodle." Such musical taunting was to become commonplace in the years ahead.

It was evident that patriots liked singing their political songs to the tune of "God Save the King" and other well-known British melodies, and loyalists enjoyed setting their barbed verses to "Yankee Doodle." (One of the first actual par-odies written to the tune of "Yankee Doodle," however, was found in the bawdy ballad opera called *The Disappointment,* published in New York in 1767. Curiously, this version had no political overtones.)

"Yankee Doodle" continually displayed its versatility throughout the Revolution. Patriots set verses to its tune to chronicle the events of war and describe heroic feats. The tune also served well as a marching song. Of course, it was consis-tently employed for parodies by the British and used by the colonists to taunt them in return. Along these lines, patriots were reported to have destroyed the printing press of James Rivington, Tory sympathizer and publisher of the *New York Royal Gazette*, and then marched off to the tune of "Yankee Doodle." It was reported that "Yankee Doodle" was played over and over again to annoy the British at Yorktown, and countless additional verses were written to describe the event.

Other songs of war and protest, set to common tunes, occa-sionally filtered from other cities to New York. This was defi-nitely a popular venue of protest as well as an effective way to transmit news of people and events. Verses were printed in newspapers or on broadsides and distributed door-to-door. The melodies were so much a part of the common culture that the songs were immediately assimilated into everyday use. Such songs probably helped to spark political actions similar to those that took place elsewhere. For example, the story of the Boston Tea Party was told in song, and New York soon held a similar protest in 1774. Then a song called "American Freedom" was written in 1775, around the time of such battles as Lexington and Bunker Hill. Its message spread quickly through verses in colonial newspapers and served to further kindle patriotic spirit. William Billings wrote patriotic words to his famous tune "Chester" in 1778, and it became a favorite anthem of revolution within the colonies. These and countless other songs are examples of the strong influence that music had in uniting the colonists, spreading the news, and inciting further active moves toward freedom.

George Washington arrived in New York on April 13, 1776, with five army regiments. The city, with its population of 20,000, was considered pivotal to the military campaign because of its location and its strategic harbor. However, chaos reigned. Washington came to a city with no British troops—the remaining ones having fled to a ship in the harbor. Also, an unusual collection of volunteers had traveled from all of the colonies to gather for the fight ahead, and they provided a strange and bedraggled sight to the observant bystander. Many civilians—both loyalists and patriots—had already fled in fear of impending battles.

Events proceeded rapidly. Washington read the Declaration of Independence in New York on July 9, 1776. Shortly thereafter, George III's statue was pulled down and made into bullets. (The statue was carted away to the strains of "The Rogue's March" played on fife and drum—the tune commonly associated with tarring and feathering.[2]) A number of new patriotic songs were written at this time and published in such newspapers as the *New-York Packet*. Of course, these new words were set to the tune of "God Save the King" in order to further taunt loyalist forces.

New York was not destined to become a patriotic stronghold during the Revolution. After a number of terrible battles, poor strategic defenses, and disastrous retreats, it became occupied by British troops for the remainder of the war and even beyond. Thousands of American soldiers were taken prisoner and were treated with brutality by British as well as Hessian troops.

The cruelty of the Hessians toward prisoners in New York was notorious and appears, again, in the verses of song. Ironically, the Hessians were also known for their music. They were accomplished upon a variety of instruments and excelled in singing and band performance. Indeed, their cultural influence was to be a lasting one after the close of the war.

Aside from patriotic and political songs, some formal musical life still existed, despite the war. It was usually directed by the British. Subscription and church concerts, musical parties, singing society activities, and band music performances were held with some regularity during this time.

Many soldiers of the British occupying forces were highly proficient amateur musicians and actors. The John Street Theatre (opened in 1767 and referred to as the city's first real theater) was renamed the Theater Royal during the occupation. It was host to the British Garrison Dramatic Club which was evidently a reasonable success.

As time went on, teas, balls, and social events were held. Music was an integral part of these festivities. Loyalist taverns featured bands that played on Saturday evenings at dinnertime. (The King's Head Tavern in Brooklyn celebrated the anniversary of the coronation not only with a dinner, but also with the singing of "Oh! The Roast Beef of Olde England," a song that was a perennial favorite for such festive loyalist occasions.[3])

Regimental bands provided entertainment, too. Despite the ravaging fire of 1776 that destroyed many homes as well as the famed Trinity Church, these groups still performed in the streets and in the church graveyard.[4]

Throughout the Revolutionary period, however, the content of musical offerings largely consisted of political verses and European imports. The development of American music did not really begin in earnest until after the war—particularly in New York.

Although the war ended in 1781, New York was not freed from British occupation until 1783, the year of Washington's famous farewell to his officers at Fraunces Tavern. The following year, New Yorkers celebrated Washington's birthday with a special dinner and a new birthday song written for the occasion. The song praised Washington ("long live great Washington") and, according to the custom of previous decades, it was set to the tune of "God Save the King." A new, free nation had formed under the guidance of an inspiring hero. New York was on the threshold of becoming free to realize its potential once again.

The New Nation

The war resulted in a great deal of hardship, deprivation, and residual political sentiments within the city. Many fled, their homes and businesses in ruin. At every turn, there was evidence of fire, pillage, and decay. Clearly, New York had a long road ahead before it could experience even a portion of its former grandeur.

Despite the brighter promise of a new and independent nation, there was still conflict in the air—the aftertaste of loyalist occupation for so much of the war. This uneasy political climate was noticeable as the new regime began replacing the old. There was a large exodus of loyalists from the city and with them went many vestiges of cultured society. Bitter resentment was directed at those who remained, and they were denied privileges of voting or holding public office.

In spite of the poor living conditions and negative political atmosphere, however, some positive forces were already at work—a tribute to the city's spirit of resilience. As a result, New York was to make remarkable progress on many fronts by the end of the century with new buildings, increased trade, and an influx of immigrants.

Again, its location made it a highly desirable center for commerce which helped to create a new economy and cultural life. It also needed to rebuild from the devastating fire of 1776 and, under the leadership of Mayor Duane, this task was begun. The fine harbor was made ready for trade once again—including the famous launching of the *Empress of China*, a ship that sailed to the Far East in 1784 to open new avenues of trade relations there. Other lucrative enterprises were to follow.

Toward the end of the century, intricate plans were begun for the systematic development of the city in order to encourage both efficient growth and effective use of land and resources. There was increased expansion northward as organized street grids were drawn and developed. Wall Street activities began informally under the buttonwood tree and in the Tontine Coffee House in the 1790s. The Articles of Confederation Congress moved to New York from Trenton—

a plum in terms of the city's status within the new nation, and the first of many great hotels was built in 1794.

Along with this growth, expansion, and formation of a newly prosperous merchant class came a rise in urban problems. An epidemic of yellow fever in 1797 as well as an alarming increase in poverty-stricken individuals produced difficulties that would not only be of strong concern in everyday life, but would also last well into the next century.

It was in this atmosphere that cultural and musical life—always existing on some level—began to blossom again. The John Street Theatre was soon filled every night. (Considering the toll that the war had taken on New York, it is amazing that the structure of the theater itself survived at all.)

The custom of writing and singing songs about events was still in fashion. Of course, military events and political themes still appeared often in many of these. Rousing verses commemorated battles, patriotism, and leaders. There were songs about peace and the new Constitution, too, despite Tory sentiments that still rumbled within the city. In fact, the musical reflections of the political atmosphere were as strong as ever during this period. Many of these songs were published in newspapers, including those that urged citizens to welcome the new and independent nation. The Constitutional Parade of 1788 prompted the distribution of two commemorative odes which were later published in the *New-York Packet*. As expected, the anti-federalists responded in kind with their own lyrics, and pressing political points continued to be debated in song long after the events of war and its immediate effects began to fade into the past. New topics eventually took over, though—elections, slavery, current heroes—foreshadowing some issues that would rise to fever pitch in the next century.

Much ado was made of George Washington and his legendary triumphs, and numerous songs were composed in his honor. (Washington was always in the news in New York, which was the site of his inauguration at Federal Hall as well as the capital of the nation, even if only for a very brief time.) The "President's March," set to Joseph Hopkinson's tune of "Hail Columbia," became the rage. Many believe that it was composed by Philip Phile for the occasion of Washington's inauguration in 1789, although there is no clear record of this. Yet the song was undeniably a favorite and has long been associated with the first president.

Music was written and performed in honor of Washington's journey from Mount Vernon to New York. Alexander Reinagle composed a chorus that was presumably sung to the great hero as he passed under the arch at Trenton. (The versatile Reinagle—composer, concert manager, and member of the Old American Company's orchestra—was said to have been a friend of J.C. Bach.[1]) This and other tributes quickly spread to New York. Ironically, Washington was received in New York to the strains of "God Save the King." The words by Samuel Low, however, were an unmistakably patriotic tribute. It is not known if music was played or sung on the occasion of Washington's famous address at Federal Hall.

Patriotism was at a new high. The "Federal Overture," which was both written and published by Benjamin Carr in 1794, is a wonderful example of this national spirit. Nine melodies were included in this work, and among them were the "President's March," "Rose Tree" (from Washington's favorite opera, *Poor Soldier*), the "Marseillaise," and "Yankee Doodle." (This was the earliest printed copy of the "Yankee Doodle" tune in America.) The overture was quite well received in New York. Carr, the original owner of the Musical Repository, was a versatile musician himself. A singer in the Old American Company, he was also a keyboardist, composer, arranger, and concert manager. His compositions were performed regularly in New York.

During this time, bands and band music also gained in popularity. A number of groups, formed during the war, continued to flourish long after peace was declared. Many Hessians stayed in the new country and organized bands and musical societies. They were well-known for their musical expertise. Members could perform, attend musical events, and even purchase instruments through these groups.

During George Washington's grand tour in 1789, it seemed that a band was ready to greet him in every town and village. Bands performed regularly in all manner of places, including pleasure gardens, theaters, taverns, and coffeehouses. (There was also some competition as to which type of entertainment would get the largest crowd—from bands, formal concerts, and puppet shows to the less cultural pursuits of sporting and gaming.) The instruments used in these bands expanded toward the end of the century. Keen interest in Turkish music led to the introduction of bass drums, cymbals, tambourines, and other exotic items into the repertoire of instruments used.

Music was again being recognized as a full-time profession. Of course, the number of extremely well-trained amateurs was also quite high. In 1789, the year of Washington's inauguration, approximately a dozen citizens were listed in a city directory as earning a living from music, although this probably represented only a fraction of those involved in some way in cultural or musical pursuits. They were from an interesting mix of ethnic backgrounds. Teachers offered instruction on a wide range of instruments as had been the custom before the Revolution. Among the many to hang out their shingles were Alexander Reinagle, Henri Capron, and Peter A. Van Hagan—all renowned in city cultural circles. Some were part-time teachers/musicians, accounts showing one grocer and one tavern-keeper among those who split their time between artistic and commercial worlds.[2] Among the more colorful individuals was William Hoffmeister (a.k.a. Billy the Fiddler), a dwarf with an engagingly large personality. Claiming to have been a friend of Mozart, Hoffmeister opened up shop as a music teacher at the corner of Fulton Street and Broadway. His students found him quite entertaining, enjoying both his stories and his remarkable attire which included seven-league boots.[3]

Concert series—never completely absent from the musical scene—were back in action, and the side business of concert management grew. As early as 1785, William Brown set subscription concerts in motion once more. Brown was evidently a performer in the first bona fide concert held in New York after the war and was known to be somewhat of an eccentric. Alexander Reinagle also became involved in subscription efforts and participated in sponsoring several series of events, including one presented at the City Tavern in 1788. This representative program offered a mixture of works by Bach, Stamitz, Haydn, and Reinagle himself. Reinagle—an ever-versatile individual—also performed in the series.[4]

Pleasure gardens, popular in New York in the 1760s, reopened. Among them were both a new Vauxhall and Ranelagh Gardens. Music was written expressly for these places, often reflecting the pastoral setting that the visitor always found so charming and restful there.

During this post-war time, many notable citizens emigrated to New York. A number of foreign musicians and composers set down their roots in the U.S. and brought their eclectic musical and individual perspectives with them. Others were associated one way or another with the management side of musical life.

The name of John Jacob Astor has always figured prominently in New York's history. Noted for his expertise in the fur trade, he used the proceeds from this business to purchase a great deal of Manhattan land. Yet he, too, circulated in the musical sphere. As a young immigrant with his meager possessions and a small purse, he brought seven flutes to the new city in the hope of setting up a musical store. (He had several years of experience abroad in his brother's music shop.) Although music was not the source of his fortune, he did sell the flutes and a variety of other instruments, opened a music shop in 1786, and even imported pianofortes[5] with a fair degree of success before devoting more time to his other enterprises. John and Michael Paff took over Astor's business in the 1790s.[6] Astor's neighbor, Thomas Dodd, manufactured his own brand of pianofortes which significantly undercut Astor's imported models in terms of price. To complete this picture, Benjamin Carr could supply music from his New York branch store to enjoy and perform on the instruments sold by all of these instrument dealers. His establishment was eventually bought by the illustrious James Hewitt.

Alexander Hamilton settled in New York and was to become a moving force not only within the city, but also within the new country. A close advisor to Washington during the Revolution, he helped create New York's first bank, ensured that New York ratified the Constitution, and acted as a prime motivational force behind the Constitutional Parade of 1788. Both the Parade and Hamilton were the focus of several odes and musical compositions during this time period.

The theater and related art forms, never completely gone even during the loyalist occupation, now began to flourish as a native enterprise. In 1785, the Old American Company theater group reorganized and began presenting performances once more, including musical events. Operas composed by and about Americans were performed, such as Hewitt's *Tammany, or the Indian,* produced in 1794. Lewis Hallam (the younger) returned to New York and ran a series of lectures—a performance tradition from pre-war times.

Theater music, particularly from the English stage, was beginning to be heard far and wide in New York, with compositions from the pens of James Hook, Thomas Attwood, and William Reeve, among others.[7]

As the turn of the century approached, the need for new performance space was recognized. The old John Street Theatre was to close shortly before the end of the century; it was too small for the needs of the expanding city. New ones soon took its place. Work on the illustrious Park Theatre began in 1795 and was completed in 1798. This would be an enduring favorite. Of course, Lewis Hallam eventually became one of its managers.

James Hewitt, long associated with the musical life of the new nation, bought the New York branch of Carr's Musical Repository in the same year as the Park Theatre's completion. He also directed the orchestra at this theater where each of 14 excellent musicians received the princely sum of $10 per week for their services.[8] Hewitt was also a prolific composer. His opera *The Patriot, or Liberty Asserted* opened in New York in 1794. He led some bands at Vauxhall's summer series where not only the concerts, but also the fireworks and the new treat of ice cream were enjoyed. Actively involved in New York's concert life, Hewitt and his friends presented one particularly fine and memorable concert which represented their varied tastes. Its program included the more traditional Haydn, Pleyel, and Stamitz works as well as a cello concerto by Phillips, a Gehot overture, and Hewitt's own "Overture in nine movements, experience of a battle."[9] Such eclecticism was not uncommon on the concert scene.

The century drew to a close with the death of George Washington in December 1799. The great hero who had led both city and country into a new era of freedom and independence was mourned throughout the land. A number of funeral marches and odes were composed in his memory, including Benjamin Carr's acclaimed "Dead March and Monody." Musical tributes were a continual part of Washington's life as well as of his memory.

The spirit of Washington and America would live on—both politically and musically—as a new century dawned.

A New Metropolis

(1800–1825)

At the dawn of the new century, New York was a city of contrasts on every level. Both urban and country atmospheres mixed in an intriguing blend. Broadway was a wide, tree-lined city boulevard with a growing number of amenities. By 1805, it had a wonderful collection of shops that would only continue to increase in number as time passed. On the other hand, the Bowery was still considered a country lane and retained some of its Dutch-style cottages, reminiscent of bygone New Amsterdam. Barefoot peddlers sold their wares at the same time the fashion conscious strolled about town in order to be seen in their finery. The very rich, the very poor, the prosperous middle-class merchants, and an eclectic mix of newcomers wove a bright social fabric as the city quickly expanded—and expand it did. New York's population doubled between 1800 and 1820.

A fairly sophisticated street grid called the Randall Plan was designed to promote growth beyond the city's former limits. A larger number of people were discovering Brooklyn, incorporated as a village in 1816. Of course, along with its expansion in population and geographical boundaries came the need for bigger and better facilities and services, and plans for banks, utilities, retail businesses, and entertainment centers were rapidly developed to begin addressing the needs of the growing population. Construction of a beautiful new City Hall was also begun in 1803.

A number of individuals made contributions to the growth and enrichment of the city in a variety of ways. DeWitt Clinton, who served several terms as mayor, ushered in a new regime. He worked to organize many civic institutions including the New-York Historical Society that is still in existence. He championed scores of social reforms in areas such as the enforcement of equal voting privileges and public schooling. (The first public school opened in 1807, private education being the only option available until then.)

On other fronts, New York's literary world boasted of such figures as Washington Irving as well as a newspaper trade that published eight dailies alone by 1807. New transportation systems were being conceived, and Robert Fulton launched his famous steamboat, the *Clermont*.

An influx of immigrants brought new energy to the city along with their diverse perspectives and styles. They brought their music with them and, during the early 1800s, melodies from abroad were quite popular. M. Carey's *Irish Melodies* was published in a number of cities including New York, and these tunes were rapidly assimilated into American culture. Such songs, including the beloved "'Tis the Last Rose of Summer," evoked a sentimentality and nostalgia that were a part of popular culture for decades.

English stage music was often heard and came from the pens of Samuel Arnold, William Reeve, and others. New Yorkers also enjoyed any form of European music that had achieved popularity in London, and a growing number of musical societies as well as individual concert promoters included these works, such as overtures by Kreutzer and Gluck, on many of their programs. Orchestras, with the Philharmonic Society counted in their number, were active from the turn of the century, and the Euterpean Club offered annual concerts for more than 45 years. Some of Beethoven's orchestral works were introduced to New York through these organizations.

Several choral societies presented frequent concerts, the most notable groups including the Handel and Haydn Society as well as the New York Choral Society, who often participated in conjunction with featured performers or at special civic festivities. The latter group performed for Lafayette during his celebrated visit in 1824.

Of course, "Yankee Doodle" was still played and sung on patriotic occasions, and other songs continued to be written about politics, war, heroes, and current events. Tammany Hall, begun as a fraternal organization in the 1790s, developed into a strong political presence, courtesy of the rather crafty and opportunistic Aaron Burr. Political opinions were strong on many issues, and heated debate often filled the air. The Hamilton-Burr duel was the extreme result of political controversy and, as always, the musical world took note. A song called "On the Murder of Hamilton" was written to be sung to the Scottish tune "Goodnight, and joy be wi' ye a'!"

"Ode for Gen. Hamilton's Funeral," by Dr. George K. Jackson, was sung at the funeral in New York.[1] Music figured into the tense time before this event, too. The rivals both attended a banquet the week before the famous duel. Arrangements for the fateful meeting had already been made, and Hamilton, who seemed in his usual humor, sang his favorite ballad, "The Drum," upon the request of his friends. Burr could only stare at him in silence.[2]

Many great structures were built during these years and, often, figured in musical life. The City Hotel, constructed in the mid-1790s at 115 Broadway, set the tone for other grand hotels that were to follow. It was the site of concerts and balls and was owned by none other than John Jacob Astor of both musical and entrepreneurial fame. James Hewitt's daughter, Sophia, made her piano debut there in 1807 at the age of seven.[3] Structures such as the massive Washington Hall (1809) would soon follow in the footsteps of the City Hotel and surpass it in size, activity, and lavish grandeur.

Theater was quite popular, and one of its grandest palaces was the lovely Park Theatre, completed in 1798. Destroyed by fire in 1820, it was later rebuilt with equal, if not surpassing, splendor. A wide range of performances were held at the Park—from Shakespeare to lighter fare. However, this and other establishments saw fierce competition—particularly in the summer—from the pleasure gardens that offered a wider variety of musical entertainment.

The popularity of pleasure gardens grew to an all-time high at the turn of the century. Although they first made their appearance in the 1760s, the Revolution inhibited patronage and, ultimately, revenue for these establishments. After 1800, however, pleasure gardens had a renewed popularity and were even more splendid. At the corner of Broadway and Leonard Street, Mt. Vernon Garden opened and led the way for a host of others. Vauxhall, first at Grand and Mulberry Streets and later on at Broome Street, was operated by Joseph Delacroix to much acclaim. Castle Garden in the Battery and Niblo's Garden at Broadway and Prince Street were two other favorites.

These gardens featured a vast array of entertainments such as fireworks, plays, concerts, and art displays. The beautiful surrounding garden atmosphere served as a tasteful pastoral setting. And, of course, the ice cream that was served there turned into quite the rage. Pleasure gardens eventually caused the tavern trade to diminish while serving as a springboard for the restaurant culture that appeared by the 1820s. Many songs were written expressly for performance at these locations, and new music was often presented. Performers included such luminaries as James Hewitt leading a band and Miss Hallam offering various song selections to the sheer delight of audiences. Pleasure gardens sharpened interest in song publication, too, helping the sheet music business to begin to gain a stronger foothold with the public.

Musicians and composers who had begun to be recognized after the Revolution gained prominence after 1800. James Hewitt carried out multiple roles within musical circles. His popular song, "The Wounded Hussar," was a raging success for decades—one of the top sellers of its time. Hewitt published it himself in 1800.[4] His musical family was highly regarded in New York and, later, in Boston. While still in New York, he functioned as band leader, composer, performer, and music publisher.

As the city grew, so did its instrument and sheet music sales. Soon after the turn of the century, there were a number of music stores doing a brisk business, including those owned by Hewitt, Gilfert, and Gibson & Davis. New Yorkers could buy an even wider variety of instruments than before through these and other establishments. Also, between 1800 and 1820, there were approximately half a dozen piano makers in New York, indicating the rising popularity of the pianoforte within home and concert hall.

As a result, the general interest in purchasing published sheet music to perform not only in public, but also for individual amusement, grew along with the instrument trade. The publishing business ultimately took the place of the formerly popular broadsides and newspaper lyrics that had acted as informal vehicles for song distribution in times past. There were a number of publishers who now produced lithographed covers with beautifully elaborate lettering on the title page. Of course, Hewitt was among them, operating from his establishment at 137 Broadway. Others included the popular firm of Firth & Hall as well as John Paff and William Dubois. The visit of Lafayette to New York set off an additional rise in the sheet music business, since a number of commemorative and patriotic songs were written and published in his honor.

The publication of songs about major events such as this was to become a permanent custom within the sheet music industry throughout its continued development.

Although the War of 1812 caused grave concern, the city did not see active combat, and its economic activity was only temporarily slowed down as a result. Citizens tracked events with keen interest, though, and when the war ended in 1815, New York celebrated with a sigh of relief. Again, music took the spotlight with songs of war and victory. James Hewitt composed and published a special musical setting for Francis Scott Key's poem "The Star-Spangled Banner" in 1816. Since there were many battles at sea, naval heroes were also duly honored in tuneful fashion. At one New York fete, a new song, entitled "Decatur, Hull and Jones are Here," was performed along with the traditional favorite, "Yankee Doodle."[5]

A financial, trade, and manufacturing center, New York became one of the leading cotton shippers to Europe. Countinghouses sprang up as a result, and the new metropolis increased its world-renowned reputation. Thus, the development and execution of plans for the Erie Canal began. DeWitt Clinton acted as a strong motivational force behind this project, begun in 1817 and completed in 1825. A great celebration was held with many new songs written in honor of this amazing achievement. At festivities held in the city after the inaugural fleet made its first trip through the new route opened up by the canal, a band played "The Meeting of the Waters" as Governor Clinton led the ceremony.[6] New paths were now open for the growth and development to come—economically, socially, and musically.

A Diverse Musical Gateway

(1825–1850)

The opening of the Erie Canal was another turning point for the city. Now a growing trade capital, it also served as a gateway to the country at large. It prospered as a center for foreign imports—goods, ideas, and culture.

The population had multiplied to 166,000 by 1825. At the same time, there was a tremendous amount of new building. Old structures—particularly old landmarks—were vanishing quickly. Northward expansion continued, and numerous attempts were made to improve public facilities. A new system was designed to provide the city with a better water supply, and a regular stagecoach created speedy surface transportation for the public. New railroad links swiftly sprang up, enhancing the sophistication of the city's transportation network. Many of the city's major streets were now lit by gas lamps—a nice touch of civilization. Even the great fire of 1835 did not keep the city down for long; building and regular activities resumed with a fierce intensity.

The city became a study in extremes. On one hand, money began to flow because of the boom in commerce and trade. Elaborate mansions were built by the rich—each one, in turn, a more pointed example of opulence run wild. Wealth became an overriding factor in high society. How this wealth was acquired, though, was frequently overlooked.

Beautiful new stores such as A.T. Stewart's and Tiffany offered an attractive diversion for wealthy patrons with time and money to spare. Additional luxury hotels were added to existing ones, providing dining, entertainment, and lodging of a superb caliber. The Astor House, built in 1836, was among the finest—particularly with its prime location at Broadway and Vesey Street, just overlooking City Hall Park. Its grandeur was almost beyond belief. (Obviously financed by the massive capital from Astor's fur empire—certainly not from his former musical pursuits—it prompted an early guest, Davy Crockett, to comment on the fate of the "poor b'ars and beavers" that had obviously sacrificed their skins for the sake of the hotel.[1]) Famous visitors at the Astor included the legendary Swedish singer Jenny Lind, whose American debut at Castle Garden was one of the foremost musical events of the century.

At the same time that the rich were enjoying the many advantages at their disposal, the poor were contending with their less than enviable lot. Crime, poverty, and corruption in the slums were growing into serious problems. With a population that seemed to pyramid daily, the custom of subdividing property for rent was born, leading to serious overcrowding. Resulting outbreaks of cholera were common given the close living conditions. Immigrants led lives of unspeakable poverty in many neighborhoods—lives that were often marred by prejudice. Ethnic and benevolent groups tried to help, but the number of immigrant poor grew too quickly for many to have any real impact. Certain slums became notorious, such as the Five Points section, located on the site of the old Collect Pond, where every crime imaginable—from robbery to beating to rape to murder—was committed on a daily basis. Street gangs were a vicious threat, and such groups as the Dead Rabbits and the Plug Uglies—who gained immediate notoriety for instigating riotous unemployment protests in 1837—had an astounding network of membership to carry out a broad range of crimes. Clearly, a better prison system was necessary, and "The Tombs" was constructed in 1838. In the midst of this constant social unrest, the world of politics became more corrupt by the minute.

Such contrasts extended to the musical and cultural scenes. There was a definite class distinction as New Yorkers sought their entertainment—musical, theatrical, and otherwise. The rich became extremely taken with the newly imported Italian opera, and the working class enjoyed circuses, exhibitions, and lighter entertainments that were increasingly popular on the Bowery. There was something for every taste and, culturally, it was an exciting time.

Rich patrons donated money for scores of worthwhile projects. Peter Cooper offered backing for the creation of an educational institute. Other funds were given to develop both the Astor and Mercantile libraries. Writers and artists were growing in number, and they formed associations including the

Bread and Cheese Club and the Century Club. This was a time when William Cullen Bryant was editor of the *New York Evening Post* and Edgar Allan Poe was spinning some of his famous works of terror. Melville and Irving were also among the many literary figures who resided in the city. A fine array of newspapers continued to be available for eager readers, and references to the musical scene began to appear in the serious critical writings of such journalists as Walt Whitman of the *Brooklyn Eagle* and Margaret Fuller of the *Tribune.*[2]

New theaters were constantly springing up: the Lyceum, City, Park, Franklin, Bowery, American, and Olympic, to name a few. The Park, already well known, continued to be among the more famous theaters until 1848. The Bowery Theatre, quite popular in its time, opened in 1826. It seated 3,000 and was the first gaslit playhouse. Although it burned down six times, it was successively rebuilt and lasted for a number of decades. More popular fare was offered at the ever-appealing Niblo's Garden and Harry Hill's Dance Hall (an establishment that thinly bordered on the sensational). Castle Garden reopened in 1824 with a band concert and was once more in the mainstream of musical life.

Opera reigned during the early part of this time period—particularly for the rich. Previously, what passed for opera consisted of a makeshift affair of brief scenes, popular tunes, and miscellaneous entertainments. Then, in 1825, Spanish singer Manuel Garcia came to New York with his troupe of opera singers, many from his family. Dominick Lynch, a vintner from the city (perhaps a latter-day counterpart to Robert Todd) was responsible for bringing this group to America. It was at the Park Theatre that an excited audience saw and heard *The Barber of Seville*—reportedly performed both in its entirety and in authentic style. Over the next season, the public got more of what it wanted—*La Cenerentola, Semiramide, Don Giovanni,* and others, with a total of nearly 80 performances. By now, New York had surpassed Philadelphia as a center for music and other forms of culture. Much of this was due to the influence and the backing of its rich and culturally hungry citizens with their passion for opera and other musical imports.

A major name in the opera world was also busy promoting Italian opera in New York. Mozart's famous librettist, Lorenzo da Ponte, had lived in the city for years while teaching Italian at Columbia College. Through da Ponte's efforts, the public was able to see *Don Giovanni* in 1825, said to be one of the first American performances of a complete Mozart opera in its original form. He also urged a group of rich patrons to support Italian opera and was the motivational force behind the building of the extravagant Italian Opera House at Church and Leonard Streets. Dominick Lynch was again instrumental in backing this project. The opening in November 1833 saw a production of Rossini's *La Gazza Ladra*. This beautiful house, often called an ancestor to the Metropolitan Opera, was a successful American performance vehicle for many Italian singers. However, the house was a financial failure and closed after only two years in operation. It was later reopened as the National Theatre. Yet this marvelous experiment whetted the appetite of the city's upper-crust for more.

The first season of Palmo's Opera House was launched in 1844. During its four years in existence, the organization introduced a number of works that were to become standard in the opera repertory, including Bellini's *I Puritani*. Shortly thereafter, in 1847, the lovely Astor Place Opera House opened with Verdi's *Ernani*. Much to the delight of the public, Italian opera concerts were launched at Castle Garden in 1845 with a star-studded list of singers who were formerly with the Italian Opera House company. Not all opera was taken quite seriously, though. Popularized versions of operas, as well as burlesques of various works, showed up frequently at theaters such as Niblo's and were enjoyed by the greater masses.

Italian opera was not the only game in town. Works from other cultures were also featured. Auber's *Le Dieu et la Bayadère* ran at the National Theatre as *The Maid of Cashmere* and, later, in 1836, at the Park Theatre as *La Bayadère*. Also, *The Bohemian Girl* by Balfe was a smashing success. It debuted at the Park Theatre in 1844 and later moved to the Bowery Theatre. It contained two songs that became known to all—"I Dreamt I Dwelt in Marble Halls" and "Then You'll Remember Me"—popular hits in the parlor song repertory.

Sheet music publishers realized a veritable gold mine in selling various vocal and instrumental renditions of memorable operatic melodies adapted for use in the parlor. In turn, famous parlor songs such as "Home Sweet Home" were incorporated into recital programs and even into some operatic productions. The business of sheet music publishing and sales was becoming increasingly more well-developed as the years passed. From the early budding businesses such as those of Astor, Paff, Firth & Hall, and James Hewitt, there followed a number of others with more lasting names—James L. Hewitt (son of James), Joseph Atwill, and Firth, Hall & Pond. Patriotic songs, operatic airs, and piano solos were among their best sellers.

Instruments were needed for parlor performances, and New York was continuing to excel in this area, too. R. & W. Nunns was the leading maker of pianos in 1830s New York. They received an award at the Mechanics Institute in 1830 for producing a superb model of a square piano. Their main rival, Dubois & Stodart, got second prize.[3]

A number of other interesting musical firsts occurred during these years. Active cultural associations introduced all types of concerts, composers, and performers to the general public—many at benefit occasions in the time-honored tradition. The Musical Fund Society, for example, was composed of both professionals and amateurs who sought to help "superannuated" musicians through performance proceeds. Their concerts, held at the City Hotel during the 1830s, often capitalized on the operatic rage. Instrumentalists, frequently included on the programs for variety, played overtures including Rossini's *Semiramide* and *William Tell* at these events.

The New York Sacred Music Society also provided a variety of programs. In 1831, it presented the *Messiah* and, in 1838, Mozart's *Requiem*. An eclectic spirit reigned in these presentations, too. One program included sacred music for voice as well as a pianist, Mr. W.A. King, who played his own fantasy on the "Star-Spangled Banner."[4]

Sacred music was of noticeable importance within the city. The Episcopal book of psalm tunes was revised and updated in 1828 to include compositions by five American composers. In 1838, on the occasion of the consecration of St. Peter's Roman Catholic Church on Barclay Street, there was a grand performance of the so-called Twelfth Mass of Mozart, with Ureli Corelli Hill leading members of the National Theatre orchestra. The appeal of this event was so great that more than 2500 people were turned away. (The church also featured a $6,000 organ built by Hall & Erben.)

In 1846, music at the newly consecrated Trinity Church witnessed a revival, and Edward Hodges formed a boys' choir to present a whole new form of repertoire. The same year also saw the installation of a new organ that touched off some controversial inaugural festivities. Evidently, Hodges and Henry Erben, the organ builder, were completely at odds. Word had it that Erben threw Hodges out of the organ loft at one point in their quarrels, and further succeeded in holding a gargantuan, if not gaudy, festival to display the new organ to the general public—much to the dismay of Hodges. There seemed little of the sacred in these proceedings.[5]

The Philharmonic Society of New York was among the most popular instrumental groups and became the oldest continuous orchestra society in the United States. Organized by a diverse group of musicians, including German pianists Henry C. Timm and William Scharfenberg, it presented its first concert in December 1842. Beethoven's Fifth Symphony, again under the baton of Ureli Corelli Hill, and Weber's Overture to *Oberon* were featured on the program. The group also played a variety of symphonic fare for an eager public and sponsored famous performers including Ole Bull, who displayed his virtuosity on the violin to sellout houses. An innovative organization, even in its early life, the Philharmonic presented the first American performance of Beethoven's Ninth Symphony at Castle Garden in 1846. During its first few years, conductors came from orchestra ranks and were rotated frequently (even during the same concert program). This practice was to change over subsequent years to a system with a permanent conductor.

During this time period, New York saw the beginnings of the age—and the antics—of the bravura pianists, their styles ranging from serious to flamboyantly bizarre. All of the more famous names in this category came from Europe, in keeping with the city's fascination with all things cultural from abroad. German-born Daniel Schlesinger, a former pupil of Ries and Moscheles, was among the best of the early imports. Again, the City Hotel was the site of his 1839 concert during which he performed a Thalberg fantasy as well as Beethoven's *Egmont Overture* arranged for two pianos, with the assistance of William Scharfenberg—an event that was instrumental in introducing more of Beethoven's music to New York. Then, with the help of additional artists, an eight-hand arrangement of Cherubini's *Anacreon Overture* thrilled the eager audience.

Other pianists such as de Meyer and Herz used more than their superb musical skills to gain notoriety and ticket sales. De Meyer hired carriages to parade up and down near the concert hall before one of his performances to simulate an eager crowd, and Herz promoted a salve that had miraculously "cured" his burned hands—all to draw in the public to New York concert appearances.

Not to be outdone in showmanship by the pianistic set, other musicians and promoters jumped on the bandwagon. In 1834, the ever-resourceful management of Niblo's Garden publicized a musical duel between English and Italian trumpet players. The former played "Robin Adair" and "The British Grenadiers" and the latter serenaded the crowd with variations on tunes from Rossini's *Otello*. The Englishman won by the vote of three judges, but each trumpet player earned $530, and local music publishers happily used this entertaining event to enjoy record sheet music sales of the tunes performed.

It is true that during this time period, New York was still fascinated with European musical trends. However, more authentic American compositions and styles were slowly taking shape—often an interesting amalgam of many cultural traditions. The Hewitt family continued to appear in the city's cultural annals. John Hill Hewitt (son of the famous James) wrote "The Minstrel's Return'd from the War" in 1825. It was sold by the family firm in Boston and New York with great success. Gradually, other homegrown songs entered the city's repertoire. Sad songs were popular in the American ballad repertoire—"The Last Farewell" and "The Dying Minstrel" among them. They were considered appropriate for ladies to perform on the parlor piano and capitalized on the sentimentality that was still in vogue. Singer Henry Russell further emphasized this trend by performing (and acting) such heart-wrenching fare as "Woodman, Spare That Tree" and "The Old Arm Chair."

Also, a new compositional/performance/character form was emerging in local environs. Early on, in 1822, British-born Charles Mathews performed a minstrel show at the Park Theatre. Not many years later, in 1828, George Washington Dixon appeared in blackface and performed what he claimed were his songs, "Long Tail Blue" and "Coal Black Rose." The public seemed to enjoy this art form which, although not entirely new, was being reinvented and enhanced. The city and the country were increasingly intrigued by the lives, troubles, and characters of black culture.

Another minstrel performer who appeared in New York was Thomas Dartmouth Rice, doing his famous "Jim Crow" routine at the Bowery Theatre. This was performed in complete dialect, dress, and blackface. During the 1820s and 1830s, these performers were often seen in variety shows and presented their acts on the same program as instrumental works, farces, or even serious plays.

Eventually, in the 1840s, minstrel bands such as the Virginia Minstrels and Christy's Minstrels joined the ranks of these individual performers in New York. All presented original material as well as parodies (e.g., "I Dreamt I Dwelt in Kitchen Halls"). Their material, often derived from slave songs, was in dialect or opera buffa form and produced something truly American in character.

Around the 1840s, songs of protest were also being performed with more serious intent. The Hutchinson Family sang "The Old Granite State," but added new verses for a performance at the Broadway Tabernacle that addressed issues of slavery and the war with Mexico. The audience that night was not particularly pleased at this serious turn of events, but a new trend was born. In the same vein as protest fare were temperance songs that also gained in familiarity, if not in popularity.

Patriotic and political material still proliferated. The city had not lost its love of honoring heroes, villains, and events. However, these songs now shared the spotlight with many other compositional styles and topics, and were becoming a less totally dominating force in the repertoire of the day than in previous times.

The eclecticism that was evident on the cultural scene continued to underline class divisions. The rich liked their opera and instrumental performances. The not-too-rich liked their dueling trumpets and bands in the streets. This division within the cultural world was highlighted most strongly—and tragically—during the Astor Place Opera riot, where a mob consisting of many gang members forced its way into the Opera House during a performance of *Macbeth*, starring William Macready. Twenty-two people were killed. The mob was partially protesting the fact that Macready's performance for the rich audience was scheduled on the same night as their favorite, Edwin Forrest, who performed the same role at a more popular house. Although indicative of the class distinctions that would continue to be a factor on the cultural scene

Castle Garden was the site of Swedish soprano Jenny Lind's American debut in 1850. *Published by N. Currier. "First Appearance of Jenny Lind in America: At Castle Garden, Sept. 11, 1850." Museum of the City of New York, J. Clarence Davies*

for years to come, such an extreme tragedy was fortunately not repeated in either theatrical or musical settings. The issue sought other forms of expression.

However, it did seem that there was one individual who could appease all the classes while turning a net profit in the bargain. In the same year as the opera house riot, P.T. Barnum opened his American Museum at Broadway and Ann Street. It had bands, exhibitions, and fantastic displays.

Barnum was also occupied with music in a more serious way. In 1850, it was through his efforts that the Swedish soprano, Jenny Lind, made her American debut at none other than New York's Castle Garden to an adoring audience of 7,000. Advance publicity for the arrival of the "Swedish Nightingale" led to songs, pictures, books, and novelties sold in her honor. Barnum left no stone unturned in assuring the success of her New York debut. Fanfare surrounding the event was enormous to the point of excess, attesting to the fact that the great promoter and showman was surely in his element. Although some tickets were priced at $3.00, there was a rush to buy at any cost. One patron paid $225 to see the performance.

Lind entertained her audience with selections ranging from "Casta Diva" to "The Herdsman's Song." To say that the crowd loved her would have been an understatement. In keeping with the eclectic concert programming of this time, two pianists played a Thalberg fantasy on themes from *Norma* on Chickering grands during the entr'acte. The evening was a tremendous success.

Again, New York had scored a cultural victory in attracting a European name to its shores. It was being increasingly featured on the musical map, and even more wonders were to follow in the decades to come.

A Time of Transition

(1850–1875)

By the time that Jenny Lind made her famous debut at Castle Garden, New York was serving as an even more popular destination for countless immigrant groups. Fleeing problems from poverty to political unrest, they flocked to the new city and brought with them a variety of rich cultures. By 1860, more than half of New York's residents were from foreign lands. Irish, German, and English were among the largest groups, but others were quickly growing in number, as well.

With this increasing international focus and ethnic mix, it seemed fitting that in 1853 the city proudly sponsored the first World's Fair to be held in America. The Crystal Palace—a beautiful domed building topped off by the famous Latting Observatory and located in what is now Bryant Park—was the site of this stellar event. Among the 4,000 exhibitions were many with musical themes, including one that contained an impressive array of pianos. The famous piano maker Henry

The Crystal Palace, completed in 1853, was the site of the first World's Fair held in America. It was here that Louis Jullien's famous concerts were performed and a display of Steinway pianos attracted much notice.
Biggs Photography

Engelhard Steinway, having opened his shop downtown in 1853, displayed one of his specially designed square pianos at the fair. It received the highest award for unparalleled sound and provided a good indication of the reputation that the firm would achieve in years to come.

Musical concerts were another enjoyable feature of the fair. French conductor Louis Jullien's light programs packed the Crystal Palace with enthusiastic crowds. A unique individual with a talent for showmanship and a creative flair, Jullien added a number of outstanding American performers to the ranks of his own orchestra. The result was spectacular. This group performed popular dances (quadrilles, schottisches, and such), music by American composers, and an occasional symphonic movement from the works of Beethoven and other serious composers. Basically, he tried to please every taste. Jullien was also noted for risking a performance of the most unusual *Santa Claus Symphony* by William Henry Fry.

Other places were joining the growing roster of concert locales. Central Park began taking shape in the late 1850s. This beautiful oasis was fashioned according to the design of Frederick Law Olmsted and Calvert Vaux. Theoretically planned as a place to encourage healthy family outings, the park was open to all, regardless of class or culture. Many outdoor entertainments were available, including a rich variety of concerts that were presented throughout upcoming years. This was an era when band music was beginning to be enjoyed fully, and one of the most popular groups was the Dodworth Band, previously acclaimed for its specially crafted marching instruments as well as its informative manual for brass players. This band held the distinction of being the first such organization to perform in Central Park.[1]

Church music continued to maintain a highly professional level of performance. Large choruses, paid soloists, and skilled organists developed and presented more complex programs within the major city houses of worship as they attracted larger and more supportive congregations.

New buildings appeared on the horizon, including many in the cast-iron style of architecture, such as the fashionable department stores of A.T. Stewart and Lord & Taylor. Development of the elevated railroad was underway, and restaurants, hotels, and stores were multiplying. Fine residences on Fifth Avenue were becoming more commonplace, even though tenements continued to spread in other parts of town. Music continually reflected this scene—through the types of compositions composed and performed, the growth of instrument manufacturing and music publishing businesses, the establishment of new concert spaces, and ongoing innovations in performance practices.

Popular repertoire fell into several categories. Ethnic songs were widely sung, particularly Irish ones, reflecting the large number of immigrants from that country. Stephen Foster's work was also in vogue, including his sentimental ballads (nostalgia was in) and Civil War songs. Family singers and group singers such as the Christy's Minstrels and the Hutchinsons performed repertoire which included topical and protest material, ranging from abolitionism and war to suffrage and temperance. (Although New York began with a strong show of support for the Union, merchants gave a second thought to the noble cause when it interfered with their lucrative trade in the southern states.) Further complicating matters were New York's legendary draft riots as well as an attempt by supporters of the Confederacy to burn down the city. Many of these events were reflected in song.

Dances for piano alone, based upon every topic from the name of a town to the bloomer craze, were sought after by the eager public as well as songs of nostalgia and sentimental subjects. Gathering around the piano and playing and singing was a favorite family pastime. These passions were fueled by the increasing availability of instruments as well as by the development of a larger number of music publishing firms.

Instruments of all sorts were not only becoming increasingly available in the city, but they were being made there, as well. By 1869, the Steinway company was leading the U.S. in the piano industry, outdistancing the well-respected name of Chickering. The presence of a piano in the home was becoming more commonplace, resulting in a profitable boom in this sector. Piano firms were also building their own concert halls as well as acting as concert sponsors. Steinway built its own 2500-seat hall in 1866, and it served as a good location for Philharmonic concerts as well as for individual recitals. Chickering moved into new quarters in 1875, complete with a concert hall that opened with none other than Hans von Bulow at the keyboard and Leopold Damrosch with the baton. Other piano manufacturers in the city included Weber, Steck, Hardman, and Sohmer—among a great many others. Some of these were names that would be familiar well into the twentieth century.

A variety of other instruments were also represented in retail circles. There were a number of woodwind makers in business such as A.G. Badger, known for fine flutes. Schreiber provided the city with brass instruments, and Gemunder offered his prize-winning violins.[2]

Music publishing was flourishing, partially due to the demand for parlor repertoire. The firms of Dodworth and Schuberth were already in existence by the 1850s. G. Schirmer and Carl Fischer were established in 1861 and 1872, respectively. Both of these firms, founded by German immigrants, produced a well-respected catalogue of serious music. Fischer specialized in band, orchestral, and choral works, and Schirmer was known for part songs as well as for the publication of many volumes of classic works. These and other publishing companies produced a varied array of published pieces for an eager public.

Wonderful entertainment centers were available to those interested in filling their leisure hours with culture and amusement. The Academy of Music, at 14th Street and Irving Place, made its debut in 1854. Here was a hall where those of taste (not to mention a certain amount of wealth) could enjoy music in style. Four thousand velvet seats and thousands of gaslights ensured that patrons enjoyed each and every performance of Italian opera in luxury and comfort. Not only could one hear opera, but also the symphony and countless other types of performances here.

For those with less disposable income, P.T. Barnum's Museum at Broadway and Ann Street (and, later, on Spring Street) offered a variety of bands, minstrel shows, spectacles, and more popular entertainments—as did establishments along the Bowery. (The charming Bowery b'hoys, out in search of an evening's fun, were a familiar sight on city streets.)

A number of world-renowned pianists performed for the New York public. As a matter of fact, the virtuosos were much in demand. Louis Moreau Gottschalk began a series of concerts in 1853 that were to continue for several years. His official debut was at Niblo's, an event that even ex-President Martin Van Buren attended.[3] As a rule, Gottschalk played many of his own pieces (a popular title being "The Banjo"), often introduced multiple piano numbers into the evening's proceedings, and unabashedly capitalized on the public's taste for hearing works concerning sentimental topics and death. Despite an unusual approach to his concert career and his involvement in many scandals, he did much to elevate performance standards in America. (He evidently also turned down a lucrative offer for a concert tour from P.T. Barnum, much to his later regret, upon the insistence of his father who was thought to dislike the tactics of the impresario/showman.)

Sigismund Thalberg was a frequent performer in New York—giving more than 50 concerts over the course of two seasons. In addition to his own works, he also specialized in performing variations on well-known melodies. (Many pianists in America loved to play Thalberg's compositions, too.) Both Gottschalk and Thalberg, just two of the more well-known names who concertized in New York, were held in extremely high regard by the ladies in their audiences—a fact which certainly did not hurt their success at the box office.

"Potpourri" concerts, featuring different types of performers, were still the custom. For example, several individual soloists would appear on the same program as a featured symphony orchestra. Also, gimmicks were not uncommon in the concert world. "Gift concerts," enticing the ticket buyer with an array of raffle prizes including such rather large items as instruments, were held at Tripler Hall and other establishments. Unusual concert spectacles were well attended, such as the performances of prodigy "infant drummer" William Henry Marsh, who was barely three years old when he achieved fame.[4]

While musical parodies and minstrel shows were consistently popular, a newer form of entertainment was gathering momentum—vaudeville. Although closely related to the popular minstrel shows, this was more of an urban mix of song, dance, and comedy. The songs and the acts were more worldly and glitzy—influenced, perhaps, by the ambience of the concert saloon. This type of entertainment was to become extremely popular for many decades. Tony Pastor received credit for being one of the first to provide the public with this form of show in 1865.

New developments were also taking place on the New York stage. In 1866, *The Black Crook* was presented at Niblo's Garden. Although there were some other examples of American works for the musical theater, this is generally acknowledged as the first real prototype of the American musical, since it incorporated a storyline with songs, action, dance, and even acrobatics that moved the plot along. An extravaganza of epic proportions, it was considered to be a groundbreaking work and enjoyed a phenomenally long run. This show paved the way for a new era in musical theater.

Classical concert calendars included a multitude of offerings from piano to voice to orchestra. Names such as Theodore Thomas were becoming commonplace in concert advertisements. This illustrious conductor led a number of groups from the Brooklyn Philharmonic Society to the New York Philharmonic Society and conducted summer concerts in Central Park. He formed his own impressive orchestra in the 1860s and, during their travels, made an indelible impression not only on the city, but also on the country as a whole well into the 1890s.

The New York Philharmonic began increasing its membership as well as its number of annual concerts. It moved into its new home at the Academy of Music in 1867 and continued to perform the European repertoire for which it was famous. It also served well as a model for orchestras in other cities.

Additional musical societies were springing up around the city. The Liederkranz and Arion societies and the Mendelssohn Glee Club were formed by the expanding German population who made a noticeable impact on musical programming. The Liederkranz had an excellent reputation and established German opera in New York with a production at the Astor Place Opera House. These societies performed a wide selection of German repertoire and elevated serious performance standards over the years. On a more popular note, German citizens originally from the Kleindeutschland section of the city heartily enjoyed their music, particularly as performed by groups at the beer gardens. Eventually, these establishments gravitated to Union Square where they became favorite haunts of bohemian society.

The Oratorio Society, another organization with an enduring tradition, was created by Leopold Damrosch in 1873. It was noted for its fine selection of works from Bach to Palestrina as well as for the topnotch quality of its performances. The Society performed *The Messiah* on an annual basis—a tradition that lingers in contemporary New York.

Culture and money were becoming increasingly inter-twined in a complex association. As Boss Tweed and the Tammany Hall crew went to work bilking the city coffers by increasingly outrageous practices, financiers such as Jim Fisk, Jay Gould, and Cornelius Vanderbilt amassed fortunes in schemes that were often ethically questionable. However, a semblance of respectability could often be acquired through cultural philanthropy, and some of these individuals occasionally bankrolled artistic enterprises with the thought of softening their previous reputations. This produced a number of intriguing results as the century progressed into its final, and probably most thrilling, quarter.

From Innocence to Gilt

(1870s Through the Turn of the Century)

The city's population had already reached a million by the 1870s, and progress was in the air. The war was over, and an optimistic future was in sight. The face of daily life was being dramatically altered by such astounding inventions as the first phone exchange (1879) and Edison's downtown electricity plant (1882). Additional wonders quickly followed.

Immigration was reaching a new high, and diverse cultures continued to bring a spark to the artistic scene. Castle Clinton was abandoned as a processing site in 1892 and relocated to Ellis Island in order to handle the growing influx of people. Geographic expansion was required to accommodate the swelling population, their dwellings, and even their places of entertainment.

The move uptown continued. The original downtown district became increasingly relegated to financial activities. This expansion resulted in many changes—more sophisticated transportation systems such as elevated trains, a greater profusion of architectural wonders, and a marked rise in new spaces for concerts and other cultural pursuits, to name just a few.

Many sites that would eventually become beloved landmarks were appearing on the horizon. Of course, songs were written about them, and stirring music was often a part of their commemorative festivities. The Brooklyn Bridge was completed in 1883, linking the sister cities together and promoting further growth of the metropolitan area. "Strolling on the Brooklyn Bridge," by Joseph P. Skelly and George Cooper, was written in its honor.[1] The Statue of Liberty, an important symbol of the age, was dedicated on October 28, 1886 with a stirring band rendition of "My Country 'Tis of Thee" performed during the festivities. Lady Liberty also inspired a number of songs and sheet music covers. Through the courtesy of ethnic organizations, landmark statues were turning up in park locations in honor of composers—Beethoven in

Central Park (1884) and Mozart in Prospect Park (1897). These were unveiled at festive celebrations that included much musical fanfare.

Other famous sites were built around this time—St. Patrick's Cathedral (completed in 1879) and the Cathedral of St. John the Divine (begun in 1892). The latter became especially known for its music and its special concerts. The Washington Square Arch (1895), Grant's Tomb (1897), the Flatiron Building (1902), and the Dakota Apartments (completed in 1884 and home to a number of famed musicians over the years) were added to the growing list.

Fine hotels and restaurants offered many choices to patrons with a variety of tastes both in cuisine and atmosphere. The original Waldorf-Astoria was built at 34th Street and Fifth Avenue and constituted a fine example of the gilded age. Delmonico's and Sherry's restaurants catered to such spectacular clientele as Diamond Jim Brady and Lillian Russell. Other popular establishments that were constantly in the news during this era included Rector's, Shanley's, and Bustanoby's.

There were headlines galore and, of course, the newspapers were always there to cover them. Prestigious structures to house these operations quickly dotted the horizon, including the famous *World* Building built in 1890 for Joseph Pulitzer. With this expanded journalistic enterprise, criticism and editorials on the arts—especially music—began appearing more frequently. H.E. Krehbiel began his commentary in the *Tribune* in 1880, along with Henry Finck in the *Evening Post* the following year. Later illustrious names in musical criticism included James Huneker of the *Sun* and the *Times*. The public looked forward to reading these columns as well as those published in a number of musical periodicals available in New York. The *New York Journal*, the *New York Tribune*, and others also began publishing songs as a part of their Sunday Supplement section—evidence of yet another partnership between music and journalism.

The presence of virtuoso pianists in New York did not go unnoticed in the commentaries, and the public greeted these figures with enthusiasm and curiosity. In the 1870s, artists such as Anton Rubinstein introduced the more modern concept of the solo piano recital, making a lasting impact on concert programming. Prior to this, instrumentalists often appeared as part of mixed programs. Hans von Bulow returned to perform in a number of tours, and Rafael Joseffy debuted in New York in 1879 at the ever-popular Chickering Hall, staying on in the city to concertize and teach. The famed Ignace Paderewski debuted in 1891, and the list of other noted personalities who appeared during this time could go on indefinitely.

Parallel with these developments on the concert stage was the rise in number of local piano manufacturers. Not only Steinway, but Chickering, Knabe, Weber, and others sponsored world-renowned artists, vied for first place in the public's affections, and tried to stay on top in the constant game of sales. Parlor music was being produced in greater profusion, and households-in-the-know needed pianos upon which to play this repertoire. "Giveaway" music, sporting piano company ads, was a catchy gimmick used by many firms to keep their brand name in mind. An increased appetite for other solo keyboard works, including dances, marches, variations, arrangements of opera selections, and miscellaneous transcriptions, kept both publishers and piano manufacturers happy. The public's interest was piqued by the increased vari-

Chickering Hall was not only the site of famous concerts, but also the address for many musical enterprises. *Biggs Photography*

Pianos were a must in every household. New York had a large number of firms with a ready supply. *Biggs Photography*

ety of musical offerings on the stage, the easier availability of instruments and, often, the newspaper commentary of the time. Music was continually woven into the fabric of daily life in every social circle.

The New York Philharmonic was still providing a good example for orchestras around the country. This group performed at varied locations in the city and flourished under the guidance of Theodore Thomas and Anton Seidl. Its rivalry with Walter Damrosch's New York Symphony Society continued, much to the interest of musical audiences who, as a result, had an even greater array of concerts from which to choose.

Schools and special programs began developing to meet the need for musical education of both children and the general public. The New York College of Music, ultimately absorbed by New York University, was one of the first schools to provide such formal training. Also, Jeannette Thurber, an enthusiastic patron of the arts, sponsored innumerable programs for children and opened a conservatory of music. She was also responsible for the series of lectures on music at Chickering Hall in 1882, delivered by noted music historian/author Henry T. Finck. Mrs. Thurber formed an opera company that was linked with both the Academy of Music and the new Metropolitan Opera, and she was a key force behind Theodore Thomas' 1883 concerts given for young people at Steinway Hall. (This series was created to assist children in the "formation of a correct musical taste."[2]) She was best known, though, for her National Conservatory of Music on East 17th Street whose most famous days were between 1892 and 1895 when Antonin Dvorak served as general director there. It was during this tenure that he composed his famous *New World* Symphony. Harry T. Burleigh and Will Marion Cook were once pupils at this school, and the roster of professors included Rafael Joseffy and Victor Herbert, among others.

Emilie Wagner founded the Third Street Settlement in 1894 with such directors over the years as David Mannes and Julius Rudel. Numerous artists received training here. The Henry Street Settlement also opened its doors around the same time. These organizations were able to reach out to the neighborhood in a personal way, providing social services, education, and artistic performances that enriched the lives of the entire community.

In 1896, Columbia University received one of a number of endowments to create a musical studies program and instituted its first professorship of music there. Edward MacDowell filled this new post, heading the list of a number of distinguished musicians who were to join the faculty in years to come.

The public school system saw an increasing amount of musical instruction from the 1850s onward, largely due to the efforts of George Frederick Bristow and his colleagues. Early on, public musical education consisted mainly of instruction from unpaid volunteers. Bristow systematically lobbied for, instituted, and developed programs and materials over the years to build an organized system. His efforts included the co-authorship of a vocal music book, the production of a series of student concerts at Steinway Hall, the promotion of musical directors' positions in the system, and the consistent introduction of fine music to the children under his tutelage. He showed a lifelong love of his profession and, fittingly, died in the classroom at the age of 72.[3]

Musical associations also continued to be formed. The Manuscript Society began in 1889 to sponsor the works of local composers. The American Guild of Organists was created in 1896 and is still headquartered in New York, providing education, resources, jobs, and materials to organists throughout the country. These and numerous additional groups were organized during this culturally fertile era.

In the meantime, the elite set was coming into its own in grand style. The "400" crowd, including such names as Astor and Vanderbilt, gave fancy dress balls, built lavish mansions, and collected and donated valuable works of art. Of course, for this latter activity, the city needed a really first-rate museum—hence, the creation of the Metropolitan Museum of Art. After its founding in 1872, it was housed at several temporary locations before moving to its present home in 1880. The building was enlarged over time, as was its cache of holdings. Financier J.P. Morgan donated innumerable works, setting the precedent for gifts from other wealthy individuals. A large musical collection, composed of lavish and unusual exotic instruments from the holdings of Mary Crosby Brown, was established around this time, as well. Eventually, the museum sponsored concerts for members as well as the general public and, through its collections and performances, would be closely associated with musical life and research. The Metropolitan's neighbor across the park, the American Museum of Natural History, was dedicated in 1877, providing the city with yet another rich cultural landmark and one that also eventually amassed a collection of native musical instruments from around the world.

Through the efforts of New York's elite, a number of other cultural institutions were formed. During the 1890s, the New York Public Library was organized through donations of the libraries of John Jacob Astor and James Lenox as well as the $5 million contribution of politician Samuel J. Tilden. This paved the way for the building of its main edifice in 1911. Throughout the years, the library acquired musical manuscripts, artifacts, collections, and related resources to assist performers and scholars in various research endeavors.

Members of New York's wealthier classes interacted closely with prominent musical figures for the benefit of each other and the city. The Damrosch family was well regarded. The father of this illustrious group, Leopold, served as conductor of the Philharmonic Society, the Arion singing society, and the Oratorio Society as well as the 1881 mega music festival in New York. He was also founder of the New York Symphony. His son, Frank, organized The People's Choral Union in 1892, enabling working-class inhabitants of the lower East Side to indulge in enjoyable singing activities, and formed the Musical Art Society (1894), specializing in the performance of a cappella repertoire. These groups, as well as a large number of other singing societies, were quite popular and added generously to the regular cultural life of the city. Frank was also a founder of the Institute of Musical Art in 1905, which later evolved into the Juilliard School of Music.

Leopold's other son, Walter, was another intriguing musical personality, stepping in as conductor of various organizations after his father's death. Walter, too, was particularly remembered for forging a link with the illustrious Andrew Carnegie to solicit the funds required for the creation of Carnegie Hall. Walter Damrosch was destined to be a busy man throughout his career both in the performance and in the politics of music.

With the beautiful new Metropolitan Museum in place as a temple of fine art, the city found itself in need of a similar edifice for music. Both Chickering and Steinway halls obviously had their limitations in terms of size. Although these buildings were appropriate for more intimate recitals, a suitable space for symphony orchestras and other large groups and produc-

Walter Damrosch, conductor of both the Symphony Society of New York and the Oratorio Society, was instrumental in gaining the support of Andrew Carnegie for the creation of Carnegie Hall. *Biggs Photography*

tions was required. Through the persuasion of Walter Damrosch, Andrew Carnegie eventually came up with the requisite $2 million to construct the building in what was considered to be on the outskirts of town at Seventh Avenue and 57th Street. (This coup was not finalized without some strong urging from Mrs. Carnegie.) The architect, William B. Tuthill, was an excellent choice for the project, being a tenor, cellist, and secretary of the Oratorio Society in addition to his chosen profession. The resulting building and acoustics were peerless. In a fitting move, Damrosch was chosen as director.

Carnegie Hall, originally called the Music Hall, opened in May 1891 with a gala concert and a performance by the New York Symphony Society. Tchaikovsky conducted at this event, as did Walter Damrosch. After this auspicious beginning, the hall went on to host many notables throughout the years. Paderewski came to the United States under the auspices of Steinway and debuted in Carnegie Hall on November 17, 1891. Although the audience was modest for this first concert, word eventually spread about this performer whose fame was quickly assured. Steinway booked a tour, and the rest was history. Thousands of other international soloists, orchestras, chamber groups, and special performing ensembles have appeared on Carnegie Hall's magical stage ever since. Needless to say, it is now synonymous with musical excellence.

Around the time that Walter Damrosch was busy trying out his powers of persuasion on Andrew Carnegie, one of the most interesting musical conflicts of the era was closing its final chapters. Here was a plot that involved culture, money, power, and class distinction and is often referred to as the "opera wars." It epitomized the extreme class consciousness of the day as well as the impact of money on art and the city in this gilded age.

The first scene of battle took place at the Academy of Music on 14th Street, the preeminent opera house in the city, patronized by the wealthy aristocracy of the day. The Academy had been the cultural haven of the old-line rich, or Knickerbocker gentry, whose ancestry (not to mention vast financial resources) could be traced back to Revolutionary times. These patrons, such as August Belmont, consistently enjoyed their opera performances from one of the 18 choice box seats. This wonderful house, managed during the 1870s by J.H. Mapleson, was the site where many internationally known singers were introduced to New York.

PROGRAMME
—— OF THE ——

MUSIC FESTIVAL

In celebration of the opening of the new

MUSIC HALL,

Cor. 57th St. & 7th Ave.,   NEW YORK.

Founded by ANDREW CARNEGIE.

MAY 5th, 6th, 7th, 8th and 9th, 1891.

The Symphony Society Orchestra,
The Oratorio Society Chorus

AND THE FOLLOWING ARTISTS :

P. TSCHAIKOWSKY, the eminent Russian composer, who will conduct several of his own works.
Frau ANTONIA MIELKE, Soprano,
Mlle. CLEMENTINE DE VERE, Soprano,
Mrs. Th. J. TOEDT, Soprano,
Miss ANNA LUELLA KELLY, Soprano,
Mrs. KOERT KRONOLD, Soprano,
Frau MARIE RITTER-GOETZE, Contralto,
Mrs. CARL ALVES, Contralto,
Mrs. CLAPPER-MORRIS, Contralto,
Signor ITALO CAMPANINI, Tenor,
Herr ANDREAS DIPPEL, Tenor,
Herr THEODOR REICHMANN, Baritone,
Herr EMIL FISCHER, Bass,
Herr CONRAD BEHRENS, Bass.
Mr. ERICSON BUSHNELL, Bass,
Frl. ADELE AUS DER OHE, Pianist.

WALTER DAMROSCH,   -   -   CONDUCTOR.

TUESDAY EVENING, MAY 5th, 1891.
OVERTURE, "LEONORE" No. III............................BEETHOVEN
ORATION AND DEDICATION.
RT. REV. HENRY C. POTTER, D. D.
FESTIVAL MARCH...TSCHAIKOWSKY
Conducted by the Composer.
TE DEUM...BERLIOZ
(First time in New York.) For Tenor Solo, Triple Chorus and Orchestra.
Soloist—SIGNOR ITALO CAMPANINI.

WEDNESDAY EVENING, MAY 6th, 1891.
"ELIJAH," Oratorio for Soli, Chorus and Orchestra........MENDELSSOHN
Soloists, { Frau ANTONIA MIELKE, Frau MARIE RITTER GOETZE,
{ Herr ANDREAS DIPPEL, Herr EMIL FISCHER.

THURSDAY AFTERNOON, MAY 7th, 1891.
OVERTURE to "FIGARO"......................................MOZART
GRAND FINALE, Act II, "FIGARO,".........................MOZART
Frau MIELKE, Frau GOETZE, Herr DIPPEL, Herr REICHMANN, Herr FISCHER.
SUITE No. III, for Orchestra...........................TSCHAIKOWSKY
Conducted by the Composer.
ARIA FROM "LE ROI DE LAHORE,"..........................MASSENET
Herr THEODOR REICHMANN.
PRELUDE AND FINALE FROM "TRISTAN AND ISOLDE,".......WAGNER

FRIDAY EVENING, MAY 8th, 1891.
THE SEVEN WORDS OF OUR SAVIOUR............HEINRICH SCHUETZ
(Seventeenth century.) (First time in America.)
For Soli, Chorus, String Orchestra and Organ.
Soloists { Frau ANTONIA MIELKE, Frau MARIE RITTER-GOETZE,
{ Herr ANDREAS DIPPEL, Herr THEODOR REICHMANN,
Mr. ERICSON BUSHNELL
TWO A CAPELLA CHORUSES: }
a. PATER NOSTER }(New. First time in America.) TSCHAIKOWSKY
b. LEGEND. }
Conducted by the Composer.
SULAMITH...LEOPOLD DAMROSCH
For Soli, Chorus and Orchestra.
Soloists, Frau ANTONIA MIELKE, Herr ANDREAS DIPPEL.

SATURDAY AFTERNOON, MAY 9th, 1891.
FIFTH SYMPHONY, C MINOR...................................BEETHOVEN
DUET...
Miss CLEMENTINE DE VERE,   Frau MARIE RITTER GOETZE,
CONCERTO for Piano with Orchestra.....................TSCHAIKOWSKY
Piano, Miss ADELE AUS DER OHE.
Conducted by the Composer.
PRELUDE,
FLOWER MAIDEN SCENE, Act II. } FROM PARSIFAL..........WAGNER
For Six Solo Voices and Female Chorus.

SATURDAY EVENING, MAY 9th, 1891.
"ISRAEL IN EGYPT" Oratorio.................................HANDEL
For Soli, Double Chorus and Orchestra.
Soloists :
Miss CLEMENTINE DE VERE,   Frau MARIE RITTER GOETZE,
Herr ANDREAS DIPPEL, Herr EMIL FISCHER, Mr. ERICSON BUSHNELL

For scale of prices and other details see page 5.

The opening of Carnegie Hall in May 1891 featured this gala series of concerts. *Courtesy of Carnegie Hall Archives*

The new millionaires, however, were relegated to the orchestra seats below, unable to infiltrate the prestigious loge or box section. Their "tainted" money, certainly not inconsiderable in quantity, was only acquired in Civil War times and thereafter. The Knickerbockers considered these newcomers to be social, and probably cultural, inferiors. Nevertheless, the new rich continued to aspire to the advantageous box seating and to all that it represented. Their attempts at breaking in, however, were consistently unsuccessful. William Henry Vanderbilt could not even buy his way into the loge seating at the Academy. Evidently, his exorbitant bid of $30,000 for an 1880-81 season box seat was rejected.[4] It was obvious that seating was a sacred matter. As one commentator was later to humorously remark: "A man's. . . opera-box is . . . his castle."[5]

In retaliation for the seeming injustice and snobbery of this system, Vanderbilt and friends, including the notorious Jay Gould, joined forces to build the Metropolitan Opera House at a site on Broadway between 39th and 40th Streets—nearer than the Academy to the Fifth Avenue residences of the fashionable set. Naturally, it was bigger, better, and more ostentatious—termed the "new yellow brewery on Broadway" by rival manager Mapleson because of its size and the unusual shade of its exterior.

The social forces at work would not allow two fine opera houses to peacefully co-exist and offer the public a choice of diverse performances. Too much power was at stake. Backers on each side wanted their house to be number one, and the public followed new developments with interest. The managers of the two houses, Mapleson at the Academy and Henry E. Abbey at the Metropolitan, were being forced into a position of open rivalry, and a contemporary news account prophesied that this rivalry would eventually be a "war of extermination."[6]

Both the Met and the Academy scheduled their openings for the same evening: October 22, 1883. Excitement was running high. The Met presented Gounod's *Faust*, and the Academy offered Bellini's *La Sonnambula*. The contest was on. One woman was reported to have attended half of each performance, caught between curiosity about the new house and adherence to the tradition of the old.

However, the splendor of the day, from the lavishness of its decor to the sheer number of its star-studded crowd of society-conscious millionaires, went to the Met. This, of course, was the turning point in the opera house war.

Mapleson eventually conceded, saying: "I cannot fight Wall Street." The Academy died several years later without much fanfare, and a new breed of power symbolically came into being on the social and cultural front—not to mention an opera house and company that would long remain cultural icons on both national and international levels.

However, money and power were not at play on such a grand scale at the other end of the economic world. As always, the elite existed in sharp contrast to its poor counterparts—so aptly depicted in Jacob Riis' 1888 work, *How the Other Half Lives*. Tenement life was certainly thriving, if one could call it that. Ethnic and social neighborhoods were becoming delineated—including the Irish in Hell's Kitchen, Little Italy near the old Five Points, and Bleecker Street with its colorful band of bohemians. Yet these tenement enclaves produced their own rich source of people, places, and styles that would contribute enormously to the musical life of New York. Famous personalities were being born in urban ghettos, many on the lower East Side. These individuals would soon be recognized for their talents after the turn of the century. Their numbers included Irving Berlin, George Gershwin, Richard Tucker, Jan Peerce, Eddie Cantor, and Fanny Brice, to name just a few.

These many groups loved their own special forms of entertainment, particularly when it touched a sympathetic chord in their experience, and music often exhibited a definite ethnic slant. Irish sentimental tunes and "coon songs" each took a turn as favorites in the public eye. Yiddish theater flourished, too, and a number of beloved composers and performers within this community greatly popularized songs from scores of productions.

The team of Harrigan & Hart, who performed their appealing variety show in the 1870s at the Theatre Comique, also made quite a name for themselves. Harrigan and musical director David Braham wrote "The Mulligan Guard" as a parody of post-war groups that still paraded around in uniform. The song spawned complete shows about the Mulligan Guard and other such groups. The work was so successful that William Pond published a volume of some of the songs in 1883. Harrigan & Hart portrayed a number of stock ethnic characters, depicting their plights in the new world in a hilarious fashion. Audiences empathized and laughed along with the situations that were so true to the everyday life of the immigrant poor. The team of Weber & Fields, who appeared at their own theater, also achieved fame with similar performances of ethnic parody and musical numbers.

Variety shows such as these foreshadowed many other kinds of developments within the music and entertainment industries on the popular level. As it was, the number of active theaters almost doubled between the years of 1880 and 1900. A variety of exciting establishments could be found around Union Square: Tony Pastor's, the National Theatre, the Dewey Theater, the Alhambra, and Atlantic Gardens, to name a few. Each one proudly advertised its particular specialty. Steinway Hall, for example, was known for its serious concerts, and Bryant's Opera House for its minstrel shows. Among the most famous was Tony Pastor's, purveyor of "polite" vaudeville. Also, Pastor had the honor of introducing Lillian Russell to the public at his theater.

Restaurants clustered in Union Square, too. Luchow's, one of the most popular and enduring, opened in 1882 with some backing from William Steinway. In an attractive locale near Steinway Hall, the Academy of Music, and the activity of the Square, Luchow's served a variety of famous cultural clientele. Steinway and his friends dined there daily, and the restaurant catered many banquets for the musically inclined. This was also the site of the initial meeting that led to the permanent founding of ASCAP—the American Society of Composers, Authors and Publishers—in 1914.

During the 1880s, a new face was also developing in the world of music publishing—one that was to emphasize its own special brand of Americana. Up until then, the public was happy with its instrumental pieces and sentimental songs, purchased from one of the conservative music publishers of the time and quietly played at home. However, a new popular song market was taking shape, and the seeds of Tin Pan Alley were rapidly being sown. Frank Harding assumed control of his family's publishing business in 1879 and started a trend by letting songwriters "hang out" in his offices, thus lending a much more informal air to the proceedings. Soon, the firms of T.B. Harms (1881) and M. Witmark (1885) were created, and they actively began to cater to the many different tastes of the public. The latter firm was a true example of American enterprise. The business was created by three brothers (the oldest of whom was 17), using a child's printing press. They turned out songs about current events and sentiments, with their first published title being "President Cleveland's Wedding March." They also led the string of publishers to the Union Square area by being among the first to open their offices there.

Charles K. Harris formed his enterprising "songs to order" business and opened up shop in New York, gaining fame with the five-million-copy hit "After the Ball" of 1892. Although such sentimental songs were still quite popular, a number of other topics were fodder for hits—places, people, events, and inventions. The choruses of these songs were especially memorable, and the public was soon set to humming them. Formula was at work here, but everyone loved it anyway. Harris even went so far as to write a "how to" book on songwriting. Other contemporary publishers of note were Jerome H. Remick Company and Leo Feist and Company.

Unlike their predecessors, these new publishing firms did not wait for the public to come to them. They went out and created an audience, sending song "pluggers" to entertainment palaces and even into the streets to literally buttonhole an appreciative market. Pluggers would stand up in the middle of a variety show and sing an extra chorus of a publisher's featured song—from a spotlighted seat in the audience, of course. This went a long way toward hooking the public's interest and increasing sheet music sales.

Many of these songwriters were former salesmen (for everything from men's ties to ladies' corsets) and thoroughly knew the art of the sales pitch. Everything and everyone was fair game. Pluggers made sure that when a musical star entered a restaurant for dinner, the orchestra would immediately strike up her latest song—another great advertisement. Department stores including Macy's had music demonstrators in the sheet music department who constantly plugged songs to the public. Music was so closely tied to advertising that it was used more often in promotions for products and as supplements to Sunday papers. Companies loved tunes that could popularize their product (e.g., "Under the Anheuser Bush" and "The Drake's Cake Walk"). New York was the mecca of this fast-paced music industry, and everyone seemed to make a profit.

Sentimental ballads reached the zenith of their popularity in the 1890s—easy to play and sing around the parlor piano.

Many of these ballads told a story ("The Little Lost Child"), and upon the invention of the song slide by a Brooklyn electrician, these sad stories could be viewed upon the screen while the singer filled in the woeful details. This was yet another innovative way that the "Alley" plugged tunes.

New York current events showed up in song and offered many a souvenir for the curious. "I've Just Been Down to the Bank" was written in 1884 about the bankruptcy of Brooklyn's Marine Bank in which even President Grant lost money.[7] This event caused a great deal of scandal which probably did not hurt sheet music sales of this title.

Greater emphasis was now being placed on the covers of the sheet music itself. Pictures of current theatrical stars were quite popular—again offering the message to buy. Also, elaborate artwork was being used more frequently on these covers. E.T. Paull, whose office was in New York, was known for his colorful, unique scenes of history, fantasy, and the like on sheet music covers. Others soon followed in this tradition.

Soon, this lucrative industry was blossoming around Union Square and, by the turn of the century, Tin Pan Alley had moved en masse to 28th Street where it received its name from Monroe Rosenfeld—newspaper reporter, songwriter, and character extraordinaire—upon hearing the maniacal cacophony of sound that spewed from the many publishers' windows up and down the street. By now, the sounds of pianos, singers, and loud debate could be heard far and wide. It was here that million-copy (or several-million-copy) hits were born, including all-time favorites such as "A Bird in a Gilded Cage" and "Let Me Call You Sweetheart."

Independent songwriters and house songwriters continued to turn out popular, catchy tunes and lyrics. Standard sing-alongs such as "Daisy Bell," "The Sidewalks of New York," and "My Wild Irish Rose" all came from this era. The songs were easy to play and sing, were memorable and, most important, were accessible to the public. New firms, including that of Harry von Tilzer, joined the ranks of Tin Pan Alley and were a resounding success.

Tin Pan Alley also helped to usher in the ragtime craze. The bouncy syncopation of this idiom led to its great success. Ragtime grew out of the plantation-type dance known as the cakewalk with its catchy rhythms and banjo sound. Supposedly, New York got its first taste of ragtime when Ben

Harney began performing it in 1896 at Tony Pastor's. Publication began in 1897, and the craze was off and running. Scott Joplin, who opened an office on West 29th Street, wrote his immortal "Maple Leaf Rag," published in 1899. This and other rags became top-selling items, and many such compositions were to follow.

The Broadway musical theater was also coming into its own, and Tin Pan Alley helped to sell songs made popular on this front, too. This was a gold mine for the music business. The 1890s through the turn of the century saw such hit productions as *A Trip to Chinatown* as well as the operetta-type shows of Victor Herbert, Reginald De Koven, and others. Musical revues including *The Passing Shows* and the early *Ziegfeld Follies* were on the stage shortly after 1900, as well as patriotic fare from the pen of George M. Cohan. The songs written for these and many other shows, revues, and extravaganzas were gobbled up by an eager public who were now well attuned to the current favorites, courtesy of the ever-industrious song pluggers.

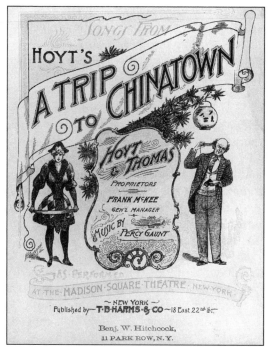

This popular show featured several Tin Pan Alley hits, including "After the Ball" and "The Bowery." *Biggs Photography*

Outdoor musical entertainment was popular. P.T. Barnum's Hippodrome at Madison Avenue and 26th Street became Gilmore's Garden, honoring the famous band master. This site would, ultimately, become the first Madison Square Garden. P.S. Gilmore turned this edifice into a wonderful indoor park, and his band performed approximately 150 concerts there. Also, Central Park and Prospect Park each provided a nice array of band and small ensemble concerts as well as other entertainments in good weather. German street bands were also quite popular during the 1890s and helped to maintain an interest in related repertoire.

Coney Island blossomed as an entertainment mecca during the 1880s. Along with the amusements and the beach were band concerts, minstrel shows, orchestra performances, revues, and other musical entertainments. This was a favorite haunt, too, of the infamous Mose Gumble, song plugger extraordinaire. A number of performers worked at Coney Island in their "pre-fame" days. Eddie Cantor was a singing waiter, and Jimmy Durante was a ragtime pianist there.

Bands directed by Gilmore, Herbert, and others did a brisk business at Manhattan Beach in the summertime for enthusiastic audiences during the 1880s. This and other popular beach locations inspired songs, too, including "On a Sunday Afternoon"—written by Harry von Tilzer after a trip to Brighton Beach (with lyrics by Andrew B. Sterling).[8]

New York moved faster and became larger. Boundaries were to widen once more. During the 1800s, Brooklyn had become a substantial entity in itself. Industry was growing fast in the Bronx and Queens, although Staten Island had managed to maintain its tranquil atmosphere. These uniquely distinct areas merged in 1898, just as the century neared its close, to become the five boroughs of New York City—enlarging the city's geographical boundaries and making it even more diverse in character. Thus, potential musical horizons enlarged, as well. Despite miserable weather, consolidation festivities included outdoor celebrations with performances by vocal and band organizations. An "Ode to Greater New York" was even composed in honor of this historic occasion.

New York—larger, complex and thriving—moved from its golden cultural age into the twentieth century. Now, music was available in some form to those in every walk of life.

From War to War

(World War I Through the 1940s)

On the threshold of the first World War, the city was humming patriotic tunes as well as songs made famous on Broadway. The nation seemed unified through song, and Tin Pan Alley was reaching another peak of commercial success. Music, the Alley, and entertainment in general, along with the business principles that governed them, were becoming noticeably more sophisticated in comparison to previous decades.

The American Society of Composers, Authors and Publishers was formed in 1914 to protect the rights of composers and to ensure them royalties for music performed in public. Victor Herbert and a group including Jay Witmark,

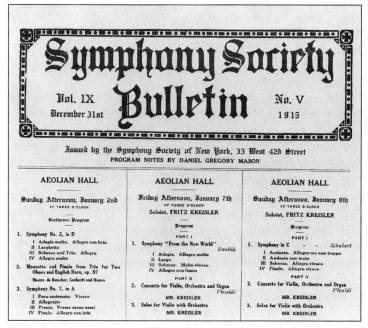

Despite vast changes on the musical scene, well-established groups and soloists still performed regularly on the classical concert calendar.

Biggs Photography

Glenn Macdonough, Gustave Kerker, and others launched this organization at the famous Luchow's restaurant on 14th Street. Within a few short years, ASCAP expanded to include various aspects of the publishing, recording, and performing worlds. Its formation was well timed, offering knowledgeable assistance to creative individuals in an age when technology and other rapid developments could have inadvertently posed a threat to their fair treatment.

Theater was popular, as could be seen by the tremendous number of new playhouses that were being built, and American musical comedy was emerging as a singular art form through the efforts of such individuals as George M. Cohan. The patriotic subject matter of Cohan's songs and shows could not have come at a better time. From "You're a Grand Old Flag" to his smash hit of World War I, "Over There," Cohan raised America's patriotic spirit. A longtime resident of New York, his "Give My Regards to Broadway" was a fitting tribute to the heart of the city.

The war was a turning point for New York, as it was for the entire country. The reality of an international conflict left its brutal impact on society at large. People became increasingly aware of world events and trends. Coupled with this was the increase in technology, causing dramatic influences on the pace and texture of cultural and social life. The innocence of the previous decades was now a memory.

Life moved faster as the "roaring '20s" got underway. Transportation was faster with the widespread use of the automobile as well as the construction of more bridges, tunnels, and subways linking the city to the outer boroughs for quicker commutes into and around town. Fast dancing, already popular with the catchy rhythms of ragtime, got even faster with the introduction of the Charleston in Broadway's *Runnin' Wild* in 1923, as well as the Lindy Hop, the Black Bottom, and others. Popular musical forms were moving faster, with jazz, dixieland, and novelty hits beginning to overshadow the slower sentimental fare of yesteryear. And entertainment moved faster— with speakeasies featuring illegal booze as well as fine entertainment in an attempt to bypass Prohibition restrictions. Flappers sported outrageous new clothes and hairdos, a controversial bohemia formed in Greenwich Village, and a hedonistic spirit dominated. The lights of Times Square and Broadway had never been brighter—both literally and figuratively.

Clubs and entertainment palaces continued to move northward in Manhattan and elsewhere. Harlem provided some unique shows and music for those who traveled to such sites as the Cotton Club and Connie's Inn. Scores of famous performers—from Billie Holiday to Duke Ellington—regularly delighted audiences with their special musical stylings. Jazz and blues sounds were capturing the public's imagination, and these new performers offered the best. Patrons enjoyed the exotic atmosphere and entertainment, and Harlem experienced a cultural renaissance that had a long-lasting impact, with its development of musical styles that would become significantly popular within the mainstream in years to come.

In the meantime, other performers, these and other jazz innovators, were playing to full houses, concert halls, dance halls, and clubs in other parts of town. Bix Beiderbecke, the legendary cornetist, debuted in New York in 1924 at a midtown dance hall and went on to acclaim for his many creative recordings. Fletcher Henderson was at Roseland, and Paul Whiteman headlined at the Palace. These were only a few of the scores of individuals and bands that were gaining in popularity during this time.

George Gershwin led a host of others in changing the face of theater and popular song, incorporating many jazz, blues, and ethnic motifs into his work. A New York native as well as a song plugger, pianist, and house composer, he learned his trade well on Tin Pan Alley, composing innumerable songs, many with lyrics by his brother Ira, for Broadway and, later, for the movies. As a serious composer, experimenting in his own unique style, he created orchestral and solo instrumental works. His famous *Rhapsody in Blue* was premiered at Aeolian Hall on 42nd Street in 1924 with Paul Whiteman's orchestra. The sound and character of this work has long been associated with the city.

Meanwhile, Irving Berlin—another veteran of the lower East Side as well as of Tin Pan Alley—was turning out an astonishing number of tunes for Broadway revues, including the *Ziegfeld Follies* and his own *Music Box Revues*. In a true rags-to-riches tale, Berlin adapted to the changing spirit of the age, becoming more successful by the year. He wrote rags during the ragtime era (e.g., "Alexander's Ragtime Band"), showtunes during the heyday of Broadway, and topical material. "Oh, How I Hate to Get Up in the Morning" served well in both wars and was still a real show-stopper later on during World War II.

Jerome Kern and Cole Porter were also busy enriching the repertoire of Broadway and popular song in general. Kern altered the face of musical theatre with *Showboat* (1927), an American musical opera that closely linked both story and score and, at the same time, dealt with some groundbreaking subject matter. Porter delighted audiences with the sly sophistication of his melodies and lyrics (e.g., "Let's Fall in Love," "Anything Goes") that became popular in the café society that he so dearly loved. Porter, a longtime resident at the Waldorf, also wrote many songs about his adopted city—"I Happen to Like New York" (1930), among others.

Theaters and vaudeville/variety houses had joined the move north and were now centered around the Times Square area. The Palace, at 47th Street and Broadway, opened during World War I and quickly became the leading vaudeville house of its day, featuring such performers as Eddie Cantor, Sophie Tucker, and Al Jolson. It surpassed the formerly popular Victoria Theatre built by Oscar Hammerstein. Meanwhile, the Winter Garden, the Hippodrome, and the Century dotted the theatrical landscape. The twenties also saw scores of wonderful musical revues, offering even more variety on the entertainment scene. The public still loved the sheet music that came from these productions, and publishers were happy to oblige with a continual supply.

Movie palaces including the Strand opened shortly before the war, and the Roxy debuted in the twenties, dazzling patrons with gaudy splendor. Beautiful decorations, a seating capacity of more than two thousand, elaborate pipe organs, and lavish orchestra pits all served to enhance the total impact of the silent flicks that flashed on the screen. These palaces provided attractive work for musicians, too. However, with the advent of talkies in 1929, some of New York's musicians and music publishing businesses traveled west. This event, too, marked a change in the nature of the city's entertainment life. Coincidentally, this was the year of the great stock market crash. Yet there was still music that catered to every taste and financial status, helping to bolster the spirits of New Yorkers, even if just for a few hours.

Big bands caught on in the twenties and maintained a significant presence within the industry over the course of the next several decades in New York. They were directed by such luminaries as Vincent Lopez (a piano-playing Brooklyn native), Guy Lombardo, Cab Calloway, Eddie Duchin, Glenn Miller, and the Dorseys. These groups and others were featured regularly at major hotels around town—the Waldorf, the Pennsylvania, the St. Regis, and the Roosevelt—as well as ballrooms and restaurants. Duchin helped to enliven the reputation of the Central Park Casino, making it one of the city's most sought-after night spots. Recordings of big band hits were eagerly bought by fans from the twenties until well after World War II.

Many smaller groups and combos began playing in a gathering of clubs on West 52nd Street where jazz and, later, swing was featured. This area eventually came to be known as "Swing Street." Fats Waller and Count Basie were among the name performers here, and the thirties saw a rise in popularity of this district that was to last for decades. Places like the Onyx, Jimmy Ryan's and Birdland were to become synonymous with this part of town for many years. A variety of new jazz and swing sounds came from this quarter that would further broaden the scope of modern musical styles.

Swing was particularly successful as performed by the large dance bands. Benny Goodman ("the King of Swing"), Glenn Miller, Woody Herman, and Tommy Dorsey were among those whose bands captured the public's fancy with this catchy style. So many events illustrated its popularity. In 1938, Benny Goodman and Count Basie headlined at Carnegie Hall at a landmark swing concert. The resulting recording is still considered to be a classic. In the same year, the "Carnival of Swing," a WNEW benefit for musician's union local 802, was held at the Randall's Island stadium. Said to be the largest live concert that had taken place in New York during this era, it had 25,000 people in attendance. The bands of Count Basie, Benny Goodman, Duke Ellington, Gene Krupa, and others appeared with such featured performers as Rudy Vallee and Ella Fitzgerald.

Along with records (a real bonanza for the music business) came radio. The public could listen to performers, bands, and hit tunes in the comfort of their homes. NBC aired its first broadcast in 1926, featuring performances by the Oratorio Society, the Goldman Band, and Mary Garden, among others. Many great musical stars were to be heard on the radio over the years—including Eddie Cantor, Al Jolson, and Bing

Crosby. New York was, again, in the forefront of this industry. However, this whole shift in listening customs, coupled with an exodus of publishers and musicians to the West Coast movieland, caused major reverberations in Tin Pan Alley. The joyous sounds that once filled 28th Street were no more. In addition, New York and its music business had become too sophisticated for the antics of song pluggers and their care-free employers from the days of yesteryear. The days of a plugger buttonholing a singer or producer under the street-light of a brownstone were gone. Instead, publishers moved to office buildings in the West 40s, and a number of them began to congregate in the Brill Building—a sort of latter-day Tin Pan Alley. Although some names from the old days remained, a more mature outlook prevailed. This was an organized business enterprise now, and Tin Pan Alley had left its adolescent years behind.

The somber feeling that had taken hold of the Depression-ridden city was made more tolerable under the leadership of Mayor Fiorello La Guardia. A versatile fellow, La Guardia chased fire engines, battled wits with an ever-growing mob presence, and was one of the first to comment that New York needed some type of central performing arts complex—an idea that was debated for a while and abandoned, but not for-gotten. (It later resurfaced when Lincoln Center was dis-cussed—a belated tip-of-the-hat to the perceptive outlook of the charismatic mayor.)

The thirties also saw the addition of many new buildings, an ironic turn of events considering the economic times. The Chrysler Building was constructed in 1930, and the Empire State in 1931—an edifice long associated with the city. (King Kong took over the building in the famous movie of the fol-lowing year.) Later on in the decade, New York was host to the 1939 World's Fair, located in Flushing, Queens. In an attempt to uplift the sagging morale of the city, as well as a world with serious political trouble, the fair emphasized its optimistic theme of the "World of Tomorrow."

Rockefeller Center emerged during the thirties. It was home to the Radio City Music Hall, the world-famous palace of entertainment. The Rainbow Room at Rockefeller Center also became a new nightclub for the rich and offered high-priced entertainment by assorted performers from Bea Lillie to the band of Ray Noble. And the Radio Corporation of America

(RCA) housed the famous NBC Symphony Orchestra that came under the baton of the notorious Arturo Toscanini.

Toscanini was one of the great names in classical music in New York during this time. He was conductor of the New York Philharmonic from 1928 to 1936. From 1937 to 1954 he directed the NBC Symphony, a group that was ostensibly created for him. The symphony was recognized for its many fine recordings over the years, thus making great music easily accessible to the public in their homes. And Toscanini was famous for his unique and somewhat volatile personality, as well, and stories of his acerbic wit and emotional outbursts spread quickly to a public eager with interest and curiosity.

The classical music scene had matured, and many great names not only performed, but also composed and taught in New York in the decades between the wars. The list is endless—Sergei Rachmaninoff, Josef Lhevinne, Bela Bartok, Kirsten Flagstad, Richard Tucker, and more. The New York Philharmonic Orchestra was, of course, a permanent fixture in Carnegie Hall, and John Barbirolli and Artur Rodzinski occupied its podium in the post-Toscanini years. Visiting orchestras also commanded its stage. Carnegie Hall was still *the* place to debut in New York—and in America. However, one could hear many fine concerts anywhere from the Brooklyn Academy of Music, to the newest Steinway Hall, to Lewisohn Stadium. Town Hall, completed in 1921, was also the site of many a famous recital.

Music was increasingly becoming an important part of the advanced educational scene. The Juilliard School of Music officially came into being in 1926 (blending the Institute of Musical Art and the Juilliard Graduate School) with quarters, during this era, on West 122nd Street. This world-renowned institution possessed an impressive faculty and trained thousands of internationally acknowledged musical artists. The Mannes College of Music (once called the David Mannes Music School) opened just around the first World War, and the Neighborhood Music School, ultimately to become Manhattan School of Music, was also growing actively during this same time. The music program at Columbia constantly expanded, and fine music departments in local schools of the City University were being created, such as the one at Queens College (1937). One could receive excellent training in many facets of music within the city's boundaries in these and many other such institutions.

The piano business, which had fallen off during the twenties due to the advent of radio and the new freedom made possible by automobiles, enjoyed a bit of a renaissance during the thirties. It was generally agreed that music was not only a soothing way to forget the troubles of the Depression, but it was also an important outlet for the youth of the nation. The piano firms of New York City did their best to support artistic programs during these troubled times. Steinway, Aeolian, Baldwin, and others sponsored radio programs to everyone's mutual benefit. The programs got aired, and the companies got extensive advertising.

Music was stressed in a number of ways in the public schools as an important activity—despite the Depression or, perhaps, because of it. A huge Music Educators National Conference concert was held in the city in 1936 with thousands of school children participating. Walter Damrosch conducted, and Mayor La Guardia and Eleanor Roosevelt were among the dignitaries in attendance.[1]

The Depression had an additional positive impact on the arts. The Federal Music Project, sponsored by the WPA, was an influential development in New York. This ensured the employment of approximately 2000 musicians in the city in a number of venues including orchestras, bands, and theaters.

Interest in music and in piano manufacturing continued as the country headed for World War II. Piano companies not only helped to maintain good cultural relations with other countries, but also such New York–based firms as Steinway and Kimball contributed their expertise by building various aircraft parts in their factories to support the war effort.[2]

By the time that World War II became a reality, New York was bursting with live music that was successful enough to fill clubs and restaurants, sell records and sheet music, ensure hit radio shows, and keep the public humming again—even in the face of new adversity.

Modern Times

(World War II and Beyond)

The war unified New Yorkers as well as the country. The music of bands and singers entertained troops overseas, soldiers waiting to leave, and those left behind. The songs, the nostalgia, and all that was associated with this time remained—in the recordings, the sheet music, the clubs, and on the radio.

At the war's conclusion, the city surged faster and faster into the modern age. Relieved that the horrors of global conflict were behind and eager to forget their accompanying atrocities and heartache, the nation sought peace, prosperity, and a fresh start. Families fled to the city's suburbs in search of the good life as urban decay became a greater reality. Family life and values were treasured. Change was in the wind and each ensuing decade would see even greater transitions. And music was somehow still a part of it all.

Radio and records were now commonplace, and the new innovation called television was fast charming additional households. Of course, radio stations, record companies, and TV studios were in New York, and these served to make music a big part of local life. People bought records of their favorite singing stars (e.g., Frank Sinatra, Rosemary Clooney) as well as the continually popular big bands. They still loved radio with its many music programs such as *Make Believe Ballroom*. And television kept the public abreast of the top-selling tunes with such shows as *Your Hit Parade* and, later, of new rock innovations with appearances by Elvis Presley and the Beatles on the *Ed Sullivan Show*.

Broadway had just been introduced to the music of Rodgers & Hammerstein with the landmark musical *Oklahoma* (1943), and the theater-going public couldn't have been happier. Leonard Bernstein also entered the picture in theatrical circles shortly thereafter with his music for *Candide* (1956) and *West Side Story* (1957)—the latter reflecting life in the slum neighborhood that would soon make way for Lincoln Center. Bernstein went on to international fame as conductor of the

New York Philharmonic from 1958 to 1969. A charismatic individual who was very visible on the New York scene, Bernstein (a West Side resident) was known for his flamboyant conducting style, his innovative concerts for young people, and his vast compositional output ranging from symphonies and chamber music to Broadway and ballet.

As always, New York could boast of ways and places to appeal to every musical taste—from folk at the Village Vanguard to classical at its new showplace—Lincoln Center for the Performing Arts.

The neighborhood immortalized in *West Side Story* had been razed to make way for Lincoln Center. This was a major event in the musical world that had been anticipated, not without controversy, as a place that would outshine all of its predecessors. The old Met gave way to a new one. Juilliard abandoned its old building uptown for striking modern facilities. The New York City Opera relocated from City Center a short distance away into its spacious theater. And the New York Philharmonic left the beloved landmark Carnegie Hall for its new home. All of the classical arts congregated in one center, and its supporters loved it while others fought the idea strongly.

Carnegie Hall almost lost its battle to survive during this transitional stage within the artistic community. Fortunately, through the efforts of Isaac Stern and others, this remarkable landmark was saved, surviving past the danger into its centennial years. There was room for both old and new after all.

Other changes continued to come even more quickly. The big bands from the hotels and restaurants gave way to rock bands in clubs such as the Peppermint Lounge and, ultimately, to more technologically sophisticated heavy metal–type groups with their mega concerts that were marvels of an advanced electronic age. Folk groups from Village hangouts eventually yielded to cabaret there and experimental musical fare in SoHo. Night clubs and jazz clubs still existed but moved to a geographically extended community, forming and re-forming into many different stylistic segments. As the city's and the nation's culture saw changes—from the free love and drug movement of the sixties, to the Vietnam protests of the seventies, to the AIDS horrors of the eighties—the city's artistic community reflected them all.

New concert halls sprang up—many in renovated locations—proving that there was a place for Lincoln Center as well as many smaller venues. From Symphony Space on the upper West Side to Flushing's Town Hall, innovative concert spaces took shape and remained. Many offered stages for new composers and performers from local neighborhoods—as well as a greater variety of choices for audiences.

Now, a variety of institutions have actively initiated concert series of a professional caliber in order to enhance their contributions to the arts. Colleges sponsor musical events in their concert spaces with name performers often on the bill. Just about every branch of the City University, NYU, Columbia, and other schools offer excellent series. Large churches, museums, and historical societies also present performances for a broad audience and cater to every musical taste imaginable.

Outdoor concerts are still popular as they were in older times. Now, the Metropolitan Opera performs before huge crowds in Central Park and in other lovely settings in borough locations. Little parks also offer something for a summer audience, such as band concerts at Damrosch Park in Lincoln Center and Forest Park in Queens that are reminiscent of bygone days. Plazas and atriums of corporate office buildings are also the frequent settings of great music. Rap, ethnic, classical, and novelty music can be heard on the streets and in the subways.

Carnegie Hall and Town Hall are in full use and are, thankfully, protected as landmarks. They do much to remind us of the city's musical heritage and continue its rich tradition of performance. Juilliard, Mannes, and Manhattan School of Music have grown from their modest beginnings into large, internationally known institutions. Well-established settlement houses are still quite active in the arts, as are many outstanding private local music schools.

Historic groups such as the Oratorio Society and the New York Philharmonic are still playing to appreciative audiences. Their founders would be proud. New singing societies, orchestras, and chamber groups are thriving all over the five boroughs, enhancing both performing and listening opportunities. Jazz, pop, cabaret, and experimental music are all alive and well throughout the city. New York's support of the arts has never seemed to diminish. Despite hard times and controversy, there has always been and still is music to suit everyone.

Much time has passed since the Dutch sang at their holiday fests and since Pachelbel performed at Robert Todd's house in

1736. The pleasure gardens and immense downtown theaters are gone. All that is left of the old life on Union Square or in Tin Pan Alley is the facade of a landmark building or two. However, despite vast changes, there are still many echoes of this distant past. Traditional performing groups remain; historic concerts are recreated; and new and fresh musical ideas are tested. Simply put, the city loves and supports its music, as it always has.

From its colonial beginnings to its highly sophisticated present, musical New York has always been a treasure trove of exciting discoveries.

CHAPTER NOTES

Chapter One: Colonial Times

[1] Edward Robb Ellis, *The Epic of New York City* (New York: Old Town Books, 1966), p. 47.

[2] Ellis, p. 122.

[3] Esther Singleton, *Social New York Under the Georges, 1714-1776* (New York: D. Appleton, 1902), p. 288.

[4] *The New Grove Dictionary of Music*, edited by H. Wiley Hitchcock and Stanley Sadie (New York: Grove's Dictionaries of Music, 1986), vol. 4, p. 417.

Chapter Two: Revolution and Independence

[1] Vera Brodsky Lawrence, *Music for Patriots, Politicians, and Presidents: Harmonies and Discords of the First Hundred Years* (New York: Macmillan, 1975), p. 40.

[2] Susan Elizabeth Lyman, "The Search for the Missing King" (clippings files under "New York City Monuments," Library of the Municipal Reference and Research Center, The City of New York Department of Records and Information Services).

[3] Michael and Ariane Batterberry, *On the Town in New York: From 1776 to the Present* (New York: Charles Scribner's Sons, 1973), p. 4.

[4] O.G. Sonneck, *Early Concert-Life in America (1731-1800)* (Leipzig: Breitkopf & Hartel, 1907), p. 182.

Chapter Three: The New Nation

[1] Frank Monaghan and Marvin Lowenthal, *This Was New York: The Nation's Capital in 1789* (Garden City, NY: Doubleday, Doran, 1943), p. 130.

[2] George G. Raddin, Jr., "The Music of New York City, 1797-1801," *The New-York Historical Society Quarterly*, Vol. 38, No. 4 (October 1954), pp. 478-479.

[3] Monaghan, p. 130.

[4] O.G. Sonneck, *Early Concert-Life in America (1731-1800)* (Leipzig: Breitkopf & Hartel, 1907), p. 186.

[5] Oliver E. Allen, *New York, New York: A History of the World's Most Exhilarating and Challenging City* (New York: Atheneum, 1990), p. 84.

[6] Arthur Loesser, *Men, Women and Pianos: A Social History* (New York: Dover, 1990), p. 444.

[7] Raddin, pp. 480-481.

[8] Loesser, p. 452.

[9] Irving Lowens, *Music and Musicians in Early America* (New York: W.W. Norton, 1964), p. 198.

Chapter Four: A New Metropolis (1800–1825)

[1] Vera Brodsky Lawrence, *Music for Patriots, Politicians, and Presidents: Harmonies and Discords of the First Hundred Years* (New York: Macmillan, 1975), p. 179.

[2] Edward Robb Ellis, *The Epic of New York City* (New York: Old Town Books, 1966), p. 199.

[3] Christine Ammer, *Unsung: A History of Women in American Music* (Westport, CT: Greenwood Press, 1980), p. 9.

[4] Charles Hamm, *Yesterdays: Popular Song in America* (New York: Dover, 1990), p. 32.

[5] Lawrence, p. 198.

[6] Lawrence, p. 234.

Chapter Five: A Diverse Musical Gateway (1825–1850)

[1] Michael and Ariane Batterberry, *On the Town in New York: From 1776 to the Present* (New York: Charles Scribner's Sons, 1973), p. 62.

[2] *The New Grove Dictionary of Music*, edited by H. Wiley Hitchcock and Stanley Sadie (New York: Grove's Dictionaries of Music, 1986), vol. 4, p. 369.

[3] Arthur Loesser, *Men, Women and Pianos: A Social History* (New York: Dover, 1990), p. 476.

[4] Loesser, p. 474.

[5] Vera Brodsky Lawrence, *Strong on Music: The New York Music Scene in the Days of George Templeton Strong, 1836-1875. Volume I: Resonances, 1836-1850* (New York: Oxford University Press, 1988), pp. 374–375.

Chapter Six: A Time of Transition (1850–1875)

[1] *The New Grove Dictionary of Music*, edited by H. Wiley Hitchcock and Stanley Sadie (New York: Grove's Dictionaries of Music,1986), vol. 4, p. 358.

[2] *The New Grove Dictionary of Music*, p. 368.

[3] Arthur Loesser, *Men, Women and Pianos: A Social History* (New York: Dover, 1990), p. 498.

[4] Vera Brodsky Lawrence, *Strong on Music: The New York Music Scene in the Days of George Templeton Strong, 1836-1875. Volume II: Reverberations, 1850-1856* (Chicago: University of Chicago Press, 1995), p. 194.

Chapter Seven: From Innocence to Gilt (1870s Through the Turn of the Century)

[1] David Ewen, *All the Years of American Popular Music* (Englewood Cliffs, NJ: Prentice Hall, 1977), p. 93.

[2] "Concerts for Young People," *The New York Times* (December 23, 1883), p. 6.

[3] Thurston Dox, "George Frederick Bristow and the New York Public Schools," *American Music*, Vol. 9, No. 4 (Winter 1991), pp. 339-352.

[4] Edward Robb Ellis, *The Epic of New York City* (New York: Old Town Books, 1966), p. 378.

[5] "Hogs and Opera Boxes," *The New York Times* (November 28, 1883), p. 4.

[6] "The Coming Opera War," *The New York Times* (July 11, 1883), p. 4.

[7] Ewen, p. 113.

[8] Ewen, p. 157.

Chapter Eight: From War to War (World War I Through the 1940s)

[1] Craig H. Roell, *The Piano in America, 1890-1940* (Chapel Hill: The University of North Carolina Press, 1989), p. 247.

[2] Roell, p. 269.

PART TWO

The Sites

Manhattan

■ DOWNTOWN/FINANCIAL DISTRICT

HANOVER SQUARE

Hanover Square (at Pearl Street)

Former site of the New-York Gazette, *a publication of "firsts"—the first city newspaper (1725) and the first to advertise the city's first documented public concert (1736)*

William Bradford was definitely an innovator. He established the first printing press in the city at 81 Pearl Street in 1693. He went on from there to create New York's first newspaper in 1725—the *New-York Gazette.* Its offices were in Hanover Square.

His was also the first paper to advertise Pachelbel's 1736 concert at Robert Todd's house. A major musical event, this was another first, too—the first documented public concert in the city. Bradford had the privilege of a six-day lead over Zenger's *New-York Weekly Journal* in advertising the event. (Zenger, incidentally, served as an apprentice with Bradford before creating the *Journal.*)

The advertisement specified that the concert was for the benefit of Mr. Pachelbel, the harpsichord part being "performed by himself." It went on to say that the other instruments (violins and German flutes) as well as the songs would be performed by "private hands." Four shillings could buy tickets to this illustrious event that took place on Wednesday, January 21, 1736.

The *Gazette* continued to advertise musical events in the years to come.

FRAUNCES TAVERN & MUSEUM
54 Pearl Street (at Broad Street)
212-425-1778

Historic atmosphere reminiscent of Revolutionary times as well as colonial days when the first publicized New York concert was held in 1736 at a neighboring residence

---

Originally built in 1719, this site was the home of the DeLancey family. It was considered to be "next door" to the house of Robert Todd, who lived on Broad Street near the corner of Pearl.

It was at Todd's home on January 21, 1736, that the first documented public concert was held—as advertised in William Bradford's newspaper, the *New-York Gazette*. For the price of four shillings, attendees could hear C.T. Pachelbel at the harpsichord along with violin, flute, and vocal accompaniments by other performers.

Robert Todd, a vintner and dabbler in all things political, social, and artistic, sponsored other such performances in ensuing years. However, his place in New York City musical history was assured by being the host of this first formally advertised concert event.

Although Todd's residence is long gone in the name of progress, the recreation of the DeLancey site, which subsequently became Sam Fraunces' Queens Head Tavern in pre-Revolutionary times (and, later, Fraunces Tavern), still remains. Although most of the original structure of the building was destroyed over the years, the site is charming and atmospheric, providing the visitor with an idea of what life must have been like when the country and its musical activities were new.

It was said that the Sons of Liberty held meetings here. (Who knows? Perhaps this was where they gathered before taunting the British with musical parodies.) Of course, George Washington also bade farewell to his officers at this site.

Now, a fine restaurant and a museum occupy the building—both replete with the echoes of history. One can learn much about early New York from the permanent and changing exhibits on display. Lectures, an occasional event with music, and related programs also offer the visitor much information as well as a sense of what life might have been like in a vanished New York.

Nearby, at the National Museum of the American Indian (One Bowling Green / 212-825-6700), some unique native instruments are part of the permanent exhibits—drums, gourd rattles, and panpipes (*siku*) as well as flutes (*sool*) and violins (*nadah benagolze*) of the White Mountain Apaches. There are also occasional programs with music pertaining to American Indian heritage and culture and an interesting selection of musical recordings at the museum's store.

CASTLE CLINTON
Battery Park
212-344-7220

Site of nineteenth-century pleasure garden with a history of musical events including Jenny Lind's celebrated American debut

Originally called the South-west Battery, this fort was one of several that were created in readiness for a possible invasion. Completed in 1811 and built on a small artificial island, it was connected to Manhattan by a causeway. (Later, it was linked by landfill to become Battery Park.) Since many citizens were worried about an attack by British forces during the War of 1812, this group of forts provided a secure atmosphere for a city that had gone through turbulent, war-torn times during the Revolution. However, no invasion occurred and no shot was ever fired in battle from the fort.

At the close of the war, the site was renamed in honor of DeWitt Clinton and used as a district headquarters for the military. After these headquarters were relocated, Castle Clinton came under the jurisdiction of the city and in 1824 was transformed into a palace of entertainment—or pleasure garden—that would ultimately be known as Castle Garden. Lafayette landed here, also in 1824, before embarking upon his tour of America. Over the years, other notable figures were received and honored at this site, including Andrew Jackson, Henry Clay, and Prince Albert.

Soon, Castle Garden became well known as a "resort" with beautiful gardens and a spectacular fountain. It was the scene of band concerts, fireworks, and various entertaining scientific demonstrations, including balloon launches. Refreshments were served, and one could walk on the promenade above its sandstone walls, which were eight feet thick.

More sophisticated entertainment was presented to the public after the addition of a roof in the 1840s. Concert operas were performed beginning in 1845, including such famous works as *The Barber of Seville*. This was also said to be the site of the first American performance of Beethoven's Ninth Symphony in 1846.

On September 11, 1850, Jenny Lind made her American debut here. A crowd of more than 6,000 witnessed this illustrious event, organized and promoted by P.T. Barnum. Lind, often referred to as the "Swedish Nightingale," presented an eclectic program to the adoring crowd. She opened with Bellini's "Casta Diva" and proceeded to sing European and Scandinavian selections. She closed with an ode to America that was written specially for this memorable occasion. At the conclusion, a "tempest of cheers" was heard throughout.

Shortly thereafter, in 1855, the site was turned into a landing depot for immigrants (prior to the use of Ellis Island). More than seven million immigrants entered through this station before it ceased operations in 1890. Eventually, after a remodeling by the noted firm of McKim, Mead & White, it became the site of the New York Aquarium, which remained until 1941. Afterwards, Castle Clinton was almost lost to the wrecker's ball. However, public outcries, along with the help of Eleanor Roosevelt, saved it from demolition.

Declared a National Monument in 1946 and restored in the 1970s, Castle Clinton currently serves as the point of departure for trips to Ellis Island and the Statue of Liberty. A small pictorial exhibit details its colorful history and, while strolling through the open-air circular structure and the surrounding paths in Battery Park, visitors can almost envision the grandeur of its bygone days as a pleasure garden.

THE MUSEUM OF JEWISH HERITAGE
—A LIVING MEMORIAL TO THE HOLOCAUST
18 First Place—Battery Park City
212-968-1800

A tribute with many facets, including musical ones

There are approximately 2,000 photos, 800 artifacts, and 24 documentary films pertaining to Jewish heritage and culture at this new museum.

The building itself is a six-sided structure, symbolizing the six million who perished in the Holocaust as well as the Star of David. Three floors of exhibits each cover a different time period—from 1880 to 1930, the Holocaust, and post-war decades.

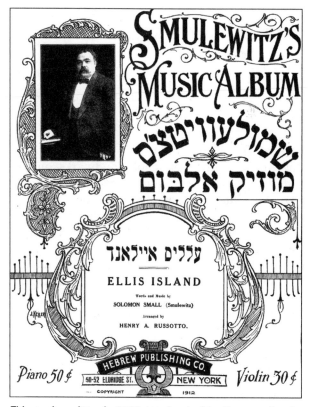

This music, written in 1912, was inspired by the many immigrants who came to this country from Eastern Europe through Ellis Island. It is included in "Jewish Life a Century Ago" at the Museum of Jewish Heritage. *Gift of the Hebrew Publishing Company/Museum of Jewish Heritage*

Musical references abound. One film, entitled "Jewish Culture on the World Stage," contains clips of such famous musician/entertainers as Al Jolson, Paul Simon, Fanny Brice, and Bob Dylan, among others. There are also numerous photographs of those in the musical world. Artifacts include a trumpet played by a man in the inmates' orchestra at Auschwitz. This activity saved his life.

If you decide to stroll further along the esplanade in Battery Park City, you may see some sculpture with musical themes (a modernistic guitar or an animal playing an instrument) in the little parks and children's area that dot this scenic landscape.

TRINITY CHURCH & GRAVEYARD
Broadway at Wall Street
212-602-0800

A rich historical and musical heritage extending from colonial times to the present day

---

This is the third church structure to occupy this site, and it is one of the most readily identifiable landmarks on the downtown landscape. The first church was raised in 1698, and it is said that the infamous Captain Kidd (a onetime New York resident) helped to build it by lending some of his ship's block and tackle equipment during construction.

With the installation of its first magnificent organ in 1741 (by J.G. Klemm), church music became a more important and visible part of city culture. William Tuckey became the first clerk of the church in 1753 and was a leading figure in teaching music. He also acted as a sponsor for concerts and performed in events outside the church. Tuckey established a wonderful singing school for children at Trinity and was a dynamic leader of the regular choir, introducing much new repertoire to both the church and the city at large.

Trinity burned to the ground during the devastating fire of 1776. The subsequent building, completed in 1790, was later declared structurally deficient and was demolished.

When Richard Upjohn's Gothic Revival edifice was completed in 1846, interest in church music was revived as well. A beautiful new organ, built by Henry Erben, was inaugurated at a huge festival attended by 18,000 people, much to the dismay of the music director, Edward Hodges, who preferred a more dignified method of celebration. However, Hodges went on to revitalize the music program at the church, bringing it back to its formerly spectacular level.

Today, the church boasts of a magnificent Aeolian-Skinner organ and a fine choir. Not only can superb music be heard at services, but the choir also gives frequent concerts.

Noonday performances by professional guest artists are also open to the public as part of a regular series. This is especially popular with those who work nearby in the financial district.

Audio tours of the church are available and, together with the small but informative museum located on the premises, visitors can obtain a vast wealth of background on Trinity, its history, and its music.

The attached graveyard, dating from 1681, contains the burial places of many famous New Yorkers. William Bradford, the newspaper entrepreneur who eagerly announced the groundbreaking Pachelbel concert, is among them.

Federal Hall National Memorial (Broad & Wall Streets / 212-825-6888) is the site where Washington took his oath of office. There are interesting exhibits here in addition to a well-established series of fine noonday performances.

WINTER GARDEN
The World Financial Center Complex
West Street (between One World Trade Center and Hudson River)
212-945-0505

Beautiful music, palm trees, and a river view

The addition of the World Financial Center to the downtown scene in 1989 added charm and vitality to the area. The Winter Garden, at the heart of the complex, is a spectacular glass-enclosed, five-story atrium decorated with 90-foot palm trees.

Between the panoramic view of the Hudson River to the west and the sweeping stairs on the eastern wall, visitors may sit awhile at one of the tables dotting the space. Here they can enjoy one of the many vocal, chamber, jazz, folk, ethnic, and popular groups regularly appearing under the arched sweep of the performance space during various times of the day. Seasonal musical treats also add a festive touch. Performance schedules are available at the information center.

> Concerts and musical events are sponsored at a variety of downtown locales, especially during the summer months. Be sure to check out the plazas in front of large office buildings, atriums (180 Maiden Lane, among them), and little parks. Flyers, available at many locations, often list upcoming events. During the winter holiday season, South Street Seaport features performances of a chorus of singers in a "living Christmas tree" arrangement.

■CITY HALL AREA

ST. PAUL'S CHAPEL & CHURCHYARD
Broadway at Fulton Street
212-602-0747

A favorite house of worship for George Washington, this colonial church was also the setting for many distinguished sacred musical presentations

---

This beautiful chapel was built in 1766 and is said to be the oldest church building in Manhattan. It clearly evokes colonial New York both in design and in atmosphere.

The church has a vast history, and some modest exhibits provide visitors with fascinating information and memorabilia pertaining to its rich past. The pew used by George Washington, a frequent worshiper here, can still be seen, as well.

St. Paul's served as the site for a number of musical events over the years, with a particular emphasis on choral performance. The Handel and Haydn Society presented a portion of

The Creation here in 1818. Lafayette enjoyed the efforts of the New York Choral Society in this setting during his famous 1824 visit. Also, in 1831, the Sacred Music Society gave New York's first complete performance of the *Messiah* at St. Paul's.

The church still hosts concerts, the most popular being the noonday series. Fine performers are regularly welcomed by audiences here, particularly by those who work nearby and can frequently attend these events.

> Theater Alley (just off Ann Street, east of Broadway) is the site of the stage door entrance to the Park Theatre (1798-1848). A popular center of cultural activity, it hosted violinist Ole Bull's American debut (1843) and staged a number of operas, including Beethoven's *Fidelio*, Donizetti's *L'elisir d'amore*, and Balfe's *The Bohemian Girl.*

ST. PETER'S ROMAN CATHOLIC CHURCH
22 Barclay Street

An old and beautiful landmark with particular musical notoriety

This is the oldest of the city's Roman Catholic parishes, and it has interesting links to New York's early musical life. Replacing an older and structurally unsafe building at this site dating from 1785, this Greek Revival–style edifice—really an Ionic temple formed of granite—was the work of John R. Haggerty and Thomas Thomas. It was constructed between 1836 and 1840. The original plot of land was purchased from Trinity parish with money donated from French and Spanish foreign legions as well as Cornelius Heeny, a partner of John Jacob Astor.

The church itself was consecrated in 1838 to much musical notoriety. Mozart's "Twelfth Mass" was performed by a chorus and the orchestra of the National Theatre, directed by Ureli Corelli Hill, whose name appears everywhere in the city's musical annals during this time. This event was so anticipated, not to mention well attended, that more than 2000 people were said to have been turned away. Both the pews and the aisles were packed with attendees, including the noted diarist George Templeton Strong, who wrote of the magnetic power of the event. It was later discovered that this frequently performed Mass was not actually the work of Mozart at all. The true composer has yet to be identified.

St. Peter's also featured a massive and quite impressive organ built by Hall & Erben. It cost $6,000—an extraordinary sum for its time.

LIBERTY POLE & COMMEMORATIVE MARKER

City Hall Park (on Broadway side of the Park opposite Park Place)

Here are echoes of political and patriotic sentiments set to music

This was the location of the city Commons during colonial and Revolutionary days. It was here that loyalists and patriots engaged in battles and demonstrations—physical, verbal, and musical—in a passionate outpouring of their differing points of view.

Eight liberty poles have been placed at this site from 1766 to 1953. The first was erected by the Sons of Liberty in honor of freedom from oppression and, ostensibly, celebrated the repeal of the Stamp Act. The crowd sang "God Save the King." This sentiment was short-lived.

Several months later, British soldiers hacked down the pole. The Sons of Liberty replaced it, and the British removed it again. This action was repeated several times until the British occupation of the city. Each time the pole was raised or destroyed, songs were sung—but they were blatantly satiric. The British would sing parodies to the tune of "Yankee Doodle," and the Sons of Liberty would sing parodies of "God Save the King." These songs both inflamed and mobilized patriots and loyalists alike. Honed to near perfection at this site of early conflict, their cutting words, set to familiar accompanying tunes, spread rapidly and symbolized the strong (and antagonistic) sentiments that raged on both sides. Throughout the Revolution, music continued to play an important part in stirring up patriotic feelings, spreading news of battles, and unifying the colonists against the opposition.

In 1921, the Sons of the Revolution, with support from the New-York Historical Society, raised a flagpole—the sixth liberty pole—in honor of the heroic patriots of the Revolution. A tablet was also dedicated near the pole in honor of those who died for liberty. The tablet remains, but the flagpole was subsequently replaced twice due to damage from the weather.

SURROGATE COURT BUILDING FACADE & INTERIOR
31 Chambers Street

Musical reflections and adornments

The figures on this building (erected between 1903 and 1908) represent the eclectic thoughts and pursuits of the New Yorker at the turn of the century. A variety of intellectual, business, historical, natural, and artistic subjects are represented.

On the Centre Street side of the building, in the facade cornice, reside eight female figures personifying different disciplines. Here, Music stands fully equal to such companions as Art and Medicine, among others. The sculptor Philip Martiny (1858-1927) created these figures.

Inside, the main entrance area is almost unparalleled in its grandeur. Again, there is a musical connection. The breathtaking marble stairways and central hall were inspired by the interior of the Paris Opéra.

THE PACE DOWNTOWN THEATER
at Schimmel Center for the Arts
One Pace Plaza (3 Spruce Street)
212-346-1715

An enjoyable musical "find"—tucked away in a busy downtown locale

This theater, seating approximately 650, is part of the Schimmel Center for the Arts. The Center itself was made possible by Michael and Lenore Schimmel, who were strong supporters of Pace University and of the artistic community. Busts of the couple along with a framed tribute are on display in the lower lobby of the Center.

A wide variety of music is available at this theater—orchestra, chamber, and solo concerts as well as opera. There is a nice blend of college, community group, and professional guest performances on the annual calendar. The Highlights in Jazz series is a real favorite, presenting an eclectic array of top jazz musicians here on a regular basis.

■TRIBECA/SOHO

TRIBECA PERFORMING ARTS CENTER
at Borough of Manhattan Community College
199 Chambers Street
212-346-8510

A versatile arts complex serving the downtown community and the city

The campus of this modern community college is the setting for a very popular downtown arts complex. Three theaters fill a variety of needs for different types of performances—both musical and dramatic.

Theater One seats 922 and, with its proscenium stage, is adaptable for larger productions and concerts. Theater Two has a modest seating capacity of 282. There is also a 99-seat "black box" that is used for readings and small showcases.

The Center specializes in multi-cultural performances as well as New York premieres. A recent performance calendar has included works by the school's artist-in-residence, composer/conductor Butch Morris, as well as leading Japanese, Turkish, and American musicians in a series of "conduction" concerts, entitled "Skyscraper"—a special performance of conducted improvisations merging Eastern and Western traditions. Other concerts have included African dance and music, a rhythm and blues group, Chinese cultural celebrations, Broadway/pop lyricists, and 1940s Village-type cabaret. This is just a small sampling of the variety of offerings each season.

The BMCC Downtown Symphony, composed of faculty, students, local residents, and others, also performs here twice a year.

KNITTING FACTORY
74 Leonard Street
212-219-3055

A performance space that has expanded into a multifaceted musical business

Created in 1987, this is a well-known favorite within the downtown musical world and beyond. The club has several performing areas within its confines—the main performance space, the cozy Old Office, and the Alter Knit Theatre.

Performers have ranged from the Ethnic Heritage Ensemble, to Steven Bernstein's Sex Mob, to the Lonesome Organist, and more. Jazz, rock, experimental, and klezmer music have been heard here and there are also poetry readings, video showings, and silent movies with special music.

The club sponsors and produces festivals, operates an agency for touring artists, and has its own recording label. This is truly a center for anything artistic.

There are numerous galleries, clubs, and museums in the Tribeca/SoHo area. Many of them sponsor musical evenings in conjunction with exhibits or special events. Since this scene is constantly changing, part of the fun is discovering an intriguing new performance each time you visit.

The Children's Museum of the Arts (182 Lafayette Street) occasionally presents musical performances for the younger set at its popular galleries.

ROULETTE
228 West Broadway (at White Street)
212-219-8242

A charming loft setting for a wide variety of musical tastes

This 74-seat space opened in 1980 and is a good example of the eclecticism of the downtown musical scene.

Several dozen concerts are presented annually covering a complete musical spectrum, including jazz, rock, experimental, and classical genres.

Occasional concert-receptions are also sponsored.

At one time, minstrel and variety shows were held at theaters in this area that are now long gone. Mechanics Hall (472 Broadway), where the Christy's Minstrels performed for many years, and Buckley's Ethiopian Opera (539 Broadway) were among the many famous houses of the day.

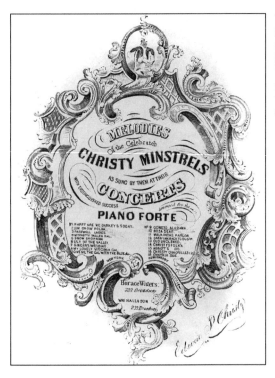

The Christy Minstrels regularly appeared at Mechanics Hall. They were one of many such groups that were popular during this time.
Biggs Photography

■LOWER EAST SIDE AND ENVIRONS

ELDRIDGE STREET SYNAGOGUE
12 Eldridge Street
212-219-0888

A landmark house of worship with musical connections—old and new

---

This lovely synagogue—the first large building constructed by the eastern European population here—was designed in 1887 and once had a thriving membership of several hundred people. It was long known for its beautiful architectural and ornamental detail.

Music has always figured in some way here. In the 1880s, there was a movement on the lower East Side to bring in the best cantors possible in order to attract new members, particularly those of means who could support the congregation, and to justify the maintenance of such a large edifice. This congregation paid $5,000 (an enormous sum for the time) to bring a wonderful cantor, Pinchas Minkowsky, from Odessa, to participate in the synagogue's first season. Opening day also featured music by soloists as well as a vocal quartet.

Eddie Cantor once lived across the street. He not only attended the synagogue, but he also had his Bar Mitzvah here.

When the site was declared a historic landmark in 1996, the synagogue celebrated with music. Performers included a pianist, a klezmer group, student singers, and others. Music ranging from cantorial selections to Gershwin ballads was featured at this event.

Now, under the sponsorship of the Eldridge Street Project, many programs, tours, and presentations are offered to schools and to the general public. Occasional musical events are featured, including cantorial concerts, klezmer events, and klezmer workshops for children.

EDDIE CANTOR HOME
19 Eldridge Street

Onetime home of famous performer

Eddie Cantor (1892-1964) could trace his roots to this lower East Side neighborhood. A world-famous performer, he appeared in the *Ziegfeld Follies* and *Whoopee* on Broadway and also could be seen in films. His energetic presentation made him a memorable character, and he was associated with such song hits as "Yes Sir, That's My Baby," "If You Knew Susie," "Margie," "Ida," and "Makin' Whoopee." Cantor received wide acclaim for his performances in vaudeville and appeared at the Palace Theater.

As time went on, Cantor achieved additional fame through his radio and television shows and was a positive influence in popularizing both songs and performers through these mediums.

While Cantor lived in this tenement building, he took acting and music classes at the nearby Educational Alliance.

IRA GERSHWIN BIRTHPLACE
60 Eldridge Street

The acclaimed lyricist, Pulitzer Prize winner, and partner of brother George Gershwin was born here

This was the birthplace of Ira Gershwin (1896-1983), the talented lyricist, who collaborated with his brother, George, on countless numbers of memorable songs for stage and screen. Some of their shows included *Oh, Kay!, Lady, Be Good,* and *Of Thee I Sing* (for which Ira won a Pulitzer Prize for drama along with fellow collaborators George S. Kaufman and Morrie Ryskind). He also worked with other composers in later years— Jerome Kern, Kurt Weill, and Harold Arlen, to name a few.

Many famous musical figures came from the lower East Side (which, until recently, was defined as including what is now known as the East Village). In addition to the Gershwins, Eddie Cantor, Irving Berlin, and Al Jolson were from this section. All rose to musical and theatrical fame.

EDUCATIONAL ALLIANCE
197 East Broadway
212-780-2300

A famous neighborhood settlement house with music in its history

---

Created in 1889 by Isidor Straus and Benjamin Altman, among others, the Alliance served as a settlement house for the nearby Jewish community.

Classes in language, music, theater, and art were offered to eager neighborhood youth, whose numbers included Eddie Cantor. Years later, Cantor expressed his appreciation for the training he received here.

The Alliance sponsors occasional concerts along with frequent art exhibits, many with multicultural themes.

An interesting "Hall of Fame" also contains photographs of those whose accomplishments were closely connected to this institution.

> The building at the intersection of Eldridge and Rivington Streets was once P.S. 20, the school attended by the Gershwins and lyricist Irving Caesar.

MUSIC FOR HOMEMADE INSTRUMENTS
262 Bowery
212-226-1558

A unique approach to music-making

This intriguing musicians' collective was started in 1975. Members design and construct instruments from wood, cardboard, household utensils, and other materials. Some of their creations include a styrocello, a carimba (cardboard tube marimba), a coba (conduit pipe marimba), a boweryphone, and fork windchimes, among numerous other examples—all recycled from found objects and the like.

Items that were once discarded as trash have been fashioned into creations that are highly respected in the worlds of art and music. These instruments have been displayed at the Lincoln

Center Library as well as at the Smithsonian Institution. The group's work has also been featured in such wide-ranging publications as the *Village Voice* and *The Wall Street Journal*, and their programs have delighted many audiences.

Special music is written for the instruments, in conjunction with the acoustical potential of the materials as well as various sonic patterns. Compositions are also influenced by multi-ethnic musical cultures and traditions as well as by the various sounds of the city. (The city produces many sounds that make a music of their own, and the director of this collective, Skip LaPlante, suggests stopping for a while at various sites to hear them—the pitch of a car driving over the Williamsburg Bridge, or the rush of sound under building overhangs such as at the World Trade Center plaza. They all make their own special music.)

Lecture/demonstrations and workshops are held at schools, where techniques of instrument building, acoustics, and musical principles are presented.

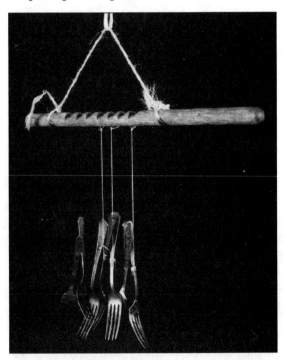

This is a set of fork windchimes, an example of the work created by Skip LaPlante and Music for Homemade Instruments.
Photo by John Berens, courtesy of Skip LaPlante

The group offers performances at special public events, street fairs, and festivals as well as at concerts in the loft where Skip LaPlante maintains more than 250 instruments within the collection.

Different materials make interesting music in many ways! Sonic Architecture (website: http://www.interport.net/~sonarc/ maintext.html) designs interactive artworks for school playgrounds as well as special exhibits at museums and parks in New York and throughout the country. These works illustrate many principles of science, ecology, architecture, and music. Mallets, chimes, and drums are shaped with metals, pipes, glass, and other materials into artistic creations that yield a variety of unique sounds.

THE VILLAGES

■THE EAST VILLAGE

THE AMATO OPERA THEATRE
319 Bowery (at East 2nd Street)
212-228-8200

Fine opera performances in a unique little theater

Created and managed by an enthusiastic couple with a love of fine music, this company has been in existence for more than 50 years. It regularly presents operas from the traditional repertory and offers many young singers a chance to perform and, often, to be discovered.

The house, itself, is unusual—with a stage that is 20 feet wide and an auditorium that only seats 107. Still, the Amato has long been a landmark company within both the neighborhood and the city—admired for its productions as well as for the charm of its setting.

THE MUSIC STORE AT CARL FISCHER
62 Cooper Square
212-777-0900

A firm with a long history whose store will delight musicians and musical enthusiasts alike

---

Musician Carl Fischer immigrated to the United States from Germany in 1872 and established his landmark music firm in New York. He sold instruments and published musical scores and arrangements in response to the active musical life of the city at that time. He was particularly interested in band music, becoming a major publisher of this genre, especially the works of Sousa. He launched a journal, *The Metronome*, for bandmasters in 1885.

Later, under the auspices of his son and son-in-law, the company became active in the publication of school music and championed works by new composers. The firm is still a family enterprise and has a solid history of more than 100 years in business, with offices in several cities in addition to its main headquarters in New York.

Originally located on East 4th Street and, later, on Fourth Avenue, Fischer has been at its present 12-story Cooper Square location since 1923. At the hub of the historic district in the Cooper Union and Astor Place neighborhood, this spacious old store carries a wide variety of music for all instruments and is a browser's delight.

FRONT PARLOR OF THE MERCHANT'S HOUSE MUSEUM
29 East Fourth Street
212-777-1089

A rare musical instrument in a historic setting

This red brick structure was built by Joseph Brewster in 1832 and purchased several years later by Seabury Tredwell, a hardware merchant. Members of the Tredwell family lived in this house for close to a century until Seabury Tredwell's youngest daughter, Gertrude, died in 1933. (Legend suggests that she was the model for Henry James' heroine in *Washington Square*.)

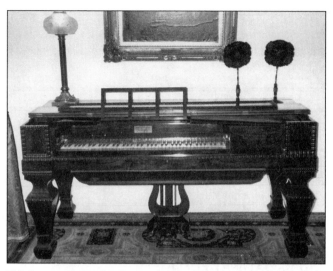

This is a rare example of a Nunns and Fischer piano, manufactured in New York in the 1840s, now in the collection at the Merchant's House Museum. *Courtesy of Merchant's House Museum, New York*

This site, listed in the National Register of Historic Places, was lovingly restored so that the public could enjoy both its beauty and history. Architect Joseph Roberto worked on it for more than 20 years to preserve its character and authenticity.

The furnishings in the house are representative of the many changes in decorating styles that the Tredwells saw over time. Since the family preserved a substantial amount of furniture and possessions throughout the years, many of the original items are on display and impressively reflect the tastes of bygone times.

The music lover will delight in the rare rosewood square-case piano (over which hangs the portrait of the original Mrs. Tredwell). It was manufactured in the 1840s by the New York firm of Nunns & Fischer, a partnership which lasted only from 1834 to 1848. (After the firm dissolved, though, the partners evidently continued to work at their trade in the city.) The piano has six and a half octaves and a cast-iron sounding board. One of its most unusual features consists of a single long organ pedal, to the left of the regular piano pedals, which activated concealed bellows to create an organlike sound when used.

This museum also serves as the site for special events, which occasionally include intimate concerts (although the square-case piano is not in use at the present time).

George Gershwin moved to 91 Second Avenue when he was six months old. This was one of the family's numerous residences throughout the years.

Fillmore East was once located at 109 Second Avenue and, although only in operation for a brief time, it exerted a profound influence on the sixties musical scene. Performers included Janis Joplin, the Grateful Dead, and Jimi Hendrix along with a spectacular light show.

YIDDISH BROADWAY PLAQUES
at entrance to the Second Avenue Deli (212-677-0606)
156 Second Avenue (at East 10th Street)

Sidewalk plaques pay tribute to the many individuals—including musicians—who were once a part of this thriving cultural tradition

At one time, more than half a dozen Yiddish theaters did a booming business in this immediate area. Some popular names—theatrical as well as musical—are honored here.

In front of the entrance to the Second Avenue Deli are star-shaped plaques set into the sidewalk with the names of these Yiddish stars of bygone times. Included are some musicians and composers—most notably, the famous baritone Boris Thomashevsky and the composer Sholom Secunda. Secunda wrote more than 40 operettas for the Yiddish theater and was known for his hit song "Bei Mir Bist Du Schon."

Gershwin was said to be inspired by many of the musical creators associated with this theatrical tradition. He especially admired the music of Joseph Rumshinsky and the work of operetta composer Abraham Goldfaden, also honored here.

The Second Avenue Deli has interesting photographs and memorabilia relating to the Yiddish theater (in addition to its fine food).

The P.S. 122 Performance Space is housed at First Avenue and East 9th Street. It serves the area as a cultural and social center with outreach programs that meet many needs. Its two theaters offer drama and dance presentations as well as some experimental music performances. Ira Gershwin is thought to have attended the school that was once located here. And on a more modern note, Jimi Hendrix was said to have lived nearby at 321 East 9th Street.

Christadora House was once a neighborhood settlement and the site where, in 1914, George Gershwin performed for the first time in public in the third-floor concert hall. He played a tango that he had composed. This building, located at 145 Avenue B (at East 9th Street), is now an apartment house.

THIRD STREET MUSIC SCHOOL SETTLEMENT
235 East 11th Street
212-777-3240

A historic neighborhood settlement that still serves the community well

Although it left its namesake locale more than 25 years ago, this school is still true to the philosophy of its founder. Created in 1894 by Emilie Wagner, this center was designed for children who would otherwise have been without such cultural and educational resources.

It continues its service to the community, now offering music courses to students of all ages. Individual and group instruction is provided along with classes in theory, composition, and chamber and jazz ensemble performance. Its concert series is presented in a 300-seat auditorium, and the school's other facilities include a well-stocked musical library and two dozen music studios. It also has a well-established outreach program for schools and sponsors many special performances for local community residents.

■GREENWICH VILLAGE

GREENWICH HOUSE MUSIC SCHOOL
46 Barrow Street
212-242-4770

A thriving music center that grew from a turn-of-the-century settlement house

---

Greenwich House was founded in 1902 by Mary Kingsbury Simkhovitch for the purpose of social outreach and reform. Programs greatly benefited an over-populated neighborhood of eager immigrants seeking new homes and fortunes in America.

The school of music has been an important part of Greenwich House since its creation in 1905 and its relocation to its present Barrow Street locale in 1914. Past students have included individuals who are famous in many walks of life—such as renowned composer John Cage and former mayor Ed Koch.

Classes and private instruction are offered for children and adults of all ages, and the organization has a highly successful arts-in-education program.

A fine selection of student, faculty, and special guest artist concerts can be heard at the school's 90-seat Renee Weiler Concert Hall as well as at the larger Hayden Auditorium, located at the main house down the block at 27 Barrow Street.

> Walk by 6 St. Luke's Place. This is the former residence of one-time mayor James J. Walker, a music enthusiast whose original ambition was to be a songwriter. However, he did pen the lyrics to the 1905 song hit "Will You Love Me in December As You Do in May?" (tune by Ernest Ball). The nearby park is also named in Walker's honor.

THE BITTER END
147 Bleeker Street
212-673-7030

Manhattan's oldest rock club is still thriving

Opened in 1960, this is billed as New York's oldest rock club still in operation, although it certainly features music of many different styles.

A number of name performers once appeared in front of its famed "brick wall." They included Carly Simon, Chick Corea, Joan Baez, and Linda Ronstadt. Peter, Paul & Mary also got their start here when folk music and coffee houses were very much in vogue.

Have some fun discovering the vast array of musical clubs that the Village has to offer. This section contains only a small sampling of what is available—there are just too many to do justice to every one. Check out the Bottom Line, the Village Gate, Knickerbockers, and Zinno's—just for starters! Each one has a unique history and a lineup of exceptional performers.

THE BLUE NOTE
131 West 3rd Street
212-475-8592

A fine club that has helped to keep the jazz tradition alive and well

---

This is one of New York's most beloved jazz clubs, having garnered its reputation from the roster of fine performers who appeared here since its opening in 1981. Dizzy Gillespie, Sarah Vaughan, the Modern Jazz Quartet, and Lionel Hampton are just a few of the bright lights of jazz who have delighted audiences at this site.

The club also features other musical genres such as blues, Latin, and pop.

Incidentally, it has a gift shop—a unique feature for a Village club.

The Music Inn (169 West 4th Street / 212-243-5715) is a small and informal store and showcase of unusual musical instruments from around the world.

NEW YORK UNIVERSITY
MUSICAL THEATER HALL OF FAME

Loewe Hall
35 West 4th Street

A splendid tribute to songwriters and musical theater greats

The lobby of this small theater, part of the New York University complex, pays tribute to a rich variety of composers and performers from the American musical theater. Attractive bronze plaques with informative details line the walls to honor individuals such as the Gershwins, Cole Porter, Eubie Blake, Lorenz Hart, Irving Berlin, Mary Martin, Comden & Green, Kander & Ebb, and George M. Cohan, among others.

NYU instituted this Hall of Fame on November 10, 1993, in conjunction with the hundredth anniversary of Broadway. At a gala ceremony presided over by Kitty Carlisle Hart and NYU's president, Jay Oliva, special awards were presented to Carol Channing and Jule Styne, and a musical tribute from current Broadway shows was performed. The plaques for the first group of inductees were dedicated at this time, including Jerome Kern, Richard Rodgers, Oscar Hammerstein II, Alan Jay Lerner, Frederick Loewe, and Ethel Merman.

In 1995, the site officially changed its name to the Frederick Loewe Theater in honor of the composer of the beloved musical scores for *Gigi, Camelot,* and *Brigadoon.* Additional plaques were unveiled, and a musical tribute to Loewe was performed.

The school views its ties to the musical theater world quite seriously, and each year it holds a Hall of Fame ceremony. The university's graduate program was the first to offer a course of studies for aspiring musical theater composers and writers.

A variety of events are regularly held at this site, sponsored by the school and by outside groups. Audiences for these performances may then enjoy the lobby's splendid tribute to those who made the American theater resound with beautiful words and music.

Music is recognized here in an artistic rendering in this busy New York University neighborhood. Two terra cotta medallions (one representing the Muse of Music, the other, Art) are attractive features on the facade of 80 Washington Square East. Dating from 1880, they were donated by Ivan C. Karp, the founder of the Anonymous Arts Recovery Society.

The Arch in Washington Square Park is a prominent Village landmark dating from 1895. Famed concert pianist Jan Ignace Paderewski appeared in a benefit concert with the Boston Symphony Orchestra at the Metropolitan Opera House on March 27, 1892, to raise funds toward the completion of construction on the arch.

The famous pianist Ignace Paderewski gladly performed at a benefit concert to raise funds to complete the Washington Square Arch.
Biggs Photography

THE NEW SCHOOL
66 West 12th Street
212-229-5690

Music and related topics for every taste

The New School was started in 1919 as the first university for adults. Considered a place for both teachers and students to meet together for the purpose of exchanging ideas and learning, it has always maintained a philosophy of providing education for all needs—even as the school evolved into a full-fledged college.

Over the years, the New School has developed into an institution with degree programs, extension courses, special lectures and workshops, and concert series. It now has more than 1500 courses and offers many types of higher degrees, certificates, and non-degree programs.

The music program has become increasingly well known, with jazz studies as a major specialty. Frequent jazz concerts and series are presented as well as recitals in other musical genres. The Mannes College of Music is now a division of the New School, providing even more musical emphasis than before.

Some interesting musical luminaries were associated with this institution in the past, too. Both Aaron Copland and John Cage once taught here!

A veritable landmark in itself, Asti's restaurant (13 East 12th Street / 212-741-9105) has a staff who serves opera arias along with dinner. Surprise guests have also been known to join in.

THE VILLAGE VANGUARD
178 Seventh Avenue South (at West 11th Street)
212-255-4037

A respected landmark on the jazz scene

This is the oldest surviving jazz club in New York with an illustrious history of great performers. Its superb acoustics, unusual pie-shaped space, fine performers, and acclaimed series of live recordings ("Live at the Village Vanguard" and others) have made this club legendary.

Max Gordon opened the club in 1934, and it served as a venue for poetry readings, jazz, swing, pop, folk, and cabaret over the years. Both the Thad Jones and Mel Lewis orchestras appeared here, as did Dizzy Gillespie, Mary Lou Williams, Coleman Hawkins, Thelonius Monk, Keith Jarrett, and Eddie Heywood, among many others.

Photographs on the walls chronicle the many performers who have delighted audiences at the Vanguard during its illustrious history.

SQUARES, PARKS, ENCLAVES AND NEIGHBORHOODS

■ UNION SQUARE

Only the ghosts of the famous Union Square musical sites remain. This was once the center of the musical world, and it is still an interesting area. A most famous nineteenth-century edifice was the Academy of Music, situated on the northeast corner of East 14th Street and Irving Place. Once an opera house for the old-line rich, it was forced out of business by the newer and more opulent Metropolitan Opera. Victor Herbert, longtime patron of Luchow's restaurant (110 East 14th Street), founded ASCAP here. Tony Pastor's Opera House (between Third Avenue and Irving Place) was where vaudeville supposedly originated, with such performers as Lillian Russell and George M. Cohan. The first Steinway Hall (107-109 East 14th) accommodated 2500 people and was once the site of New York Philharmonic concerts as well as numerous recitals by piano virtuosi. Nearby, Chickering Hall (northwest corner of Fifth Avenue and 18th Street) opened in direct competition to Steinway with an inaugural series performed by Hans von Bulow. All are gone. Only the Decker Piano Building remains (33 Union Square West). A beautiful architectural example of bygone times, its days as a piano firm are long gone, too.

■ STUYVESANT SQUARE AREA

ST. GEORGE'S CHURCH
East 16th Street and Rutherford Place

Historic church where Harry T. Burleigh once sang

This historic church is famous on its own as well as for one of its most memorable former soloists, Harry T. Burleigh.

Founded in 1749, the original St. George's served as the first chapel for Trinity Church parish, an institution that figured often in New York's musical history. St. George's relocated and grew into one of the wealthiest churches in the country, providing a fine musical program to complement its religious services.

Harry T. Burleigh (1866-1949) attracted fame and respect for himself and for the church on several counts. One of scores of applicants, Burleigh was selected for an open baritone soloist's position in St. George's choir, becoming the first black singer to be employed there. He remained in this spot for 52 years, nobly rising above occasional incidents of prejudice.

A student at the National Conservatory of Music, he became acquainted with Antonin Dvorak and was responsible for introducing him to the beauties of black spiritual music. This influence is strongly evident in Dvorak's *New World* Symphony, written during his stay in America.

Burleigh was acclaimed for his many beautiful settings of traditional spirituals, his choral and solo arrangements, and his own compositions. His creative setting of the lovely spiritual "Deep River" was a classic then as well as now. Burleigh also served as a music editor at Ricordi for more than 30 years and as a soloist for Temple Emanu-El for 25 years.

DVORAK SITES
(Street name, plaque at house site, statue of the composer)
East 17th Street (between First and Second Avenues)

Famed composer of the New World *Symphony and other lasting compositions once lived and worked in this vicinity*

Antonin Dvorak (1841-1904) was invited by Jeannette Thurber to act as both school director and professor of compo-

sition at her innovative National Conservatory of Music, joining
the ranks of such illustrious faculty members as Rafael Joseffy,
Victor Herbert, James Huneker, and Henry T. Finck, among others. (The conservatory was located at 126-128 East 17th Street,
now part of the Washington Irving High School site.)

During his time in New York, as well as while vacationing
at a Czech community in Spillville, Iowa, Dvorak observed
the many facets of music in America while continuing to compose. He integrated many of these newly discovered sounds
into his works. Harry T. Burleigh, a singer and student at the
conservatory, introduced him to black spirituals for which
Dvorak felt an especially powerful attraction, and some of his
compositions—particularly the *New World* Symphony—
reflected these themes. He was also intrigued by American
Indian sounds and incorporated pentatonic motifs common to
this idiom into his work.

Dvorak produced a significant body of compositions during
his American stay, including two string quartets, a violin
sonatina, a cello concerto, and some piano pieces. However,
his most famous creation from this time was most certainly
the Symphony No. 9, *From the New World*. It reflected the

Antonin Dvorak was director of this conservatory between 1892
and 1895. *Biggs Photography*

essence of the composer's fascination with the sounds of native America. The New York Philharmonic premiered the symphony under the baton of Anton Seidl at Carnegie Hall on December 16, 1893.

Dvorak Place

East 17th Street, between First and Second Avenues, was renamed Dvorak Place in honor of the Czech composer.

Plaque at House Site

Dvorak's home at 327 East 17th Street was unable to achieve the landmark status that it deserved. After a controversial series of events, the original structure was demolished, and the current building is now being used as a medical facility. However, a bronze plaque at this site serves as a distinguished remembrance of this brilliant man.

The inscription was adapted from a hundredth birthday commemorative plaque and notes three of the most beloved works written while Dvorak was living at this site: the *New World* Symphony, the *Biblical Songs*, and the Cello Concerto.

The plaque, the marble mantlepiece, and some additional items were salvaged from the original house prior to its demolition. Plans are being discussed for a small Dvorak museum where these pieces can be appropriately displayed for the public to enjoy. A prospective site for this display is the Bohemian National Hall at 321 East 73rd Street, built in 1896. Ironically, Antonin Dvorak helped to raise funds for the building of this hall through his performances. If sufficient backing can be garnered for this project, supporters foresee a Czech cultural center and an ethnic restaurant here in addition to the Dvorak display.

Statue of the Composer

Just a short distance from the house site is the newly installed statue of Dvorak in Stuyvesant Square Park. Located in the northeastern portion of the park near the 17th Street entrance, it was dedicated on September 13, 1997. This bronze statue, created by sculptor Ivan Mestrovic, had awaited a permanent home for 30 years. Donated to the New York Philharmonic in 1963 by the Czechoslovak National Council of America, it remained on top of Alice Tully Hall at Lincoln Center where original plans for a roof garden with statuary

Ivan Mestrovic's statue of Antonin Dvorak was installed in Stuyvesant Square Park in 1997, near the site of his former residence and the school where he was director in the 1890s. *Photo by Todd Weinstein, courtesy of Dvorak American Heritage Association/Stuyvesant Park Neighborhood Association*

were abandoned. The statue is said to have been the last work of Mestrovic, who was a student of Rodin.

The New York Philharmonic Orchestra presented the statue to the Dvorak American Heritage Association. This group worked closely with the Stuyvesant Square Neighborhood Association to raise funds not only to restore and maintain the statue, but also to commission the creation of the new green granite pedestal from Jan Hird Pokorny.

The unveiling ceremony was attended by a large crowd of spectators, and a host of honored guest speakers were featured, including representatives of various cultural associations, the Czech ambassador, the mayor of Prague, and the city's first lady, Donna Hanover. Musical selections by Dvorak were performed by the Harmonie Ensemble/New York and guest vocal soloists. A gala concert followed at St. George's Church.

■GRAMERCY PARK AREA

The beautiful Gramercy Park area has a few interesting musical stories. The Players Club at 16 Gramercy Park South was organized in 1888 for men active in the arts—music included. Walter Damrosch was among its members. He was not only a famed conductor, but also the catalyst for the creation of Carnegie Hall. Nearby at 34 Gramercy Park South, John Ringling (of circus fame) once maintained an apartment in which he installed a massive pipe organ.

Theodore Roosevelt was born at 28 East 20th Street. This faithfully reconstructed house is open for public tours, and it is the site of frequent concerts (212-260-1616).

■CHELSEA AREA

The Kitchen (512 West 19th Street / 212-255-5793) presents a variety of new and experimental music by emerging composers and performers.

HOTEL CHELSEA
222 West 23rd Street (between Seventh and Eighth Avenues)

A site that has always been associated with the arts

This ornate landmark structure has long been associated with the artistic community. One of New York's first cooperative apartment buildings, it was converted to a hotel in 1905.

Designed and built by Hubert, Pirsson & Company between 1883 and 1885, its twelve stories made it one of the taller structures of its time. The facade includes the famous iron balconies with their elaborate flowery ornaments as well as unusual dormers and roofline, giving the building its character and an easily recognizable profile. A grand staircase and an eclectic lobby both add to its unique personality.

Although long associated with literary figures, a number of composers and musicians have also lived at the Chelsea. Perhaps its most famous composer was Virgil Thomson, who resided at the hotel from 1940 until his death in 1989. In addition to his compositions (the most well-known being *Four Saints in Three Acts*, with text by Gertrude Stein), he was a noted critic for the New York *Herald Tribune*. Fellow resident and composer George Kleinsinger wrote the musical *Shinbone Alley* (starring Eartha Kitt), as well as a favorite children's symphony, *Tubby the Tuba* (popularly narrated by Danny Kaye).

Folksinger Bob Dylan reportedly wrote songs at the Chelsea, as did the now-forgotten street figure Moondog, who penned unconventional fare. A number of rock groups and singers lived here, too, including Janis Joplin, the Jefferson Airplane, Jimi Hendrix, and Pink Floyd, to name a few. Sid Vicious, notorious member of the English punk rock group The Sex Pistols, killed his girlfriend, Nancy Spungen, at the Chelsea and later died there of a heroin overdose.

> During the 1860s, 23rd Street, between Sixth and Eighth Avenues, had a number of musical and theatrical establishments. The Grand Opera House, at the northwest corner of Eighth and 23rd, was among the most famous. Owner Samuel N. Pike ensured a successful opening, but the Academy of Music drew most of the attention. Jim Fisk and Jay Gould bought it, and thereafter it lived a checkered life—serving up all kinds of entertainment until it was finally demolished as a movie house near the time of its centennial anniversary.

■OLD TIN PAN ALLEY NEIGHBORHOOD

OLD TIN PAN ALLEY SITE

West 28th Street (between Broadway and Fifth Avenue)

Where publishers, songwriters, and pluggers were once happily in business

Although the music business in New York existed as a lucrative enterprise around Union Square, it reached new heights of glory as firms gravitated to the area of West 28th Street and its close environs. It existed in this locale from approximately 1893 to 1913, but enjoyed its heyday at the turn of the century. By this time, Charles K. Harris had a five-million-selling hit in

This music was a good example of the tunes published in Tin Pan Alley. This score was written by Monroe Rosenfeld, the man who gave the Alley its name. *Biggs Photography*

"After the Ball," and other tunes such as "The Band Played On" and "Sweet Rosie O'Grady" were being hummed in the streets. Life was carefree, music was popular, and profits rang out as never before.

It was here that the illustrious Monroe Rosenfeld—newspaperman, composer, gambler, and general all-around character—coined the name Tin Pan Alley. He said that the noise on the street sounded like tin pans clanging—the sounds of demonstrators at their tinny pianos and office noise resounding through the windows on this street of old brownstones.

It was also here that songwriters sold to publishers, "pluggers" aggressively operated to promote songs to performers and anyone who would lend an ear, and the American songwriting enterprise blossomed into a serious money-making machine.

Stroll down this street and try to imagine the turn of the century with its non-mechanized music business. Some of the buildings themselves remain, although the character of their tenants is much different than it was a century ago.

Here are a few of the firms, along with their addresses, that operated during this golden era:

28th Street

Leo Feist, Inc.	#36	(1900-1902)
Harry von Tilzer Music Publishing	#37,42	(1902-1907)
P.J. Howley Music Company	#41	(1905-1907)
Jerome H. Remick & Company	#45	(1905-1908)
Shapiro, Bernstein & Company	#45	(1899-1904)
M. Witmark & Sons	#49-51	(1893-1898)
Paul Dresser Publishing Company	#51	(1905-1906)

29th Street

M. Witmark & Sons	#8	(1898-1903)
F.A. Mills	#32, 45, 48	(1895-1908)

The Gershwin Hotel (7 East 27th Street / 212-545-8000) is near the old Tin Pan Alley neighborhood and is the namesake of the songwriter who once worked in this famous area.

■ HERALD SQUARE AREA

> The Hotel Pennsylvania (West 33rd Street and Seventh Avenue) achieved great fame in the 1930s and 1940s with its big band entertainment. Glenn Miller's band popularized the song "Pennsylvania 6-5000," which was the phone number of the hotel. It still bills itself as having the longest-running phone number.

MADISON SQUARE GARDEN/THE PARAMOUNT
Seventh Avenue at West 33rd Street
212-465-6741

A sports center that doubles as a concert space

Mega concerts can be heard at the 5600-seat Paramount as well as at the larger Garden. From rock to Barbra Streisand, these events are usually sellouts. While heading for the box office, take a look at the bronze insets in the floor. Of course, many of these are in honor of sports figures. However, both Billy Joel and Elton John are immortalized here, too, for their past performances at this site.

■ MURRAY HILL AREA

PIERPONT MORGAN LIBRARY & MUSEUM
33 East 36th Street
212-685-0610

Fine musical research collections and concert series are a part of this venerable cultural institution

Originally the library of the illustrious financier J. Pierpont Morgan (1837-1913), this 1906 building was designed by McKim, Mead & White (with an addition by Benjamin W. Morris completed in 1928, after Morgan's death and the site's conversion to a public reference library). Morgan attached the main structure to his residence in order to store his vast collections of books and art.

Now a museum and research library, this landmark contains many old and rare musical manuscripts, including works dating back to the thirteenth century as well as autograph scores and personal papers from such composers as Beethoven, Gounod, Chopin, Mozart, Mendelssohn, and Wagner, among others. Thousands of pieces of correspondence from the pens of great composers are also maintained here.

These archives comprise an important resource for scholars and performers. Occasional exhibits of portions of the music collection are also made available for public viewing, and concerts are often presented in conjunction with these displays.

■BRYANT PARK AREA

FORMER SITE OF AEOLIAN HALL
33 West 42nd Street

Once a favorite concert hall and the site of some landmark performances

---

This was once a forerunner on the concert scene in New York. So many greats appeared on its stage—the Symphony Society as well as the Philharmonic Society, Fritz Kreisler, Harold Bauer, Ossip Gabrilowitsch, and others.

It was also here that George Gershwin's famous *Rhapsody in Blue* was premiered on February 12, 1924, with Paul Whiteman's orchestra and Gershwin as the soloist. It was a part of the concert entitled "Experiment in Modern Music," a concept created by Whiteman.

The site is now occupied by a building of the City University of New York Graduate School.

The main research branch of the New York Public Library (Fifth Avenue between West 40th and 42nd Streets / 212-930-0800) was designed in 1911 and is recognizable by its stunning architecture and its familiar pair of lions by the front steps. There are some works pertaining to music within specific collections here. Occasional concerts, many presented in conjunction with events, are also held at the Celeste Bartos Forum. (See also "Library for the Performing Arts at Lincoln Center.")

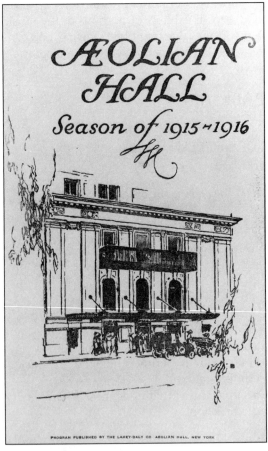

ÆOLIAN HALL
Season of 1915~1916

PROGRAM PUBLISHED BY THE LAHEY-DALY CO AEOLIAN HALL, NEW YORK

Aeolian Hall was once a center of concert activity, featuring famed soloists and orchestras. It was also the site of the premiere of George Gershwin's *Rhapsody in Blue* in 1924. *Biggs Photography*

BRYANT PARK

Sixth Avenue (between West 40th and 42nd Streets—behind the library)

Music has always been a part of this historic location

This was the site of the Crystal Palace from 1853 to 1858. A spacious edifice designed in the style of a greenhouse, it was modeled after a similar structure in London and also contained an observatory. The "Exhibition of the Industry of All Nations," a sort of world's fair, was held here and contained displays of all types—approximately 4,000 of them. Music was, of course, represented.

The Steinways entered the American Institute Exhibition here in 1855. They achieved much recognition from this event, and it helped to boost subsequent piano sales.

There was also a great deal of musical entertainment at this site. Louis Jullien, a French conductor, led an orchestra of European and American musicians. Their concerts were quite popular (as was Jullien's personality), and their repertoire consisted of everything from Beethoven to Fry's *Santa Claus Symphony*.

Regrettably, this remarkable structure burned down in 1858, and a great deal of loss resulted for the exhibitors. (The Steinways, alone, lost six pianos—not a small investment in those days.)

This tract of land was eventually converted into a park, named after William Cullen Bryant, in 1884. It was renovated several years ago after falling on hard times. The transformation was spectacular. Many outdoor concerts are now offered here in both daytime and evening during the warm weather. Special series featuring young performers and ensembles are particularly popular.

MIDTOWN

■ THEATER DISTRICT AND VICINITY

JOE FRANKLIN'S MEMORY LANE
Northeast corner of Broadway and West 42nd Street

Honoring a champion of song nostalgia

This street sign was dedicated on November 17, 1997, in honor of Joe Franklin, the longtime host of radio and television whose career has been dedicated to preserving and sharing the treasures of popular song. Often called the "King of Nostalgia," Franklin hosts a regular show, "Memory Lane," on WOR-AM radio that succeeds in keeping the wonderful memories of the songs, the performers, and their stories alive for his listening audience.

A ceremony for the dedication of the new street sign was attended by dignitaries from the Mayor's office, Madison Square Garden, several boroughs, and Guardian Angels

Joe Franklin, host of the WOR radio show "Memory Lane," was the recipient of a street sign in his honor at 42nd Street and Broadway. Curtis Sliwa, WABC talk show host and founder of the Guardian Angels, was present at this illustrious occasion on November 17, 1997.
Photo by Sam Teicher

founder Curtis Sliwa. Franklin was also presented with plaques and other honors in addition to the Memory Lane street sign.

Located in the heart of the "new" Times Square and just a short distance from Franklin's office (which is crammed with records and nostalgic song memorabilia), this is an appropriate tribute to a man who not only has done so much to preserve American popular song and the memory of those who have performed its repertoire, but who also is very much a part of New York itself.

Be sure to check out the New Victory Theater (209 West 42nd Street), once owned by Oscar Hammerstein, and the New Amsterdam Theater (214 West 42nd), which was formerly home to the *Ziegfeld Follies* and also saw performances by George M. Cohan and Eddie Cantor. These and other renovated theaters on the block are part of the effort to revitalize Times Square. They also offer a glimpse of musical entertainment sites and atmosphere in the early part of the century.

TOWN HALL
123 West 43rd Street (between Sixth Avenue and Broadway)
212-840-2824

From Rachmaninoff to cabaret

This historic concert hall opened on January 12, 1921. Designed by the firm of McKim, Mead & White, it is a four-story building that was created in the Georgian Revival architectural style. The interior contains a simple, yet elegant, lobby and a Colonial Revival–style auditorium that seats approximately 1500 and is known for its superb acoustics. The popularity and status of this hall grew quickly after Aeolian Hall was abandoned in 1925.

Town Hall was built by the League for Political Education, a women's group that desired a suitable public center in which to present lectures on political and social issues. Over the years, speakers included such personalities as Winston Churchill, Anais Nin, Eleanor Roosevelt, Jane Addams, and

Thomas Mann. The hall not only became a popular lecture center, but it also served as a clubhouse for League members. "America's Town Meetings of the Air" were broadcast from Town Hall between 1935 and 1956. These programs aired debates by world leaders on a variety of issues.

Many international musical figures performed on its stage, including Sergei Rachmaninoff, Andres Segovia, Dizzy Gillespie, Joan Sutherland, Marian Anderson, Duke Ellington, Eubie Blake, Nelson Eddy, and a host of others. It often served as the site for a famous debut. A wonderful collection of famous performers' photographs, with accompanying historic recital/lecture programs, is on display on the first balcony level and offers concertgoers pleasant and informative viewing during an intermission.

Regular performances have been presented here by such groups as the American Opera Society and Clarion Concerts as well as by the New Traditions performance series of drama, film, jazz, and ethnic/contemporary musical offerings—all designed to appeal to a variety of artistic tastes. The annual Cabaret Convention plays to packed audiences here each season.

Town Hall was acquired by New York University in 1958 and achieved landmark status in 1980. It saw extensive renovations that were completed in 1984 and cost $1.5 million. Today, with its eclectic calendar of events, it still serves as a popular concert and meeting hall.

RODGERS & HAMMERSTEIN WAY
West 44th Street between Seventh and Eighth Avenues

A landmark street in the world of musical theater

This street was named in honor of the famous team who created an astounding number of Broadway hit musicals. From their first collaboration in 1943 on *Oklahoma!* to *South Pacific*, *Carousel*, and others, their productions enjoyed great success in and around this area.

The memorable hit songs from these shows have become an integral part of the American musical repertoire. From "Some Enchanted Evening," "If I Loved You," and "June is Bustin' Out All Over," to "Getting to Know You," "People Will Say

We're in Love," and "Shall We Dance," each one has been played, sung, and recorded many thousands of times over.

Oklahoma! opened to rave reviews at the St. James Theatre right here on West 44th Street. *The King and I* and *Flower Drum Song* were also produced at the same house. (Stroll by and check what's playing now.)

Many of these shows have been revived on The Great White Way and have, once more, made the names of Rodgers & Hammerstein synonymous with Broadway musical theater for a new generation.

> Richard Rodgers' achievements were further recognized when the theater at 226 West 46th Street was renamed in his honor.

IRVING BERLIN PLAQUE
The Music Box Theatre
239 West 45th Street (between Broadway and Eighth Avenue)

A tribute to a musical great in the theater that he created

Irving Berlin (1888-1989), who grew up in the poverty-stricken Russian Jewish community on the lower East Side, represents one of the greatest success stories of Tin Pan Alley. Without the benefit of a formal musical education or numerous other advantages, he composed thousands of memorable songs, including "Alexander's Ragtime Band" and "Always," and became known to millions during his long career. His hits were popular on stage, screen, radio, and recordings. He also created a successful sheet music publishing firm.

This all-time legend is honored in a recently mounted plaque at the Music Box Theatre—the theater that Berlin built with producer Sam Harris. The plaque was installed at a formal ceremony in December 1994 with Berlin's three daughters and various members of the songwriting and theatrical community in attendance.

Designed by Neil Estern, president of the National Sculpture Society, the plaque contains a bas relief of the composer and an inscription that includes the titles of the Berlin songs that had their first performances at the theater—among them, "Easter Parade" and "Heat Wave."

The plaque can be seen just inside the front door of the theater's lobby, near the box office. For the price of a ticket to the current production, you may also see a permanent display of memorabilia associated with Berlin's musical revues, located in the lower-level lounge of the theater.

GEORGE M. COHAN STATUE
Broadway and 46th Street (south end of Duffy Square)

Still giving his regards to the street he immortalized in song

This quintessential showman—vaudevillian, actor, director, manager, and songwriter—is honored with a statue that gazes upon his beloved Broadway.

Despite being told early on by a music instructor that he was unteachable and by a New York music publisher that his songs were unprintable, he persevered until achieving fame as a songwriter. His many lasting hits include "Give My Regards to Broadway," "You're a Grand Old Flag," and "Over There," for which he received a special Medal of Honor from Franklin D. Roosevelt in 1940.

Born in 1878, Cohan lived in New York City until his death in 1942. Through his efforts, the American character and spirit became readily definable in musical theater during the early part of the twentieth century. His most famous shows included *Forty-Five Minutes from Broadway* and *Little Johnny Jones*. He wrote, produced, and starred in many of his own hit musicals.

This eight-foot-tall bronze sculpture, created by Georg Lober, portrays Cohan, complete with hat and cane, as if casually strolling down the street that he immortalized in song. Several of his popular hit song titles are inscribed on the pedestal of the statue.

The statue was unveiled in 1959 by Cohan's four grandchildren at a late-night ceremony which was attended by thousands of entertainers, theatergoers, cops, city officials, and Broadway types. Oscar Hammerstein II presided, and George Jessel acted as master of ceremonies. The enthusiastic crowd sang "Give My Regards to Broadway" just after midnight in a grand tribute to this favorite songwriter and New York figure.

COMMEMORATIVE SCULPTURES

The I. Miller Building
Northeast corner of Broadway and West 46th Street

Stars from the worlds of opera and musical comedy are depicted here

This location once housed the store of the famous shoe manufacturer I. Miller and was a regular haunt of theatrical and musical folk. The proprietor decided to take a vote to determine who was the most popular female star in each branch of the theater with the ultimate plan to commission statues in their honor. The final selections were Rosa Ponselle for opera, Marilyn Miller for musical comedy, Ethel Barrymore for drama, and Mary Pickford for film.

Alexander Calder created four life-size marble statues representing each of these women. They are set in gold-lined niches just above the street level of the building on the 46th Street side. Rosa Ponselle was a star at the Metropolitan Opera, and she is portrayed here in her title role in *Norma*. The other musical figure, Marilyn Miller, is shown here as the captivating main character in the 1925 Ziegfeld production *Sunny*.

The statues were unveiled on October 20, 1929, before a crowd of 3,000 spectators. Mayor James Walker, a theatrical enthusiast and an amateur songwriter himself, presented the concluding address. Both Marilyn Miller and Rosa Ponselle participated in the ceremony.

> The High School for the Performing Arts was once located at 120 West 46th Street. The lives of young musicians and performers who attended the school inspired the movie *Fame*. This institution is now a part of La Guardia High School of the Performing Arts near Lincoln Center.

> Scott Joplin, composer of "Maple Leaf Rag" and other ragtime hits, ran a boardinghouse, along with his wife, at 252 West 47th Street during the pre–World War I years.

MANNY'S MUSIC
156 West 48th Street
212-819-0576

A music store and museum with a rich history

Manny Goldrich, a young and enterprising horn salesman, opened this store in the mid-1930s. Since then, it has become one of the most popular music stores in New York with a professional line of instruments from guitars to keyboards to drums and more.

Just about anyone who is famous in the music world has visited here at one time or another for instruments, music, technical advice, and camaraderie, including Count Basie, Duke Ellington, Ella Fitzgerald, Jimi Hendrix, Carly Simon, Whitney Houston, and scores of other greats.

Manny's also bills itself as a music museum, and its collections help it to live up to that reputation. There are walls of photographs signed by the celebrities who have frequented Manny's from its opening until now. There is also a display of memorabilia, including a wall of autographed guitars from the likes of Les Paul, KISS, and John Mellencamp, among others. The store has also been known to host events such as guitar clinics for very appreciative audiences.

Manny's is always packed with musicians and browsers and is well worth a visit for its stock of merchandise as well as for its atmosphere.

> West 48th Street, on Manny's block, is a music lover's delight. Enjoy the many stores nearby, including Sam Ash Music and Rudy's Music Shop.

BIX BEIDERBECKE PLAQUE
1600 Broadway (between West 48th and 49th Streets)

Site of jazz great's New York debut

Bix Beiderbecke became a jazz legend during his brief lifetime (1903-1931) and was a familiar figure on the orchestral and early recording scene. An innovative stylist, the beautiful phrasing and tone of his cornet solos earned him fame for a distinctly individual approach.

His 1924 recording of "I Need Some Pettin'" with the Wolverines—a group that he organized in Chicago the previous year—ranked high on the list of jazz favorites. Ever versatile, he was featured on both cornet and piano in "Big Boy," recorded with the same group.

Beiderbecke performed with other orchestras, most notably with Paul Whiteman and Jean Goldkette. With the latter group, his cornet solo helped to sell a million records of "I'm Looking Over a Four Leaf Clover." He was also featured with the legendary Hoagy Carmichael on the 1928 recording of Carmichael's "Washboard Blues."

This building was once the home of the Cinderella Dance Palace—one of many such establishments on the New York entertainment scene during the 1920s. Beiderbecke made his New York debut here on September 12, 1924, with the Wolverine Orchestra.

BRILL BUILDING

1619 Broadway (at West 49th Street)

A latter-day Tin Pan Alley

Often referred to as the Tin Pan Alley of modern times, the Brill Building has always been associated with sheet music publishing, songwriting, and entertainment. It was built in 1931 and named not after a musician but, rather, after Morris Brill, whose clothing store occupied the ground floor of the building. Its tenants were legendary, including the publishing firms of Mills Music, Southern Music (the building's first tenant), Famous Music, and T.B. Harms as well as such individual luminaries as Tommy Dorsey. Visitors read like a musical "who's who" during the peak age of recording, hit parades, and modern popular song. It would not have been unusual to see the likes of Duke Ellington, Frank Sinatra, Rosemary Clooney, or Benny Goodman in the halls or elevators en route to meet with any number of songwriters, arrangers, and music publishers whose offices were located on one of its busy floors.

However, with the advent of rock and roll, the sheet music business fell upon bad times and, as a result, so did the building. By the 1970s, it had hit an all-time low, and there was even some thought that the building might be lost in the inevitable march of progress. However, within a few short years, Lorne Michaels, Woody Allen, and other film and television talents discovered the Brill, turning it into a center for the entertainment world. Its resulting renaissance is reflected in its restored facade and beautifully refurbished brass and mirrored lobby. The sheet music business still lives on at this address, although strictly in retail form, through the very popular Colony music store at street level.

This was once a latter–day Tin Pan Alley, filled with many firms and publishers in the music business. *Photo by Sam Teicher*

COLONY MUSIC
1619 Broadway (at West 49th Street)
212-265-2050

A fine blend of music and memorabilia

Appropriately housed on the ground floor of the Brill Building, this store sells a wide array of popular sheet music, scores, and new CDs as well as collectible records, music, posters, and other musical mementos.

Framed sheet music from years gone by is on display. There are also showcases chock-full of memorabilia that are tantamount to a pop music museum. (Many are for sale!) On display are items—coins, books, dolls, lunchboxes, keyrings, cups, etc.—that were originally created to promote Elvis, the Beatles, the Bee Gees, the Monkees, Ricky Nelson, and a host of other stars.

Rock, pop, and nostalgia enthusiasts will enjoy browsing here.

Nearby is the Gershwin Theatre at 222 West 51st Street—named in honor of the great New York songwriter and composer.

The Irish Arts Center at 553 West 51st Street (212-757-3318) offers classes, workshops, lectures, and performances of traditional Irish music.

W.C. HANDY PLACE
West 52nd Street and Seventh Avenue

A tribute to "the father of the blues"

W.C. Handy (1873-1958) was a versatile figure in the music world—performer, composer, and publisher. A cornetist and singer, he performed and recorded with Jelly Roll Morton and other name figures.

Often referred to as "The Father of the Blues," he certainly popularized this form of music. His songs included "Memphis Blues" and the hit "St. Louis Blues," and his New York publishing firm was responsible for turning both his tunes and those of other songwriters into commercial successes.

A beloved figure in the world of music, he was given a concert at Carnegie Hall in his honor, celebrating his sixty-fifth birthday. His life story was also movingly portrayed on the screen in 1958.

This locale is near the former location of many clubs that featured combos and soloists specializing in jazz and blues. Handy's works and the style that he made popular were most certainly heard here often.

ROSELAND BALLROOM

239 West 52nd Street
212-247-0200

One of the most famous ballrooms of all time

This famous dance palace opened in 1919 at its original location at 1658 Broadway. Considered more elegant than regular dance halls, it served as a wonderful venue for jazz and dance bands to perform along with their guest soloists.

Fletcher Henderson was the house bandleader, and he was said to have created the "big band" sound here in the 1920s along with his noted musical director, Don Redman. National radio broadcasts from this location helped to make it even more famous beyond local boundaries.

The famous "battle of the bands" took place here on October 6, 1926, between the house band and Jean Goldkette's group. It was so popular that it was repeated one week later, and recreated ten years later.

Many illustrious musicians appeared here, including Bix Beiderbecke (with Jean Goldkette's band) as well as Count Basie, Louis Armstrong, Earl Hines, and Ella Fitzgerald. This was also the site of Goldkette's farewell engagement with his famous band.

The building was demolished in 1956, and a new ballroom was built at 239 West 52nd Street. This later incarnation of Roseland specialized in ballroom dancing for a while. Now it features rock, but it still has evenings devoted to the ballroom tradition.

Check out two excellent stores: Chas Colin (315 West 53rd Street / 212-581-1480) specializes in music for brass and jazz, and Frank Music (244-250 West 54th Street, 10th floor / 212-582-1999) carries an extensive stock of classical music. They are both well known in musical circles.

■ROCKEFELLER CENTER AREA AND GENERAL MIDTOWN VICINITY

The recently renovated Roosevelt Hotel (East 45th Street & Madison Avenue / 212-661-9600) is the site of the lounge where Guy Lombardo and his orchestra broadcast his famous New Year's Eve performances for so many years.

ROCKEFELLER CENTER MUSICAL SITES
West 48th through 51st Streets (between Fifth and Sixth Avenues)

A complex with shops, restaurants, sculpture, murals, gardens, and entertainment centers

This is a major attraction for visitors, particularly at the holiday season. The famous Channel Gardens is then ablaze with lights and crowned by the imposing Christmas tree, near which skaters dance and glide. In the warmer months, there are flowers and fountains with an outdoor restaurant. Music is always featured at this location as well as at the various plazas and public spaces that dot the complex.

Rockefeller Center also has some interesting musical history and attractions.

NBC Studios
30 Rockefeller Plaza
212-664-4000

Tours are available at the famous National Broadcasting Company's facilities, home of the oldest permanent radio and television network in the country. Although there are a number of popular shows that now emanate from this location, many of its best-known musical connections are from its past. Vaudeville entertainers, singers, and other musicians were featured on its earlier broadcasts, here and at its previous location. Some of these well-known names include Rudy Vallee, Eddie Cantor, Al Jolson, and Bing Crosby.

One of the network's most successful musical figures was Arturo Toscanini. The NBC Symphony Orchestra was created for this illustrious conductor by David Sarnoff, head of NBC. Toscanini, former conductor of the New York Philharmonic, led the NBC Symphony from 1937 to 1954, helping to make great music accessible to millions through radio broadcasts and famous recordings. His studio still exists on the premises.

Before heading upstairs for the tour, check the west wall of the main lobby. Music is depicted, along with Poetry and Dance, in the mural *American Progress* by Sert.

The Rainbow Room / Rainbow & Stars
30 Rockefeller Plaza
212-632-5000

Located in the same building as NBC is one of the most famous restaurants and clubs in New York. Both the Rainbow Room and its companion club, Rainbow and Stars, are noted for their fine entertainment. Orchestras have always been a fixture here. Such famous groups as Ray Noble's band and the Casa Loma Orchestra once played here. Orchestra music is still provided in keeping with this tradition.

At the Rainbow and Stars club, top entertainers appear, offering the best in cabaret, popular, and standard repertoire. Name stars such as Rosemary Clooney continue to delight listeners in this lovely art deco setting.

Taipei Theater
Sixth Avenue at West 49th Street
212-373-1850

This theater is located in the concourse of the McGraw-Hill Building. Music from the Chinese tradition is presented in an exotic atmosphere, along with dance and theater performances. More traditional musical concerts are also occasionally presented.

Radio City Music Hall
Sixth Avenue at West 50th Street
212-247-4777

This famed art deco entertainment hall opened in December 1932—a lush palace seating 6200. Although its life as a vaudeville theater was short, it quickly succeeded with a combination of a live stage show and a feature film.

The live show was always spectacular with a symphony orchestra, ballet, and the world-famous dancing troupe, the Rockettes. The Music Hall's Wurlitzer theater organ was said to be among the world's largest and was always a regular feature at each performance.

Declared a landmark in 1978, the hall underwent a massive renovation. It is now used for special concerts and performances (from rock concerts to such events as the revival of *Porgy & Bess* in 1983). The Rockettes still dance at the Christmas and Easter holiday spectaculars.

Outside, high above the main entrance at Sixth Avenue and 50th Street, check out the facade. There are plaques representing song, along with drama and dance (by Hildreth Meiere). Additional plaques are under the marquee and depict scenes from vaudeville (by Rene Chambellan).

"SWING STREET" SIGN & SIDEWALK PLAQUES
West 52nd Street (between Fifth and Sixth Avenues)

Memories of the heyday of jazz clubs in this area

This strip of midtown once boasted a unique collection of jazz clubs in the 1930s, '40s, and '50s. So many names in the jazz world were featured in these establishments that it seemed fitting to pay them tribute in the locale where many of their stellar reputations were born. Thus, the block was renamed "Swing Street."

On the north side of the street, the sidewalk contains a number of inset granite plaques, installed in 1979 in honor of individual Swing Street jazz performers, including Sarah Vaughan, Coleman Hawkins, Billie Holiday, Charlie Parker, and Dizzy Gillespie, among others. These plaques—collectively called "Jazz Walk"—are located near the CBS Building. (Look carefully, since pedestrian traffic has taken a bit of a toll, and the plaques are somewhat easy to miss!)

ST. THOMAS CHURCH
1 West 53rd Street
212-757-7013

A well-established musical program in a busy Fifth Avenue locale

This historic church is a joy to visit. The architecture, stained glass, and ornamental details are fascinating.

A perfect setting for music, both visually and acoustically, a variety of concerts are presented here regularly. The famous St. Thomas Choir of Men and Boys performs a varied repertoire here frequently. Visiting choirs, small ensembles, guest performances, and a series of organ concerts are all a part of the artistic schedule. (The fine Aeolian-Skinner instrument has undergone a number of revisions and has an inspiring sound produced by more than 9,000 pipes.) The church also sponsors one of the more popular performances of the *Messiah* in the city during the holiday season.

City Center (151 West 55th Street) was once home to the New York City Opera and other musical groups. It is now a dance center, although concerts are occasionally featured.

Nearby, one can find so much exciting music in a variety of settings. The Donnell Library Center (20 West 53rd Street), a branch of the New York Public Library, has sponsored a quality concert series in its auditorium for many years—from classical to popular fare. The Summergarden at the Museum of Modern Art (14 West 54th Street) offers lovely music in its outdoor sculpture garden. Check the schedules at all of the area churches—from St. Patrick's Cathedral at East 50th Street and Fifth Avenue to the Fifth Avenue Presbyterian Church at West 55th Street—for special performances in inspiring settings. There are also many atriums in this locale—the IBM Building (East 56th Street and Madison Avenue), Trump Tower (East 56th and Fifth Avenue), and others. They often have choral groups for special occasions, piano music, and additional types of performances.

THE PLAZA HOTEL
Fifth Avenue (between West 58th and 59th Streets)
212-546-5493

A site with Victorian splendor and a musical history, too

This opulent landmark hotel, built in the 1890s, overlooks scenic Central Park. From permanent residents, to hotel guests, to those who frequented the establishment for dining and entertainment, the list of the famous associated with the Plaza reads like a "who's who." Lillian Russell, Enrico Caruso, the Beatles, and many others all stayed here.

George M. Cohan evidently spent several hours a day at the Oak Room before shows for many years. He was at the Plaza so frequently that people actually thought he lived there, which was not the case. After he died, the Lambs Club officially dedicated the northwest corner of the restaurant in his memory.

Eddie Duchin, the famous pianist and orchestra leader, lived at the Plaza with his wife and entertained there at the Persian Room. "The Incomparable Hildegarde" also performed on piano at the Persian Room. Other performer/musicians who appeared here over the years included Robert Goulet, Dinah Shore, Lainie Kazan, and Carol Channing.

Celebrities still patronize the hotel, and music can still be heard there. The Oak Room buzzes with musical activity. And the Palm Court features salon music, reminiscent of an elegant, bygone era.

FLORENCE GOULD HALL
55 East 59th Street (hall entrance and box office)
at the Alliance Francaise
212-355-6160

Concerts from baroque to twentieth-century with a French flavor

This wonderful concert hall was created in 1988 and is a part of the Alliance Francaise, the center for French culture and education that reached its centennial year in 1998. The Alliance Francaise is dedicated to sharing various aspects of French culture with New Yorkers as well as to serving the French population here—fostering friendship among all groups. A superb library, classes in all aspects of French culture, and an acclaimed series of concerts and performance events make this a popular, educational, and entertaining institution.

Florence Gould Hall is an attractive, 400-seat concert space with wonderful acoustics, state-of-the-art equipment and facilities, a Steinway piano, and reception accommodations. Named after the philanthropist who was well known for her love of France as well as all of the arts, this space has been praised for its exceptional design and artistic appointments— a worthy tribute to a beloved and generous individual.

Concerts are regularly performed here by visiting French as well as American musicians and artists. Repertoire ranges from baroque works for harpsichord to modern compositions for chamber ensemble. A sampling of events on the concert schedule includes: Le Quatuor, a string quartet with a comedic presentation; Concert Royal, a group specializing in baroque works; and New York/Paris/New York, a series of both French and American chamber music by such groups as the Parisii Quartet and the Wanderer Trio. Pre-concert lectures and soirees often accompany the musical fare. Theater and dance performances are also a part of the cultural attractions here.

Florence Gould Hall may be reserved by outside groups for special musical and cultural performances. The Little Orchestra Society and the New York Theater Ballet both perform here as well as a number of other independent groups.

In addition, a smaller facility, the Edward Larocque Tinker Auditorium, is a part of the Alliance Francaise. It seats 120 and has been used for lectures and cabaret events as well as meetings and corporate functions.

Florence Gould Hall at the Alliance Francaise, the site of fine chamber and solo concerts, many featuring French repertoire. *Photo by Jacqueline Chambord, courtesy of the French Institute/Alliance Francaise*

■CARNEGIE HALL AREA AND ENVIRONS

SITE OF CHICKERING HALL
27-29 West 57th Street

A reminder of New York's former status as a piano center

Chickering was one of the leading companies in New York during the flourishing years of piano manufacturing and sales. Founded in Boston in 1823, the Chickering company expanded into other cities, including New York, over subsequent decades. The firm was recognized long before Steinway opened up shop in America, and its product was heartily endorsed through the years by such performers as Louis Moreau Gottschalk.

Frank Chickering managed the New York operation which opened in 1859 and was destined to be in constant competition with Steinway. The gold medal that the Chickering piano won at the Paris Universal Exhibition in 1867 as well as the Imperial Cross of the Legion d'Honneur bestowed upon Frank Chickering by Napoleon III both went a long way toward keeping this competitive spirit alive between the two firms.

Chickering owned and operated a concert hall on 18th Street and Fifth Avenue that opened its doors in 1875 with a concert by Hans von Bulow. However, changes in the market resulted in the sale of the hall in 1901 and the company's subsequent absorption into the American Piano Company as one of its divisions. However, a new Chickering recital hall was opened at this 57th Street location in 1923 to honor the firm's hundredth anniversary.

Pianos do not make beautiful music here any longer. Yet replicas of the gold medallion and the Imperial Cross (the latter said to be a symbol of the American Piano Company) can still be seen atop the edifice—an echo of a time when the piano business was in its heyday.

STEINWAY SHOWROOM & CONCERT HALL
109 West 57th Street
212-246-1100

A showroom, museum, and concert hall all under one roof

Steinway has had a long history since its founder, Henry Engelhard Steinway, began his business in a loft on Varick Street in 1853. (See "Steinway Factory" in the Queens section.)

The original Steinway Hall was located on East 14th Street and was quite a beautiful space. Seating 2500, it accommodated the New York Philharmonic and world-famous performers who played to capacity crowds. When this building closed in 1890, Steinway Hall relocated to its current address.

Visitors can get a real sense of the company and its piano from a visit to the showroom here with its informative exhibits on display. Scores of lovely instruments can be viewed, and the helpful sales staff can answer any questions regarding the purchase of a fine piano.

Browsing here on the first floor is fascinating—where one can see photographs, memorabilia, awards, and various other items that trace Steinway's history and development. Patent letters from 1869, tools once used in the workrooms, and various piano mechanisms all provide interesting information on the process of piano manufacturing, as well as on the exceptional design of the Steinway product itself. Many photos of Steinway artists line the walls, too—a testament to their love of this instrument.

The showroom also houses an amazing collection of artworks pertaining to music. There are busts of Rachmaninoff, Rubinstein, Paderewski, and additional figures. Paintings depict Wagner at his Steinway and Beethoven communing with nature as well as scenes evoked by such works as Liszt's *Hungarian Rhapsody No. 2*, Sibelius' *Finlandia*, Wagner's *Tristan and Isolde*, and others. There are also portraits of various composers and Steinway family members.

The building contains an intimate, beautifully appointed recital hall that is available for reservation by outside groups and individuals.

CAMI HALL
165 West 57th Street
212-397-6900

A lovely concert space across from a famous neighbor

This 200-seat hall was formerly known as Judson Hall in honor of Arthur Judson (1881-1975), a savvy concert manager in New York from the 1920s through the 1970s. Judson formed Columbia Artists Management, Inc. (CAMI) for which the hall was eventually named. Many groups and individuals rent the hall for recitals, opera, chamber music, and auditions.

The building, dating from 1917 and designed in the Italian mannerist style, was once home to Louis H. Chalif's School of Dancing.

CARNEGIE HALL COMPLEX

154 West 57th Street
212-247-7800

Practice, practice, practice!

This is probably the most famous concert hall in the world. Notable debuts here have included those of Arthur Rubinstein, Jascha Heifetz, Enrico Caruso, Van Cliburn, and Marian Anderson, among countless others, and its list of past performers is staggering. Every major orchestra has appeared here—the Philadelphia Orchestra, the Chicago Symphony, the London Symphony, and the Vienna Philharmonic, to name just a few.

Jazz has also had a long history at Carnegie—from Ella Fitzgerald, Charlie Parker, and Fats Waller to the ground-breaking 1938 "swing" concert featuring Benny Goodman and Count Basie. (The recording from this event is considered to be a jazz classic.) The Carnegie Hall Jazz Band was formed in 1991 and has continually performed for enthusiastic audiences. There have been folk and pop concerts, dance perfor-

This is a depiction of Carnegie Hall on opening night in 1891.
Courtesy of Carnegie Hall Archives

mances, comedy sessions, lectures, rallys, and special events—not just formal classical recitals! This is an eclectic center with a revered history.

Walter Damrosch had more than a little part in bringing about the creation of Carnegie Hall more than a hundred years ago. Near and dear to the heart of his father, Leopold Damrosch, was the hope of finding a new concert space for his groups—the Oratorio Society and the New York Symphony Society. Upon Leopold's death, Walter assumed both his father's responsibilities and goals. He approached Andrew Carnegie who, although not primarily a music philanthropist, was not altogether unsympathetic to the subject. Once Damrosch finally obtained support from Carnegie, the rest was history.

The architect for the building was William B. Tuthill—the perfect choice. Not only was he a musician himself, but he was also the secretary for the Oratorio Society. His heart was in this project in so many ways. Peerless acoustics, beautiful design, and richly ornate detail were the result and made this concert hall one that was destined to be truly outstanding.

Carnegie Hall, originally known as the Music Hall, opened on May 5, 1891, with Tchaikovsky as a featured guest conducting the New York Symphony Society orchestra in his *Marche Solennelle*. That particular evening was the first in a five-day music festival, marking the hall's introduction to New York's musical world. This much-anticipated occasion earned Carnegie Hall high marks on all counts.

Although Damrosch meant for Carnegie to be the home of his New York Symphony Society, the rival group—the New York Philharmonic Society—also took up residence here in 1892. Eventually, the groups merged in 1928 to become the New York Philharmonic, with Carnegie their official home until the advent of Lincoln Center in the 1960s. The Philharmonic has had a list of legendary conductors, including Arturo Toscanini, Bruno Walter, and Leonard Bernstein, who helped the orchestra earn its fine reputation within these walls.

An impressive structure that seats almost 2800, Carnegie Hall has seen performers from Vladimir Horowitz to Eubie Blake and from Andres Segovia to Paul Whiteman's band. Its style is truly diverse. Ignace Paderewski made his American debut here in 1891, a figure who remained synonymous with musical excellence for years to come. (He performed three concerts in the space of a week. Although the first one was modestly received, the audience rushed the stage by the third.) World premieres of works here have abounded—ranging from Dvorak's *New World* Symphony to Gershwin's *An American in Paris.*

Carnegie Hall had a close brush with the wrecker's ball in the late 1950s. Fortunately, Isaac Stern spearheaded an effort to save the building, ultimately earning it landmark status and sparking a massive renovation prior to its centennial anniversary. It is now more popular than ever, happily co-existing with Lincoln Center and offering concerts by every renowned soloist, orchestra, and group imaginable.

The hall was renovated in 1986, reopening with a splendid celebratory concert. Luminaries such as Isaac Stern, Peter Duchin, Yo-Yo Ma, Vladimir Horowitz, and Zubin Mehta with the New York Philharmonic all contributed toward making this a wonderful event. Leonard Bernstein even conducted a work that he wrote specially for the occasion. A massive centennial celebration was held in 1991 with many orchestras and performers from around the world.

Still a superb acoustic gem, the hall's lush interior is reminiscent of nineteenth-century New York splendor. Historic photos and memorabilia are located throughout, and visitors can enjoy behind-the-scenes tours in addition to a full choice of concerts.

Above the ground floor, a tower of individual studios, rehearsal halls, and small performance spaces has served musicians and creators of every specialty. Constructed after the main hall in the 1890s, this space is a maze of artistic wonders. Edward MacDowell and Leonard Bernstein are among the many famous names who were once tenants and used these working spaces, helping to fill the corridors with the joyous sounds of music.

Visitors can attend pre-concert lectures, professional workshops, family and children's concerts, and a variety of other activities. Dining facilities and a gift shop are available for concertgoers, as well.

Just as it has been for more than a hundred years, an appearance at Carnegie Hall is the mark of musical honor and achievement.

Weill Hall

This intimate concert space was opened in 1891, the same year as the main hall. Once referred to as the Chamber Music Hall, it was continually in use for a variety of events. Toscanini tested recording possibilities there, and both NBC and CBS broadcast live radio shows from this site during the 1930s.

Popular as a showcase for young musicians after its renovation in 1947, what came to be known as Carnegie Recital Hall underwent yet another remodeling in 1986, at the same time as the main hall. This wonderful space, seating more than 250, was then restored to its original 1890s appearance. Renamed for Joan and Sanford I. Weill, whose generosity made the renovation possible, this is a perfect location for intimate concerts, chamber music groups, and specialty performances.

The Rose Museum

Opened in 1991 in conjunction with Carnegie Hall's centennial, this inviting space on the second floor of the complex presents a number of changing exhibits focusing upon various aspects of the Carnegie Hall world. Previous exhibits have honored Tchaikovsky in America, the early years of Leonard Bernstein, the piano sonatas of Beethoven, the Gershwins, and other topics. A permanent display traces the history of the hall.

Named after its major benefactor, the Susan and Elihu Rose Foundation, this museum was formed for the purpose of sharing the contents of the Carnegie Hall archive with the public, who generously donated photos, letters, programs, records, memorabilia, and artifacts to its collection. Now, the archival collection boasts of 2500 square feet of material. It maintains such unusual items as Benny Goodman's clarinet and Toscanini's baton in addition to many other rare pieces.

Listen carefully at subway stops around the city. The Metropolitan Transportation Authority sponsors a program entitled "Music Under New York" which now features more than 100 individuals and groups at various transit locations. Music ranging from classical and jazz to bluegrass and ethnic is presented by these fine performers for the enjoyment of the public.

57TH STREET SUBWAY STATION
"N" AND "R" LINES
(57th Street and Seventh Avenue)

This artwork signals arrival at a famous destination

How do you get to Carnegie Hall? On the subway, of course!

Check the names inscribed on the white ceramic tiles here on the mezzanine walls (north and south). They are a veritable "who's who" of the music world. Performers' names are listed with their debut/performance dates at Carnegie Hall. They're all here—Ignace Paderewski, Beverly Sills, Duke Ellington, Maria Callas, Tony Bennett, the Philadelphia Orchestra, the Chicago Symphony, John Philip Sousa, Arthur Rubinstein, and countless others. (Speakers and political figures are also included.)

The north wall contains a striking porcelain enamel mural by Josh Scharf, entitled "Carnegie Hall Montage." Completed in 1994, this modernistic creation captures the eclectic essence of the hall's illustrious roster of past performers.

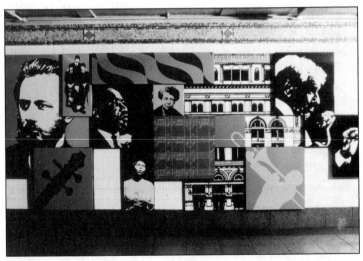

"Carnegie Hall Montage," completed in 1994 by Josh Scharf, portrays various performers from the Hall's illustrious past. *An original artwork owned by MTA New York City Transit and commissioned by the Metropolitan Transportation Authority/Arts for Transit*

Walk by the Osborne Apartments at 205 West 57th Street. Home to many musical figures over the years, this was where Leonard Bernstein wrote *West Side Story.*

This is one of scores of tiles lining the walls of the subway mezzanine that honor past celebrities who have performed at Carnegie Hall. *An original artwork owned by MTA New York City Transit and commissioned by the Metropolitan Transportation Authority/Arts for Transit*

JOSEPH PATELSON MUSIC HOUSE
160 West 56th Street
212-582-5840

A well-stocked classical music store

Just around the corner from the main entrance of its famous neighbor, this well-known music store has been in business for more than 50 years and has served the Carnegie Hall community and the city well. Housed in a historic building with a charming atmosphere of bygone days, Patelson's carries a fine range of classical (and some popular) music for instruments, ensembles, and vocalists as well as scores, books, periodicals, and related items. If browsing doesn't yield the item you're looking for, a knowledgeable staff member will gladly help.

Stroll by the Hearst Magazine Building at 951-969 Eighth Avenue (between 56th and 57th Streets). Among the many regal sculptures on the facade is Music, featured with her sister, Art, at the front entrance to the building.

BELA BARTOK PLAQUE & BUST
309 West 57th Street

The composer's last New York residence

This popular Hungarian composer (1881-1945) was known for his extensive research into the native folksongs of his homeland, both individually and in partnership with Zoltan Kodaly. The flavor of these folksongs permeates many of his works, giving them a distinctive sound.

Bartok toured the United States in 1927 and 1928 before returning to his country. However, he began experiencing increasing danger in Hungary because of the political situation there. Bartok's antifascist views brought numerous attacks from both Hungarian and Romanian newspapers. Fearing for the safety of his manuscripts, he sent them overseas to safety. Subsequently, he made a return visit to the United States and, after concluding his affairs in Europe, he emigrated permanently in 1940.

During his years in America, Bartok successfully completed a large body of research and was appointed a research assistant at Columbia University. He concertized with his wife and composed several major works. He received a commission from Yehudi Menuhin to write a work for violin. The "Sonata for Solo Violin" was introduced by Menuhin at Town Hall on November 26, 1944, to extremely favorable critical acclaim. He also composed the "Concerto for Orchestra" (commissioned by Serge Koussevitzky) as well as the "Piano Concerto No. 3."

Bartok's New York residences included addresses in Forest Hills and Riverdale. He frequently traveled to the country, though, in an effort to improve his failing health. Bartok lived at this address on West 57th Street during the last year of his life.

BROADCAST MUSIC, INC.

320 West 57th Street
212-586-2000

A well-respected performing rights licensing organization and research center

Broadcast Music, Inc. is a licensing organization that was founded in 1940 to protect the creative works of writers and publishing affiliates in its membership.

BMI publishes booklets and other helpful written materials for those within the industry. It also hosts numerous workshops, showcases, and related presentations and grants awards to composers.

This organization also maintains extensive archives for research purposes. Collected by Carl Haverlin, the first president of BMI, these holdings include autographs, scores, letters, and memorabilia of the great composers as well as of American and jazz music figures.

MUSEUM OF THE AMERICAN PIANO

211 West 58th Street
212-246-4823

The lure and lore of the piano

This is a small museum dedicated to the study of all aspects of the piano. Rare instruments, photographs, and memorabilia are on display tracing piano history from the eighteenth and nineteenth centuries onward.

The museum collects early and unique pianos for their historical significance as well as for their technical and musical features.

Special exhibits focus on different aspects of this most popular of instruments. Recently, the topic of early keyboard history (up to 1829) was featured. An original Muzio Clementi square piano, dating from around 1798, was a highlight.

Informative lectures and demonstrations are given in conjunction with these displays. Tours are by appointment.

Classes and lectures on the technical elements of the piano are offered regularly, not only for the layman, but also for those wishing to pursue careers in this area.

In addition, owner Kalman Detrich, an expert in the field, restores and repairs pianos of all kinds. The caliber of the work is world-class, and he has numbered Ella Fitzgerald, Duke Ellington, and Itzhak Perlman among his many famous clients. Those who would like to sell or purchase a fine piano are also invited to contact Mr. Detrich.

> This area has many piano centers. Check out Beethoven Pianos and Faust Harrison, both on West 58th Street. Then there is Piano Piano on West 55th Street. Keep strolling—you will probably discover others!

> The St. Thomas Choir School is located at 202 West 58th Street and is affiliated with St. Thomas Church on Fifth Avenue. Along with academic studies, the boys who attend this institution receive fine musical training and the opportunity to perform in liturgical and related settings.

CENTRAL PARK

STATUE OF THOMAS MOORE
Near East 60th Street and the pond

A tribute to a versatile poet, lyricist, composer, and singer

Although Thomas Moore (1779-1852) is probably most famous as a poet, he was also well noted as a lyricist, musical composer, singer, and entertaining personality. His songbooks became quite popular in New York among Irish immigrants and others.

Moore is perhaps best known for the song "The Last Rose of Summer" which was included in his *Irish Melodies* series, written between 1808 and 1834. He not only penned the lyrics for this series, but also many of the tunes. This was one of the most beloved collections of its time in the city and elsewhere, and its various printings enjoyed prolific sales.

Moore's other works include a large selection of popular songs written in 1802 and 1803, as well as *Sacred Songs* (1816) and *A Selection of Popular National Airs* (1818).

He wrote the libretto for one opera, *The Gipsey Prince* (1801), and collaborated on the words and music of yet another, although unsuccessful, comic opera.

This bronze bust over a granite pedestal was sculpted by Dennis B. Sheahan in 1879. It was dedicated on May 28, 1880, at a ceremony attended by 500 spectators. Upon receiving this gift to the city from the Friendly Sons of St. Patrick Society, the mayor made an acceptance speech during which he stated that Moore's "most lasting fame will rest upon his songs."

DELACORTE MUSICAL CLOCK
Near East 65th Street and Fifth Avenue

A whimsical creation that both depicts and plays music

Children of all ages love this delightful creation. A wonderful collection of bronze animals presents a musical performance of nursery rhymes each hour. They perform 32 different songs on a rotating basis, and their repertoire includes "Three Blind Mice," "Hickory, Dickory, Dock," and numerous other old favorites. Two monkeys, sitting atop the clock, lead the festivities, striking the bell with hammers. Their companions, six other members of the animal kingdom, gather on the platform below and appear to dance and play their instruments. An interesting assortment, they include an elephant with an accordion, a goat with pipes, and a hippopotamus playing the violin. A kangaroo and her baby share the horn. The rhythm section consists of a bear on the tambourine and a penguin on the drum.

These lovable figures were created by Andrea Spadini. The design was by Fernando Texidor, and the architect was Edward Coe Embury.

George T. Delacorte, philanthropist and publisher (Delacorte Press and Dell Books) as well as a fancier of animated European clocks, commissioned the work. It is a marvel of synchronized parts with platforms for the animals, a heating system, and an intricate Schulmerich Carillons electrical bell system.

The clock was officially unveiled on June 24, 1965.
Note: The clock can also be quickly visited during the upper East Side tour.

Stroll a bit west, enjoy a ride on the carousel, and hear its nice selection of lilting tunes. Speaking of tunes, Tavern on the Green (near the West 66th Street entrance) offers fine dining and great musical entertainment.

STATUE OF ROBERT BURNS
South End of the Mall

A poet and lyricist who contributed much to the preservation of the Scottish folksong tradition

---

Scotland's national poet was also responsible for making major contributions to his country's musical heritage. Robert Burns (1759-1796) dedicated the latter portion of his life to preserving the traditions of the Scottish folksong, and his contributions to the preservation of his country's native music were many. Long an admirer of the land's rich oral heritage, Burns set about collecting songs and materials for inclusion in *The Scots Musical Museum* (1787-1803) and *Select Collection of Original Scottish Airs* (1793-1818). Burns wrote lyrics for hundreds of songs within the collections, and these form the large majority of Scottish national songs, which he endeavored to raise to a fine, high art. Perhaps his best-known song is "Auld Lang Syne" which is, however, now sung to a different tune than the original.

This bronze statue on a granite pedestal was a gift from Scottish Americans. It was sculpted by Sir John Steell and dedicated on October 2, 1880, at formal ceremonies attended by 5,000, including many dignitaries. Grafulla's band provided music for the occasion and, at the conclusion of the proceedings, the crowd sang "Auld Lang Syne."

BEETHOVEN MONUMENT
The Mall—opposite the Bandshell

In honor of the great composer

This striking monument to the composer Ludwig van Beethoven is located along the Mall near the Bandshell. It was a gift to the city from the Beethoven Maennerchor in honor of the group's twenty-fifth anniversary in 1884. This organization was one of many local German choral societies that were popular in the nineteenth century. An extensive celebration was planned for the occasion, which was attended not only by members and their families, but also by choral groups from other cities. These festivities included a large parade with a band, a concert (featuring several works by Beethoven, of course), fireworks, dinners, speeches, and elaborate gifts from the visiting choirs. A procession with 200 carriages of attendees traveled to Central Park on July 22, 1884, for the official ceremony to unveil the statue.

The piece was created by the sculptor Henry Baerer, who came to New York from Germany in 1854. Atop the monument itself is a bust of the composer. At its base is a life-sized, flowing figure in bronze holding a lyre. This figure is intended to personify the spirit of music.

BUST OF VICTOR HERBERT
The Mall—opposite the Bandshell

Famous operetta composer and one of the founders of ASCAP

This lovely bronze bust, commemorating the beloved composer and longtime New York resident, is situated near the park's bandshell. Victor Herbert (1859-1924) was a cellist, conductor, and composer who gained popularity in the early 1900s for writing such lovely songs as "Ah, Sweet Mystery of Life," "Kiss Me Again," and "Toyland." These and other memorable melodies were performed in his popular operettas, including *Naughty Marietta*, *Sweethearts*, *The Red Mill*, and *Babes in Toyland*. A versatile man, Herbert also wrote serious music, served as conductor of the Pittsburgh Symphony Orchestra, and was bandmaster of the Twenty-second

Regiment Band (succeeding P.S. Gilmore). The latter group occasionally appeared in Central Park under his baton.

Herbert was quite active in the musical community in New York City. His grave concern about composers' rights and remuneration led him to become one of the founders of the American Society of Composers, Authors and Publishers (ASCAP) in 1914.

The bust, a gift to the city from ASCAP, was created by Edmond Quinn and initially rejected by the Municipal Art Commission for placement in its present location. (Evidently, the Commission did not consider Herbert important enough for the spot.) However, these differences were resolved, and the bust was unveiled by Herbert's daughter Ella at a ceremony in Central Park on November 30, 1927. The festivities were attended by hundreds of stage and musical figures, including Sigmund Romberg and Irving Berlin. Mayor James Walker accepted the gift on behalf of the city, recalling Herbert's many contributions to the world of music. A replica of the statue was also placed in the foyer of the old Roxy Theater.

This bust of Victor Herbert, beloved operetta composer, was a gift to the city by ASCAP, an organization that he helped to create.
Daniel McPartlin/
New York City Parks
Photo Archive

NAUMBURG BANDSHELL
On the Mall

Site of much enjoyable musical entertainment over the years

Although this present bandshell was built in 1923, the first concert ever held in the park was in 1859. Three years later, an actual "band stand," designed by Jacob Wrey Mould, was completed for concert use. It was located just west of the present bandshell.

Evidently, the park was a popular place for performances because plans were underway during this time for an additional bandstand—a floating one for use in the lake. Although this structure was designed but never built, occasional concerts by a 10-piece cornet band were given on a boat for the enjoyment of promenaders on the Terrace and in the Ramble.

Elkan Naumburg, a banker and music patron, had planned for several years to gift the city with another "band stand." At the age of 88, he realized his wish. At a ceremony held on September 29, 1923, ten thousand spectators witnessed the formal dedication of the new structure. The gift was accepted by acting Mayor Murray Hulbert, Park Commissioner Francis D. Gallatin, and City Chamberlain Philip Berolzheimer.

Newspaper accounts tell of festivities that included a concert by the 60-piece Franz Kaltenborn orchestra, with Kathryn Lynbrook of the Chicago Opera acting as soloist. Edwin Franko Goldman, the famous bandmaster, composed a march dedicated to Mr. Naumburg— "On the Mall"—which he conducted on the occasion. Mr. Naumburg was also honored with a special procession and the gift of a large flag of New York.

The Bandshell was designed by William G. Tachau, nephew of Mr. Naumburg, and built by Mark Isaacs & Sons. Classical in composition, it is made of Indiana limestone. It has a curved staircase to one side and bears the inscription: "To the City of New York and its Music Lovers."

There are lots of opportunities to hear great music in this beautiful park during the warm weather. Rumsey Playfield (72nd Street, east of the Bandshell) is the site of Summerstage, where a wide variety of concerts from pop to opera can be heard. The Great Lawn (center of park between 80th and 85th Streets) is the perfect spot to enjoy the Metropolitan Opera or the New York Philharmonic Orchestra on a nice summer evening.

STRAWBERRY FIELDS

Near West 72nd Street and Central Park West

A tribute to John Lennon—popular Beatles performer and composer

This beautiful garden, created out of extremely eroded ground, was opened in 1985 and serves as a memorial to John Lennon. The popular composer and member of the "Beatles," the hit rock group of the '60s, was murdered by a deranged fan outside of the Dakota, his famous apartment building, in December 1980.

Strawberry Fields is a tear-shaped plot of land that occupies two and a half acres just inside the Women's Gate of the park. Its name was derived from one of Lennon's most popular songs, "Strawberry Fields Forever."

Originally, conservative members of the City Council intended this spot to be used in commemoration of Bing Crosby, and a great deal of controversy ensued. However, approval was finally granted for the Lennon memorial.

Yoko Ono, the widow of John Lennon, provided most of the funds for the garden ($600,000 for construction and a $400,000 endowment for maintenance). She also sent out an appeal for donations of rocks and plants that allowed landscape architect Bruce Kelly to include 161 varieties of plants as a representation of every world nation. The city of Naples donated a star-shaped mosaic, inscribed with the word "Imagine" (another hit song), which was embedded in the pavement of the garden's walkway.

Lennon was known for his efforts on behalf of world understanding; therefore, it is fitting that this area is also referred to as an "international garden of peace."

Also, check out the whimsical Sgt. Pepper sculpture nearby, depicting the famous Beatles as they are popularly remembered.

Note: This site can also be quickly reached during the upper West Side tour.

What promised to be a beautiful concert evening in 1983 was disturbed by some youthful offenders. In an effort to create something positive for all, the Diana Ross Playground (near the West 81st Street entrance) was given to the city and named for the illustrious singer and former Supremes member who was the featured performer that evening.

When visiting the northern park (easiest during the Northern Museum Mile tour), check the Frances Hodgson Burnett Memorial Fountain at Conservatory Gardens (near 104th Street and Fifth Avenue)—a memorial to the author of *The Secret Garden*. A little boy plays the flute while a young girl listens. Accepted for the children of New York by Mayor Fiorello La Guardia, it was unveiled by sculptor Bessie Potter Vonnoh's granddaughter, Verity.

Nearby, Sunday afternoon concerts are held from May through October at the Harlem Meer Performance Festival on the plaza in front of the Charles A. Dana Discovery Center (enter at 110th Street and Fifth Avenue). Multicultural performances have delighted audiences for a number of recent seasons.

THE EAST SIDE

■ TURTLE BAY, EAST SIDE AND NEARBY ENVIRONS

Opened in the 1920s, the Palm restaurant (837 Second Avenue / 212-687-2953) was said to be one of maestro Arturo Toscanini's favorite dining establishments.

STUDY FOR SIBELIUS MONUMENT

United Nations
First Avenue near East 46th Street
East side of visitor's plaza

A striking symbol of musical and international harmony

This stainless steel sculpture was created in honor of the composer Jean Sibelius by Eila Hiltunen (Pietinen) and signed in 1964. Standing four and a half meters high, it resembles the pipes of an organ and represents a study of a larger monument to Sibelius that stands in a Helsinki park.

Sibelius wrote seven symphonies containing numerous sections that have been likened to the sound of the Finnish wind. During stormy weather, the sculpture purportedly emits a low sound similar to these symphonic themes.

The piece was presented to the United Nations by the government of Finland at a ceremony on September 9, 1983. It was

This sculpture by Eila Hiltunen is in honor of the composer Jean Sibelius and was a gift to the UN by Finland.
UN Photo 163 160/Yutaka Nagata

gratefully received on behalf of the UN by Secretary General Javier Perez de Cuellar. Placed in a position of honor near the General Assembly, it is a beautiful example of Finnish art as well as a wonderful symbol and expression of harmony—so appropriate for an organization dedicated to world peace.

JAPAN SOCIETY
333 East 47th Street (between First and Second Avenues)
212-832-1155

A cultural center within the UN area that offers fine musical programs

This organization was formed in 1907 to promote understanding between the United States and Japan. Appropriately located in this international neighborhood, the society offers a variety of lectures, exhibits, and concerts pertaining to Japan as well as an active educational outreach program.

There is a beautiful 278-seat theater on the premises, the Lila Acheson Wallace Auditorium. Here, one can attend concerts of many types of works pertaining in some way to Japan. Music is performed on both traditional and modern instruments, and contemporary compositions and jazz are also featured. Opera with Japanese themes as well as lectures and special presentations with musical significance are occasionally scheduled.

A variety of changing exhibits provide a glimpse into the cultural riches of this exotic land. Music is often woven into these presentations, including a recent celebration of Japanese theater which included a display of musical instruments.

> Take a quick side trip to Beekman Place to admire the beautiful surroundings. Irving Berlin lived at number 17 for many years. An annual holiday tradition, his admirers would stand outside this home and serenade the composer with his great hit "White Christmas."

EAST 48TH & 49TH STREETS
Between Second and Third Avenues

An area of musical personalities

A number of musicians—not to mention actors—have lived in this lovely residential area. It is worth a stroll just to admire the architecture and enjoy the atmosphere and historical detail. Here are a few things to note.

Turtle Bay Gardens consists of back-to-back rows of houses with a common garden, including 227-247 East 48th Street and 226-246 East 49th Street. Over the years, this location was favored by a number of famous musical residents—Broadway composer and lyricist Stephen Sondheim, conductor Leopold Stokowski, and singer/actress Mary Martin.

Nearby on East 49th Street, the house occupied by the Zimbalist family was located at numbers 225-227. Efrem Zimbalist, Sr. was a celebrated violinist who achieved fame both in Europe and in America. A composer and faculty member at the Curtis Institute in Philadelphia, he was married to Alma Gluck, a soprano who appeared with much success at the Metropolitan Opera. They resided at this site for several years beginning in 1926, the year that the house was built. Alma Gluck's daughter, author Marcia Davenport, also lived here, and several of her novels dealt with musical topics.

Two contrasting sights are nearby, just slightly outside the boundaries of Turtle Bay. The Waldorf-Astoria Hotel & Towers (301 Park Avenue between East 49th and 50th Streets) was once home to sophisticated songwriter Cole Porter ("Night and Day," "I Happen to Like New York," etc.) His piano is now used in the hotel's Cocktail Terrace. Right across the street is the strikingly beautiful St. Bartholomew's Church (east side of Park Avenue between 50th and 51st Streets). A wide variety of musical and cultural programs are sponsored here.

TURTLE BAY MUSIC SCHOOL
244 East 52nd Street (between Second and Third Avenues)
212-753-8811

Learning to make the beautiful sounds of music

This eclectic music school, the only one of its kind serving the midtown East Side community, was founded by Eleanor Stanley White in 1925 with only six students on its rosters. The school, incorporated in 1928, has grown into one of the most successful entities of its kind.

Nestled in a quiet corner of the neighborhood in an 1860 brownstone, the school has a number of well-equipped studios and a concert hall. It offers a broad range of classes for all age groups. Everything is available, from introductory music groups for two-year-olds, to chamber music for adults, to special teen classes, to community sings. Private instrumental instruction is given by a staff of professional musicians with impressive credentials. The school provides outreach programs, special performances for medical and nursing facilities, and music therapy, among its many offerings. Concert performances are given at the school, and many are open to the public.

ST. PETER'S CHURCH & MIDTOWN ARTS COMMON
Citicorp Center
619 Lexington Avenue at East 54th Street
212-935-2200

Worship—jazz style

One of the most well-known Lutheran churches in the world, this congregation has a special ministry that reaches out to the jazz community. The Jazz Ministry was officially created by Pastor John Garcia Gensel in 1965. Popular as well as unusual, it reaches out to jazz musicians with a sensitivity to their special needs. In turn, many world-renowned names have contributed their talents to this congregation and have also been honored here.

The church offers Jazz Vespers, special concerts, jazz marathons, festivals, jazz services, and unique memorials.

Past participants in these services and events read like a jazz "who's who" from Duke Ellington to Tommy Flanagan. Billy Strayhorn donated his piano to the sanctuary of the church, and it has been happily put to good use by a number of keyboard artists.

In a more traditional mode, St. Peter's boasts of a beautiful Klais organ, the first to be placed in a church in the United States. Not only is it a superb instrument possessing 42 ranks of pipes, but it is also an artistic visual accompaniment to the striking design of the sanctuary itself. Classical organ recitals are frequently presented.

Art shows, midday jazz concerts, musical theater, and other special events are also presented in the numerous informal facilities within the complex. These are quite popular and reach out to the surrounding residential, business, and professional communities.

Citicorp Center (between Third and Lexington Avenues and East 53rd and 54th Streets) is a mix of shops and eateries. Frequent concerts are held in its open public area—an example of building space that is put to good cultural use.

■UPPER EAST SIDE

LADIES' PARLOR
Abigail Adams Smith Museum
421 East 61st Street (between First and York Avenues)
212-838-6878

A music room with rare instruments in a historic setting

Set in a quiet East Side area, near the river and in a neighborhood all its own, is this hidden treasure—a landmark structure that provides a wonderful look at the atmosphere of early nineteenth-century life in New York City. In addition, it contains some superb examples of musical instruments from this time period.

The building was originally intended for use as a carriage house on the estate purchased in 1795 by Colonel William

Stephens Smith. Colonel Smith, married to the daughter of President John Adams, was an aide-de-camp to George Washington. Construction on both the mansion and the carriage house was completed in 1799 after the Smiths had sold the property.

In 1826, the carriage house was remodeled into the new Mount Vernon Hotel by its owner, Joseph Hart, after the mansion was destroyed by fire. This day hotel was intended for New Yorkers wishing to escape city life for the peace of the "country."

The museum is designed to resemble the Mount Vernon Hotel as it appeared about 1830. A music room occupies one half of the upstairs Ladies' Parlor. A small collection of fine instruments is on display here, reflecting the early New Yorker's love of music as both cultural interest and leisure pastime.

An unusually ornate harp, created by the world-famous instrument maker Sebastian Erard (1752-1831) and imported from his shop in England, is one of the most attractive pieces. It is decorated in a fine classical motif and was built sometime between 1810 and 1820. There is also a unique Spanish cedar flute, dating from this same time period.

The music room in the Ladies' Double Parlor at the Abigail Adams Smith Museum contains a rare 1820 barrel organ, an attractive Sebastian Erard harp, and an unusual piano by John Kearsing of London (on loan from the Museum of the City of New York) that dates from the early 1800s.
Photo by Martin Beckerman, courtesy of Abigail Adams Smith Museum

The Abigail Adams Smith Museum maintains a rare piano in its own collection, dating back to 1790, that is not currently on display. The action and keyboard were manufactured in England, but the case was created in New York by Thomas Tomkison of Dean Street in what is now SoHo.

The piano on display is on loan from the Museum of the City of New York and dates from 1825 to 1830. It was manufactured by John Kearsing of London for John J. Rickers of 187 Broadway (as inscribed on a gold leaf decal above the keyboard). This unusual instrument is designed in the Empire style and created of rosewood, ormolu, brass, ivory, and gold leaf. Additional decorative motifs include carved feet with acanthus leaves.

A rare barrel organ, from approximately 1820, was made in France. Cylinders containing various songs were inserted into the mechanism, and the tunes could be heard by cranking a handle. Inside the top cover is a list of its available songs which includes the ever-popular "Yankee Doodle."

The museum also hosts musical programs relating to this nineteenth-century period, both as part of an annual summer series and during its popular holiday candlelight tours.

There are numerous cultural organizations, houses of worship, and small museums on the upper East Side, other than those included in this tour. Many host occasional concerts, often in conjunction with special events. Keep alert for performance notices during your travels.

TEMPLE EMANU-EL
1 East 65th Street (at Fifth Avenue)
212-744-1400

Impressive musical performances and a fascinating musical history

---

The largest Jewish house of worship in the world, this structure was completed in 1929 and dedicated in 1930. An imposing edifice both inside and out, it seats 2500 and is known for its imaginative architecture and design. Approach it from Fifth Avenue in order to experience its truly imposing grandeur.

Temple Emanu-El offers a number of musical concerts, lectures, and programs. Its Young Artists series, co-sponsored with the Friends of Young Musicians Foundation, presents fine soloists in full concert programs. It has also offered gala tributes to composers, such as Mendelssohn, and has been the setting for performances by stars from the Metropolitan Opera.

Many fine liturgical works are performed here, and the Temple is also known for its annual ecumenical concert, presented in conjunction with other houses of worship in the area.

Note: The Delacorte Musical Clock in Central Park can be visited quickly from this site. See section on Central Park for description.

KOSCIUSZKO FOUNDATION
15 East 65th Street
212-734-2130

Chamber music, recitals, and musical competitions held in an attractive setting

This lovely townhouse was built in 1917 according to the design of Harry Allan Jacobs. Its original owner, socialite James J. Van Alen, was a son-in-law to Mrs. Astor.

This has been the home of the Kosciuszko Foundation since 1945. The Foundation, founded in 1925, is named after Tadeusz Kosciuszko, the Polish soldier who distinguished himself through his heroic participation in the American Revolution. The organization is dedicated to the preservation of Polish education and culture through its exhibits, lectures, and musical offerings.

Music is one of the highlighted interests of the Foundation. Its chamber music, solo, and other special recitals are open to the public and are presented in an extremely attractive concert space. Works by Polish composers are featured as well as a broad range of repertoire from other traditions. String ensembles, vocal trios, a saxophone quartet, and flute, piano, and vocal soloists were recent concert offerings. A favorite chamber music concert series highlights conversations with the performers and is broadcast on local radio station WQXR-FM.

In addition, the Foundation sponsors the annual Chopin Competition, which it created in 1949 and inaugurated at a

special ceremony—all in honor of Frederic Chopin on the
hundredth anniversary of his death. Over the years its winners have included Van Cliburn.

RITA FORD MUSIC BOXES
19 East 65th Street
212-535-6717

An internationally known collection of musical wonders

___

This charming and unique store is a neighborhood institution with an international reputation. Although its founder
and proprietor, Rita Ford, passed away in 1993 at the age of 92,
her shop retains its original exotic quality. Often referred to as
a museum in its own right, it possesses an extensive collection
of music boxes ranging from rare, handmade antiques (some
dating back well into the 1800s) to unusual modern pieces.
The shop handles made-to-order requests and will service and
restore old music boxes.

The range of boxes on display includes huge antique Swiss
mechanisms that play more than a dozen classical airs.
Others are in the shape of pianos, violins, eggs, nutcrackers,
and toys. Many traditional music boxes with a variety of
exquisite designs are also available. The repertoire played on
these beautiful creations includes classical, popular, and traditional melodies.

The store displays a photograph of Rita Ford presenting
Richard Rodgers with a gold carousel music box that played
the waltz from *Carousel*—a popular combination of style and
song through the years.

During its long history, the store has provided service to
such celebrity customers as the White House, Beverly Sills,
Mrs. Nelson Rockefeller, and the King of Saudi Arabia (who
once ordered 20 matching boxes created to play his country's
national anthem).

This is well worth a visit just to browse and to admire these
unique musical gems.

HUNTER COLLEGE OF THE CITY OF NEW YORK
Musical Sites
695 Park Avenue (at East 68th Street)
212-772-4000

A diverse selection of concert halls presenting all types of musical events

Hunter College has long been associated with the arts. Its music program has a fine reputation, and its theater program is well respected within the community.

Not only has the college had a history of presenting professional concerts, but it also sponsored a Concert Bureau for many years. At one time, subscribers to annual concert and arts series numbered approximately 200,000. Musical figures such as Vladimir Horowitz were presented at the Assembly Hall. City financial crises eliminated the Bureau, but Hunter's tradition of high-quality professional concerts and performances has survived. Now, there are several refurbished concert spaces in which to enjoy a wide array of lovely events.

The Sylvia and Danny Kaye Playhouse

A donation of one million dollars from Sylvia and Danny Kaye helped to transform the former Hunter College Playhouse into an up-to-date space. Danny Kaye was beloved by audiences for his acting, comedy, singing, and love of music. Sylvia Kaye's talents as a musician and writer have long been acclaimed. She wrote music and lyrics for many films in which her husband appeared, including *The Kid from Brooklyn* and *The Secret Life of Walter Mitty*, among others. Their generous donation helped to complete this gem—with enhanced acoustics, superb facilities, and an elegant interior, including velveteen-covered seats in the same hue as Sylvia Kaye's favorite lipstick.

The first few seasons featured guest performers including singers Martina Arroyo and Sherrill Milnes, pianist Claude Frank, the Moscow String Quartet, the Atlas Camerata Orchestra, La Gran Scena Opera, and the JVC Jazz Festival.

Even prior to the renovation, this theater was always popular for musical events. Recitals by such renowned figures as Vladimir Horowitz, Regina Resnik, Daniel Barenboim, and Pinchas Zukerman were among many featured. Now the 664-

seat space is even more attractive within the musical world, and its concert calendar is full of varied and quality events.

Reopened in 1993, the theatre was named in honor of this talented couple. It is also now home to such performing groups as the Clarion Music Society.

Ida K. Lang Recital Hall
North Building—Room 424

The children of Ida K. Lang, a graduate of Hunter College's class of 1915, donated the funds to develop this 145-seat hall that was opened in 1995. Created in a striking design by the architectural group of Abramovitz-Kingsland-Schiff, it is perfectly suited for solo, chamber, and ensemble recitals.

Located in the North Building, home to the school's music department, this hall has fine acoustics along with wonderful equipment for sound recording. Two Steinway concert grand pianos are an added attraction to these splendid facilities.

The inaugural concert was performed by the internationally acclaimed Cassatt String Quartet. Other well-known soloists and groups have subsequently appeared here.

Concert series are available to the public.

Frederick Loewe Theater
In October 1997, the former Little Theater (sometimes called the Black Box) was refurbished through the generosity of the Frederick Loewe Foundation as well as other donors and renamed in the composer's honor. This attractive 138-seat theater is used for a variety of dramatic, musical, and special presentations and is situated in Thomas Hunter Hall.

At the dedication and ribbon-cutting ceremony, students performed a medley of songs by Frederick Loewe, the creator of beloved musical scores such as *Camelot* and *My Fair Lady*.

ASIA SOCIETY
725 Park Avenue (at East 70th Street)
212-288-4646

An elegant concert hall that offers traditional ethnic and intercultural concerts

---

This organization was formed to acquaint Americans with various aspects of the Asian world. Its eight-story modern center houses a large number of artworks from a variety of Asian cultures and includes the collection amassed by John D. Rockefeller.

Many forms of Asian music and performing arts have been introduced through the efforts of the Society. Here, Ravi Shankar made his American debut, and the Royal Musicians and Dancers from the kingdom of Bhutan began their first international tour. In addition to the traditional music of varying Asian cultures, more contemporary programs are presented, such as the works of Philip Glass and other twentieth-century composers.

The beautifully appointed Lila Acheson Wallace Auditorium is the setting for a wide assortment of concerts, lectures, and programs. An example of the versatility of these offerings is the Crossovers series that analyzes and celebrates the inspiration drawn from each culture by the others, with such performers as jazz great Billy Taylor and pianist/composer Jon Jang. Additional concerts and series have focused on Pakistani vocal music, qawwali (devotional music from the Sufi culture in Pakistan), and Sarangi (bowed lute) repertoire.

A fine interview series, spotlighting various topics, has featured discussions with musicians including cellist Yo-Yo Ma.

BOHEMIAN NATIONAL HALL
321-325 East 73rd Street

A former ethnic social hall with plans—including some musical ones— for the future

---

The Bohemian Benevolent and Literary Association, under the direction of Jan Hird Pokorny, has been organizing an effort to restore the 1896 Bohemian National Hall to its former grandeur. Mr. Pokorny (who designed the pedestal for the Dvorak statue in Stuyvesant Square Park) has already restored the facade of this historic building. Now he is gathering support for renovation of the interior of the structure.

Once a thriving center for the Czech and Slovak community, the building had a restaurant, ballroom, and recreation facilities.

If the renovation efforts are realized, the hall will be the home of a small Dvorak museum collection, including the mantelpiece and original plaque salvaged from his former house on East 17th Street, among other artifacts. Proposals for the future also include facilities for cultural events as well as an ethnic restaurant.

The Café Carlyle at the Carlyle Hotel (35 East 76th Street / 212-744-5737) has featured pianist/singer Bobby Short for decades, making this site a true musical landmark.

■ MUSEUM MILE, CARNEGIE HILL AND ENVIRONS

METROPOLITAN MUSEUM OF ART
(Musical Collections and Sites)
Fifth Avenue at 82nd Street
212-535-7710

A treasure trove of musical instruments, concert spaces, and musical events

Musical Instrument Room
This area is not to be missed. The core of the collection was built from holdings amassed by Mary Crosby Brown between the 1880s and World War I. She was probably the foremost instrument collector of her generation. Rare specimens of instruments from a variety of categories represent diverse cultures from around the world. Subsequently, items donated by other individuals were added.

One of the many highlights of the European collection is the oldest piano in existence. It is a 1720 model produced by Bartolommeo Cristofori, the inventor of the piano. (It is still in working condition!) Other keyboard instruments—many with ornate decorations—are on display. For example, a late seventeenth-century harpsichord with a gilt exterior and figures supporting its case is a real showpiece. Other unusual keyboard items include a clavicytherium from the early seventeenth century—an upright harpsichord with period paintings; a "glassichord" built into a table; a portable pipe organ from 1575; a 1581 double virginal with decorative paintings; and nice examples of Erard and Broadwood pianos.

Flutes and recorders, some dating from as early as 1700, are on display. There are bassoons of all sizes, oboes, saxophones, bass horns, ceremonial horns, and ophicleides of extremely unusual shapes.

A 1936 euphonium contains an unusual variety of delicately engraved decorations, including several composers, George Washington, and nudes.

There is a large selection of harps. Both a decorative barrel piano and organ are on special display, as is the oldest extant pipe organ from Thomas Appleton of Boston (1830). Stringed instruments abound, such as basses, cellos, and violins (including models created by the famed Antonio Stradivari from 1694 and 1717).

Many paintings relating to music as well as other items (e.g., a model of a stringed instrument craftsman's workshop) complement this astounding display.

There is a special collection of instruments from Eastern and Native American cultures. From India and environs, plucked stringed instruments (sarod, sitar, etc.) are shown. Other unusual items include Tibetan horns from the sixteenth century; a Burmese *mi-gyaung* (a stringed instrument in the shape of a crocodile); a moon guitar from Thailand; and a Javanese *slento*, or mallet instrument, in a dragon-shaped frame.

There are also a number of Asian ritual instruments and colorful pieces from Korea. A nice selection of North African drums can be viewed. Among the diverse collection of North American native pieces is a stopped pipe from the Northwest coast and whistles used by Sioux Indians.

Additional musical pieces and paintings with musical themes are scattered throughout the museum—always a joy to discover.

Grace Rainey Rogers Auditorium
David Mannes first initiated a series of free concerts at the Met in 1918. The tradition of holding concerts at the museum grew as time passed, and the museum now hosts chamber groups, soloists, orchestras, baroque music recitals, and lectures on various forms of music by leading conductors, critics, and performers.

The Rogers Auditorium provides a lovely setting for these events with an intimate space that seats 700. It has served as the site for the New York debut of many performers including the likes of Peter Serkin.

Other Musical Offerings
Special concert series are occasionally held in various other locations in the museum including the Medieval Sculpture Hall, the Garden Court, and the imposing Temple of Dendur.

Also, a quintet is featured on Friday and Saturday evenings in the Great Hall Balcony Bar.

Just a block or so from the museum, at Madison Avenue and East 81st Street, is Frank E. Campbell's Funeral Chapel—an establishment with a worldwide reputation. Services were held here for such famous musicians as Tommy Dorsey, Arturo Toscanini, and John Lennon.

REGINALD DE KOVEN HOME
1025 Park Avenue (between 85th and 86th Streets)

The composer of "Oh, Promise Me" once lived here

Reginald De Koven (1859-1920), the composer of the enduring song "Oh, Promise Me," lived at this site, an attractive 1912 mansion. John Russell Pope designed the home especially for De Koven and his wife, creating the look of an English Jacobean manor.

De Koven studied composition in many European capitals and created comic, light, and folk operas during his career. His most famous work was *Robin Hood* (1890), a romantic and comic opera that ran for a number of years. "Oh, Promise Me" was a major hit from this production and went on to enjoy additional fame as a wedding favorite.

A plaque was placed on this building in 1989 by the New York Landmarks Preservation Foundation in honor of De Koven.

THE LIEDERKRANZ
6 East 87th Street
212-534-0880

Home of the famed musical society

This organization, the oldest German-American choral and social society in the city, was formed in 1847 and made its official debut on May 17th of that year. Originally consisting of a small group of German men, it set out to preserve the native musical culture of their homeland through the singing and performance of works by such composers as Mozart and Beethoven. Its membership grew to as many as 1500 early in this century.

The Liederkranz combined with the Arion Society in 1918 to form an even stronger organization that emphasized the enjoyment of fine classical music, provided free musical instruction to talented youngsters, and offered many concerts by German composers.

Today, the society still sponsors and hosts a vast array of musical events including operas, concerts, and competitions. Many are available to the general public. The Liederkranz Foundation offers scholarships and sponsors deserving young musical artists. Past presidents of the society have included such luminaries as William Steinway. Diverse personalities from Theodore Roosevelt to Victor Herbert have been members of this organization.

This building was formerly the residence of John S. Phipps. It was designed by Grosvenor Atterbury in 1904. On the east side of the building is a six-foot-high bronze statue, "Polyhymnia." It is composed of two life-sized figures who are said to represent German song. A maiden holds a lyre in her hand and stands behind a boy who appears to be singing. The statue was created by Giuseppe Morretti and donated by the Ladies' Society of the Liederkranz in honor of the group's fiftieth anniversary. Five hundred club members attended the banquet and the unveiling of the statue which was placed in the corridor of the society's former headquarters at 115 East 58th Street. It was placed in the east yard following the relocation to East 87th Street in 1949.

Inside, there are countless musical articles, including a statue of Arion and a bust of Richard Wagner in the lobby. Numerous commemorative plaques and scores of photographs of singers are on display throughout the building which houses recital halls, meeting rooms, a library, and administrative offices.

SOLOMON R. GUGGENHEIM MUSEUM
Musical Programs
1071 Fifth Avenue (at 89th Street)
212-423-3500

From classical to jazz

This unique modern structure, completed in 1959, was designed by Frank Lloyd Wright as a home for the contemporary art collection of Solomon R. Guggenheim. Here, one can enjoy works by Chagall, Miro, Picasso, and a host of other modern masters. The museum was restored in 1992, and its exhibits are continually growing and enhancing in scope.

The Guggenheim also sponsors a vast array of musical and cultural programs. Its striking Peter B. Lewis Theater has hosted programs ranging from the music and cultural traditions of India to lectures on the interrelationship of opera to history and politics. A series entitled Works and Process was founded in 1984 by Mary Sharp Cronson and specializes in presentations that examine the creative process—from new works by contemporary composer Ned Rorem to discussion/performances of new productions launched by the New York City Opera.

The weekly WorldBeat Jazz Series, held in the rotunda, offers a fine selection of performances by renowned jazz figures—a popular musical attraction at the museum.

Nine East 91st Street was once the home of John H. Hammond. Benny Goodman was a frequent visitor here and evidently participated in the musicales for which the Hammonds were well known.

Check out the Wales Hotel (1295 Madison Avenue / 212-876-6000). It has a beautiful turn-of-the-century atmosphere and offers daily classical music for its guests as well as a Sunday chamber music series.

92ND STREET Y

1395 Lexington Avenue
212-427-6000

A center for musical performances, education, lectures, and special events

This branch of the Y was formed here in 1874, and its Tisch Center for the Arts has many outstanding musical programs. Varied concert series are offered and include world-renowned performers—from Nadja Salerno-Sonnenberg to Jaime Laredo to Dick Hyman. Every type of music is performed here in an imaginative style—including classical, jazz, pop, cabaret, and folk. The exquisite chamber music series is a favorite, and internationally acclaimed groups such as the Guarneri String Quartet have been a part of it in addition to scores of others. At the same time, such series as "Lyrics and Lyricists," celebrating the work of popular songwriters, have played to a packed house. All of this under one roof!

The acclaimed Kaufmann Concert Center is a wonderful setting for performances, lectures, readings, and various presentations and is a real favorite both in the community and in the city at large.

The School of Music provides private instruction on a variety of instruments, ensemble coaching, and classes in many different musical disciplines. Thousands of people—both young and old—have participated in its programs and workshops over the years.

The unusual wood frame home at 160 East 92nd Street dates to 1853 and is unique in terms of Manhattan residential architecture. Popular singer, film and stage star Eartha Kitt once lived here. She appeared at the Village Vanguard and on Broadway in *New Faces of 1952*.

DILLER-QUAILE MUSIC SCHOOL
24 East 95th Street
212-369-1484

An East Side institution with a solid history in musical education

This school was founded in 1921 by Angela Diller (1877-1968) and Elizabeth Quaile (1874-1951), both teachers at the David Mannes School (now the Mannes College of Music). Together, they created a series of piano instruction books that became famous over the years.

These books are still used here (and elsewhere), and all faculty members receive training in Diller-Quaile principles.

At its current locale since 1954, the school still carries on the tradition of fine musical education for both children and adults. A staff with impressive credentials provides both private and group instruction on a variety of instruments, and special classes are offered, including chamber groups and an opera workshop for adults. Approximately 1300 students are enrolled here.

A resident string quartet composed of faculty members performs at the school's recently renovated 1,000-square-foot performance space. Additional student and faculty concerts are also presented.

■ NORTHERN MUSEUM MILE AND SURROUNDING ENVIRONS

MARIAN ANDERSON PLAQUE
1200 Fifth Avenue at East 101st Street

Longtime residence of the famous Metropolitan Opera star who was recognized for her achievements as a musician and a humanitarian

Marian Anderson (1897-1993) was a talented and versatile contralto who performed a variety of works over her long career and led the way for other black artists to break racial barriers in many major performance venues.

During the 1920s, she made her Carnegie Hall debut and performed with the Philharmonic. In the 1930s, she made the news when an audience of 75,000 came to hear her sing at the Lincoln Memorial after being denied access to Constitution Hall on racial grounds. During this decade, she also performed at the White House.

The first black performer to join the permanent ranks of the Metropolitan Opera, she debuted in 1955 in a production of Verdi's *A Masked Ball.*

In 1958, the same year that she moved into this building, Ms. Anderson was selected as an alternate delegate from the United States to the United Nations. She was often recognized for her many achievements over the years and was the recipient of a Presidential Medal of Freedom, a Congressional gold medal, and a Grammy Lifetime Achievement Award.

Marian Anderson lived here from 1958 to 1975. This commemorative plaque was placed by the Historic Landmarks Preservation Center.

MUSEUM OF THE CITY OF NEW YORK
Musical Collections and Exhibits
1220 Fifth Avenue (between West 103rd and 104th Streets)
212-534-1672

A rich resource for those interested in music and the history that surrounds it

Formed in 1923, this fascinating collection was designed to organize and preserve the rich history of the city in all of its forms. Rooms from mansions long gone, prints, paintings, and artifacts all provide a sense of the past—the musical past included.

There are permanent exhibits, such as the one celebrating the Broadway theater, that are rife with musical displays. This particular exhibit features photos, costumes, drawings, sheet music, and memorabilia from such productions as *The Black Crook* (an early example of the musical comedy form), *The Mulligan Guard* (famous Harrigan & Hart revues), *In Dahomey* (the first full-length African-American musical on Broadway), *Kiss Me Kate*, *Showboat*, and others. In addition, there are items such as portraits of Cole Porter and Victor Herbert, Gershwin's practice keyboard, and a photograph of George M. Cohan, to mention just a few things. Items pertaining to everything from Broadway shows to minstrel shows to vaudeville are on display.

There are special exhibits on music and musical figures such as a centennial tribute to the Gershwins and a retrospective on the life of Paul Robeson. Photographs and descriptive information on The People's Hall of Fame recently honored some grassroots musicians who performed everything from Chinese opera, to traditional Puerto Rican music, to Harlem blues/jazz, to oldtime gospel, to klezmer classics.

Special concerts are often linked to the exhibits. Past performances have included music played and sung at the time of New York's consolidation as well as selections used at ethnic parades.

The period furnishings boast of a Robert & William Nunns rosewood piano and an elegant harp from the early nineteenth century, and several musical miniatures in the antique dollhouse display.

The theater research collection is extensive, containing thousands of items, many pertaining to musicals—costumes, sketches for set designs, memorabilia, scores, playscripts, programs, and much more. The museum holds the largest such collection in the United States. Researchers may apply for appointments to use these archives.

Note: The Frances Hodgson Burnett Memorial Fountain near West 104th Street in Central Park's Conservatory Gardens can be most easily reached from this site. Check the section on Central Park for a description.

> Visit El Museo del Barrio (1230 Fifth Avenue / 212-831-7952), and check for special musical events at its Hecksher Theater.

DUKE ELLINGTON STATUE
Fifth Avenue at 110th Street (Duke Ellington Circle)

A dramatic tribute to one of New York's—and the world's—most memorable jazz greats

This is one of the most impressive works of art ever designed in tribute to a musician. Sculptor Robert Graham created this amazing 25-foot bronze monument, coated in a dramatic black patina with a portion of gleaming bronze on its disk.

The nine muses are arranged in three tiers supporting the disk, atop which rests a full grand piano. Standing next to the keyboard is an eight-foot statue of this very elegant musician and composer.

Dedicated on July 1, 1997, the ceremony was attended by hundreds of musicians, politicians, and local citizens. Included in this group were Mayor Rudolph Giuliani, former mayors David Dinkins and Ed Koch, Ellington's sister and granddaughter, and cabaret star Bobby Short, who was responsible for organizing the fundraising and support for this project.

Ellington's music was featured with selections by both groups and soloists, including a performance by the famed Wynton Marsalis.

The traffic circle where the statue sits was renamed in honor of Ellington in 1995.

Note: The Harlem Meer summer concerts can be most easily reached from this site. Check the section on Central Park for a description.

THE WEST SIDE

■ LINCOLN CENTER AREA

VINCENT YOUMANS PLAQUE

Mayflower Hotel and Conservatory Restaurant
Central Park West at 61st Street (northwest corner)

Composer of "Tea for Two" was born at this site

Vincent Youmans (1898-1946) was one of the great composers of the American musical theater. His remarkable works are classics that continue to remain a part of the standard repertoire of popular song.

This plaque marks the site where Youmans was born on September 27, 1898. Presented on September 28, 1970, it was a gift in his memory from his many friends and admirers. It lists a number of Youmans' most famous songs including "Tea for Two," "Without a Song," "Carioca," "I Want to Be Happy," "Hallelujah!" and "No, No, Nanette."

Prior to the unveiling of the plaque, more than 50 devotees attended a champagne breakfast at Stampler's (the restaurant then located on the ground floor of the building). Attendees included Youmans' son and daughter, songwriters Johnny Mercer and Irving Caesar, the presidents of ASCAP and BMI, the City Commissioner of Cultural Affairs, and the famous movie choreographer Busby Berkeley.

This site, in the Mayflower Hotel building, now houses the Conservatory Restaurant, a favorite within the musical community and located a stone's throw from Lincoln Center.

AMERICAN SOCIETY OF COMPOSERS, AUTHORS AND PUBLISHERS (ASCAP)

One Lincoln Plaza (Broadway near West 63rd Street)
212-621-6000

Famous performing rights licensing organization

Victor Herbert was one of the founders of this illustrious organization, whose concept was first discussed at an informal meeting at Luchow's restaurant in 1914. Designed to protect composers, lyricists, songwriters, and publishers of music, the society ensures that fair royalties will be granted for the performance and use of copyrighted works. ASCAP provides the bridge between author/creators and those who publicly perform or otherwise make use of their works.

Today, there are more than 70,000 members of ASCAP. It continues to broaden in scope and now sponsors a wide variety of awards and grants for original composition and related musical endeavors. It also supports educational programs and publishes several reference works pertaining to composers and their music.

ASCAP is still the guardian of Irving Berlin's special piano—an interesting model. This instrument was built with a unique transposition lever—a rare device on a traditional piano, particularly in Berlin's day.

Nearby is the Radisson Empire Hotel (44 West 63rd Street / 212-265-7400) that houses a wonderful restaurant/jazz club, Iridium, featuring top-notch performers. The hotel foyer also has a display of mini opera sets for Mozart's *Cosi Fan Tutte* and Verdi's *Un Ballo in Maschera*, among others.

Right down the street, on Columbus Avenue near West 62nd Street, is The Music Store and The Flute Center of New York—where you can purchase music for all instruments and obtain assistance with flute repairs and maintenance.

THELONIOUS SPHERE MONK CIRCLE
Junction of West 63rd Street and West End Avenue (Phipps Houses)

Tribute to groundbreaking jazz pianist and composer

Before heading to Lincoln Center, take a quick detour west on 62nd Street to West End Avenue and round the corner to West 63rd Street. Here is another famous neighborhood musical site.

Thelonious Monk was a jazz innovator who not only possessed an individualistic approach, but also led the way for new styles within this idiom.

He began as a house pianist at Minton's Playhouse on West 118th Street, once quite a popular night spot and currently slated for reopening. Here, he performed with many visiting musicians and helped to create the "bebop" or "bop" style. Monk was first recorded in 1941 as a member of the Minton's House Quartet.

Monk went on to perform with such famous groups as the Coleman Hawkins Quartet and the Dizzy Gillespie Orchestra in a number of locations. He also played solo and led many of his own jazz ensembles. Performance venues ranged from the Village Vanguard to Town Hall. As a composer, his works were complex and unique—as was his keyboard style. His most popular tune is "'Round Midnight." As one of only three jazz musicians to appear on the cover of *Time*, his accomplishments attracted the attention of those beyond musical circles.

Monk was a longtime resident of 243 West 63rd Street, and this location was named in his honor in 1983.

LINCOLN CENTER FOR THE PERFORMING ARTS
West 62nd to 66th Streets (main plaza on Columbus Avenue)
212-875-5000

A cultural complex for all of the arts

The beautiful Lincoln Center complex—with its majestic concert halls, sweeping plaza, fountain, sculpture pool, and outdoor café—was first planned amidst a flurry of controversy.

As early as the 1930s, Fiorello La Guardia suggested a center where all types of music could be performed. The idea was discussed by numerous individuals but, years later, it was Robert Moses who was credited with being the catalyst for the project.

Moses chose the present Lincoln Center site with hopes of revitalizing the area, even though he was the focal point of sharp criticism. (This area, formerly known as San Juan Hill, was once the site of the tenement life immortalized in the production of *West Side Story*.) However, with the aid of financial backers including members of the Rockefeller family as well as a charter granted in 1955, construction began in 1959. The main portions of the complex were completed between 1962 and 1968 with several additions to follow in later years.

Of course, Lincoln Center eventually became the largest performing arts center in the United States. In the decades since its creation, it has served not only as a cultural mecca, but also as a pivotal force in regenerating the upper West Side.

Now, the public can enjoy the culture as well as the atmosphere. While waiting for a concert, one can stroll through the plaza (where summer performances are often held) and see fountains and outdoor sculpture, or visit one of the on-site cafés or gift shops that are a part of the complex. Tours of the entire facility, as well as of individual halls, are also available to the public.

The New York State Theater
212-870-5570

Here, on the south portion of the main plaza, near Columbus Avenue, is the home of the New York City Opera as well as the New York City Ballet. Designed by architect Philip Johnson (who had the needs of George Balanchine's group in mind), it seats approximately 2700 in its horseshoe-shaped interior. Opened in 1964, the hall underwent some reconstruction in 1982.

This is the Lincoln Center site at the groundbreaking ceremony on May 14, 1959. *Photo by Bob Serating, courtesy of Archives of Lincoln Center for the Performing Arts, Inc.*

This is a view of the main plaza buildings at Lincoln Center for the Performing Arts, a few short years after the complex was constructed.
Photo by Susanne Faulkner Stevens, courtesy of Archives of Lincoln Center for the Performing Arts, Inc.

The New York City Opera originally performed at City Center, making its debut in 1944 with *Tosca*. Formed with a philosophy differing from that of its neighbor, the Metropolitan Opera, it features many new young American singers. Rather than promoting "name" stars, it prefers to emphasize the ensemble approach in casting its roles. (However, many individuals have risen from its ranks to achieve fame, Beverly Sills being one of the most notable.)

The company offers standard repertory, classic musical theater pieces, and premieres of new productions. Over the years, the company has produced works by Handel, Mozart, and Bizet as well as those by Rorem, Menotti, and Sondheim, to name just a few. Conductors of note have included Erich Leinsdorf and Julius Rudel.

The New York City Ballet was founded in 1948 by George Balanchine and Lincoln Kirstein. It, too, offers a wide range of traditional as well as modern productions and is especially well 1known during the holiday season for its sumptuous and beloved performance of *The Nutcracker*.

A wonderful abstract work of art is featured on the right wall of the staircase leading from the lobby. Entitled "Ancient Song," it is a huge creation of gold leaf by

Yasuhide Kobashi—an example of the many artworks in Lincoln Center that honor music.

Damrosch Park/Guggenheim Bandshell
212-875-5000

Directly to the west of The New York State Theater (still bordering West 62nd Street on its outer perimeter) is this beautiful outdoor concert space, occupying 2.3 acres of the complex. It was completed in 1969 and designed by Eggers & Higgins. A paved public space surrounded by attractive landscaping and a lush backdrop of trees accommodates seating for 2500. The centerpiece is the Guggenheim Bandshell where free concerts are presented in the warm weather by such groups as the eminent Goldman Memorial Band.

The park was named after Frank Damrosch, one of the founders of the Institute of Musical Art—now the Juilliard School of Music, also located within the Lincoln Center complex. The bandshell was created in honor of Daniel and Florence Guggenheim who were active in a variety of musical circles.

This is also the site of the Big Apple Circus which regularly sets up its tent in the park for its innovative performances.

> Outdoor arts festivals can also be enjoyed near the fountain in the central plaza of the complex. The summer months are usually bursting with musical activity here—from bands to ethnic music to performance art, and more.

The Metropolitan Opera House
212-362-6000

Just north of Damrosch Park, fronting on the western portion of the main plaza, is the famed "Met." This world-renowned company moved here from its previous home on 39th and Broadway in 1966 and serves as the central focus of the plaza building group. The company and its opera houses have continually made headlines over the years.

The Met's original house opened in 1883 with a production of Gounod's *Faust,* an evening that was crucial in the infamous "opera wars." When prime seating at the Academy of Music became a major issue between "old" money and "new," the nouveau riche entrepreneurs decided to build their own opera house—more lavish, more attractive, and more celebrated than the Academy. The Met grew to such prominence that it eventually forced the Academy into ruin.

The list of international opera greats who have sung on the stages of both the old and the new house is staggering. Enrico Caruso debuted there in 1903. Other names include Lawrence Tibbett, Rise Stevens, Eleanor Steber, Birgit Nilsson, Franco Corelli, Sherrill Milnes, and Leontyne Price. Conductors at the Met have included the likes of Arturo Toscanini and Gustav Mahler. Its managers have ranged from Giulio Gatti-Casazza, formerly of La Scala, to Rudolf Bing, formerly of Glyndebourne and Edinburgh.

Numerous opera premieres have been offered through the years, and a variety of programs to support young artists, opera education, and the arts in general have been promoted by the Met.

This current house, designed by Wallace Harrison, opened to much fanfare with a world premiere of Barber's *Antony and Cleopatra*, a critical failure. However, the new house as well as performances by Justino Diaz and Leontyne Price attracted much notice.

A lavish hall seats 3788, and large onstage and backstage facilities are a real plus. An innovative electronic subtitle system allows patrons to use this service individually, if they choose. Sweeping staircases, chandeliers, and plush appointments recall the grandeur of attending operas in days gone by.

Artworks and displays that pay homage to the world of music abound. The most striking is Marc Chagall's mural—"Le Triomphe de la Musique"—on the south mezzanine wall. A huge splash of figures from the performance world are featured—singers, dancers, jazz and folk musicians, and even Chagall, his wife, and Rudolf Bing are portrayed.

The north wall has "Les Sources de la Musique," portraying not only scenes from opera, but also composers and historical/mythological musical figures—Wagner, Bach, Beethoven, Verdi, Orpheus, and King David among them.

Other artworks scattered throughout the premises include a monument to Debussy on the grand tier and a veritable museum of paintings, sculptures, and representations of opera notables on the lower level, including likenesses of Caruso, Callas, Pons, and numerous others.

Avery Fisher Hall
212-875-5030

Avery Fisher Hall is slightly northeast of the Metropolitan Opera House, also facing the main plaza. It was the first edifice to be completed within the complex.

September 23, 1962, saw the opening of Philharmonic Hall featuring Leonard Bernstein conducting the New York Philharmonic. Disappointment with the orchestra's new home, particularly with its acoustics, made a bit of a difficult start for the new complex. (The New York Philharmonic, the oldest orchestra in the country, had long been associated in the public's mind with the venerable Carnegie Hall where it had made its home since 1892. This space was, of course, a hard act to follow—acoustically, physically, and nostalgically.) Fortunately, this situation was turned into something quite positive.

Philharmonic Hall was renovated during the 1970s to enhance its acoustical facilities. Renamed in 1973 in honor of a leading manufacturer of hi-fidelity equipment (who provided a substantial gift), it was redesigned by Cyril Harris and Philip Johnson, rebuilt, and reopened in 1976.

The inaugural concert was conducted by Pierre Boulez, and the acoustics and interior design were accepted well. (A few refinements were added in 1992 to even further perfect the sound.) Ever since, it has happily served as the home to the famed New York Philharmonic as well as the host to thousands of major orchestras, festivals, and individual performing groups from around the world. Its annual Mostly Mozart Festival has become a fixture on the regular concert calendar of New Yorkers. Its acoustics, its fine interior seating more than 2700, and its grand atmosphere are considered to be among the best anywhere.

Many works of art complement the music that is heard within this hall. Richard Lippold's shimmery mobile, "Orpheus and Apollo," and Dimitri Hadzi's modernistic work inspired by a Mozart string quartet are among them. Antoine Bourdelle's bronze "Tragic Mask of Beethoven" on the Grand Promenade and Rodin's head of Mahler are also part of the "musical art" here.

The New York Philharmonic Orchestra is in residence at Avery Fisher Hall and is the oldest such group in continuous existence in the country. The Philharmonic Society was founded in 1842 and directed by Ureli Corelli Hill, a well-known conductor and musician of the time. Its inaugural concert took place at the Apollo Rooms, where Beethoven's Fifth Symphony was on the program, among other works. The orchestra also performed the American premiere of Beethoven's Ninth Symphony at Castle Garden in 1846. It soon became a model for other groups, with the quality of its performances and its range of programming far exceeding that of other American orchestras. It further prospered under the leadership of such conductors as Theodore Thomas and Anton Seidl. Specializing in German compositions at one time, it broadened its repertoire with successive conductors to embrace a wide range of works, including many premieres. One of its early rivals, the New York Symphony Society, founded in 1878 by Leopold Damrosch and directed for many years by his son, Walter, subsequently merged with the Philharmonic in 1928. (The Symphony Society had the distinction of performing at the opening of Carnegie Hall in 1891.) The orchestra has had many famous conductors including Gustav Mahler, Arturo Toscanini, Bruno Walter, George Szell, Pierre Boulez, Zubin Mehta, Dimitri Mitropoulos, and Leonard Bernstein, among others. Bernstein made history when he stepped in at the last minute to substitute for Bruno Walter, who had been taken ill. Bernstein led the orchestra during its move to Lincoln Center and further popularized the group through televised performances and innovative children's concerts, to name only a few of his accomplishments. Currently directed by Kurt Masur, the orchestra is one of the most renowned in the world.

New York Public Library for the Performing Arts
212-870-1630

Slightly recessed in the western portion of the complex and tucked between the Metropolitan Opera House and the Beaumont/Newhouse edifice is the New York Public Library for the Performing Arts. This building, completed in 1965, is a combined research facility, circulating library, exhibition gallery, and concert venue.

Research and circulating collections serve patrons interested in music, dance, and theater. Additional resources are available in media and recordings. The library also has significant historical holdings, including original scores by Mozart, Griffes, Gottschalk, Haydn, Mahler, and other composers. Its historic recordings, correspondence, sheet music, newspaper files, programs, rare books, and photographs are of valuable assistance to researchers in all of the arts.

The Vincent Astor and Amsterdam galleries mount a variety of new performing arts exhibits on a regular basis. These allow the visitor to view scores, memorabilia, and special collections pertaining to the worlds of music, dance, and theater.

The Bruno Walter Auditorium, named for the famous conductor, presents frequent musical concerts, recitals, and other types of performance art for the general public.

> Just west of Avery Fisher Hall is a beautiful sculpture pool and outdoor mini-plaza for strolling and relaxing. This area provides a "front yard" for two intimate spaces—the Vivian Beaumont Theater and the Mitzi E. Newhouse Theater—stages for dramatic and small ensemble productions.

Samuel B. & David Rose Building

On the other side of the plaza stairs (north side of the plaza in front of the Beaumont/Newhouse complex) is this 28-story building, completed in 1991—one of the newer additions to the complex family. It contains offices, rehearsal studios, and dormitories that serve the Lincoln Center community.

Walter Reade Theater
212-875-5600

This lovely space is home to the Film Society of Lincoln Center. Its intimate seating capacity of 268 is perfect for the unique offering of films presented here. Occasionally, a silent film series will also provide live accompaniment, either by piano or selected musical ensemble.

Lectures on music and occasional chamber music and other concerts are also offered here.

Juilliard School of Music
212-799-5000

Originally, Juilliard consisted of two schools—the Institute of Musical Art, formed in 1904 by Frank Damrosch, and the Juilliard Graduate School, founded in 1924. The schools fused in 1946 to form the Juilliard School of Music. This world-renowned conservatory moved to Lincoln Center in 1969 from its previous location on Claremont Avenue.

As an independent professional school, this is the first major institution of its kind in the United States to offer programs in all of the performing arts—music, opera, drama, and dance.

Its illustrious list of graduates includes Van Cliburn, Leontyne Price, and Itzhak Perlman. Its faculty list, past and present, reads like a "who's who" in the performing world—Rosina Lhevinne (piano), Ivan Galamian (violin), Roger Sessions and Elliott Carter (composition), and Leonard Rose (cello). Past presidents have included John Erskine, Ernest Hutcheson, and William Schuman. The composer Peter Mennin led the school into its new home at Lincoln Center.

The building, itself, has spacious classrooms and studios, the two-story Lila Acheson Wallace Library with modern equipment and historic holdings, art galleries, and a dramatic entranceway.

The school offers bachelor's, master's, and doctoral degrees in a variety of specific areas within each major discipline.

Juilliard has four auditoriums to accommodate a wide variety of performances. The Juilliard Theater has 1,000 seats. Paul Recital Hall, with its 292 seats, is appropriate for recitals and smaller performances. There is also the Drama Workshop and, finally, Alice Tully Hall—which is best known to the public.

Concerts, operas, small recitals, and dramatic productions are just a few of the types of events that are available for all to enjoy.

Juilliard has a well-stocked bookstore that is open to the public.

Alice Tully Hall
212-875-5050

This cozy recital hall, actually a part of the Juilliard School of Music, was added to the north end of the Lincoln Center complex in 1969. It seats 1096 and its warm atmosphere and perfect acoustics are a welcome setting for solo recitals, chamber music concerts, arts festivals and the like.

The hall was made a reality by a generous gift from Alice Tully, dramatic soprano and granddaughter of the founder of Corning Glass.

The Chamber Music Society of Lincoln Center calls this home. The group, founded by Charles Wadsworth in 1969, consists of nine members who perform chamber works in various combinations on a regular basis.

The hall also hosts Jazz at Lincoln Center, the New York Film Festival, Serious Fun, and a wide variety of special recitals.

The foyer contains a wonderful bronze piece by Antoine Bourdelle—"Beethoven à la Colonne" (1901).

Leonard Bernstein Place

West 65th Street, between Amsterdam Avenue and Columbus Avenue, divides the two portions of Lincoln Center. This street was named in honor of Leonard Bernstein—appropriate not only because of its Lincoln Center location, but also because of its close proximity to Avery Fisher Hall.

A multi-talented musical figure, Leonard Bernstein (1918-1990) made his smashingly successful New York Philharmonic debut when he filled in at the last minute for an ill Bruno Walter. Later, he served as the conductor of this orchestra from 1958 to 1969, becoming known for his dramatic style with the baton, his vast musical talent, a wholehearted enthusiasm for a wide range of works, and his audience savvy. Bernstein was conductor of the Philharmonic when it moved to Lincoln Center, and he was at the podium for the inaugural concert at Avery Fisher Hall.

The first American-born conductor of the Philharmonic, Bernstein championed a number of new works, instituted the very popular Young People's Concerts, and increased the orchestra's popularity through television.

As a classical composer, he was known for his orchestral, chamber, and vocal pieces. However, he achieved far-reaching fame for his theatrical scores, which included *West Side Story* and *Candide.*

Detour west for a minute, and you'll see The Fiorello La Guardia High School of the Performing Arts (Amsterdam Avenue between West 64th and 65th Streets). Part of the public school system, it offers intense training in music, theater, and fine art—all along with a regular academic program.

RICHARD TUCKER PARK
Intersection of Broadway and Columbus Avenue
(between West 65th and 66th Streets)

A tribute to a renowned Metropolitan Opera star

Richard Tucker (1913-1975) was revered as one of the leading tenors of his time. As a young man, he sang on the radio and in synagogues before embarking on an international career in opera.

Tucker sang more than 30 lead roles with the Metropolitan Opera during his 30-year association with the company, and he was often compared with Caruso. His final role at the Met was in *I Pagliacci,* which he performed several weeks before his untimely death. His funeral was held onstage at the opera house.

A bronze bust of the singer, created by Milton Hebald and commissioned by Tucker's family, is at the center of the small park bearing his name. The park is appropriately located just across the way from Lincoln Center for the Performing Arts.

The bust was formally presented by Tucker's widow on April 20, 1980, at a ceremony attended by singer Robert Merrill, Mayor Ed Koch, former Mayor John V. Lindsay, and various family members and friends. This sculpture is similar to one that was installed in the singer's honor in Tel Aviv.

ELAINE KAUFMAN CULTURAL CENTER
AT THE ABRAHAM GOODMAN HOUSE
129 West 67th Street
212-362-8719

A center for musical performance, education, and research

This cultural complex, built in 1978, houses the Merkin Concert Hall, an acoustic gem seating 457 and high in popularity among performers. Many groups and individuals rent the space for concerts, and the hall also sponsors several concert series and serves as the site for live radio broadcasts. Also housed in this complex is the Ann Goodman Recital Hall, a setting for more intimate programs.

The on-site Lucy Moses School for Music and Dance provides a variety of classes and performance opportunities for the young. The Special Music School of America is also on the premises.

Other facilities within the complex include the Birnbaum Music Library, containing diverse musical materials, particularly those pertaining to Israeli culture. Approximately a dozen classrooms, two dozen music rooms, dance studios, and an art gallery complement this institution's offerings.

The cultural center is also home to numerous performance ensembles.

■ UPPER WEST SIDE

THE DAKOTA APARTMENTS
One West 72nd Street

An example of elegant West Side apartment life with an illustrious history of musical residents

---

This apartment house was completed in 1884 and was thought to be so far away from the center of town that it may as well have been located in the Dakota territory—hence, its name. It was considered to be the first real luxury dwelling of its kind. The apartments in this commanding edifice are known for their high ceilings, beautiful woodwork and decorations, and spacious interiors.

A number of famous individuals from the musical world have lived here over the years—Leonard Bernstein, musicologist/critic Edward Downes, Judy Holliday, and Judy Garland, among others. Of course, one of the building's most famous musical residents, John Lennon of the Beatles, was tragically shot and killed in front of this building by a deranged fan.

Note: You can make a quick trip to Central Park's Strawberry Fields (West 72nd Street entrance to the park) from here. This is the garden created in memory of John Lennon. See the section on Central Park for a description.

VERDI SQUARE & STATUE
West 73rd Street at Broadway and Amsterdam Avenue

An opera composer and his title characters

This little square displays an innovative sculpture in honor of Giuseppe Verdi. Atop the monument is a regal, full-sized statue of this famed opera composer. Surrounding him at the base of the structure are four full figures from his most popular operas—the title characters from *Otello*, *Aida*, and *Falstaff*, and Leonora from *La Forza del Destino*.

The monument, created by Sicilian sculptor Pasquale Civiletti, is created of white carrara marble on a granite base. Its inscription reads: "Erected by the Italian community through the efforts of Chevalier Charles Barsotti, editor of the Italian daily newspaper, *Il Progresso Italo-Americano*."

The sculpture was unveiled in 1906 at a festive ceremony attended by 10,000 spectators and preceded by a parade of Italian societies up Fifth Avenue from the Washington Square Arch. Various representatives of the Italian-American community as well as an emissary of the King of Italy were prominent guests. There were numerous speeches as well as performances of some of Verdi's works by both chorus and orchestra.

A highlight of the ceremony was the release of a balloon by Barsotti's grandchild, which carried the veil from the statue. Doves were then set free, and showers of roses and other flowers descended upon the crowd. This beautiful spectacle was arranged in the colors of the Italian flag.

The statue was restored in 1997 and rededicated at a ceremony attended by the sculptor's great-granddaughter as well as many city dignitaries. Verdi's music was performed by members of The New York Grand Opera Company.

This site is an official New York City Scenic Landmark.

THE ANSONIA

2109 Broadway (between West 73rd and West 74th Streets)

The home of famous musical residents—past and present

The brainchild of copper and manufacturing heir William Earle Dodge Stokes, this ornate 17-story structure has long been a favorite of the New York musical community. Stokes wanted to create the most wonderful hotel imaginable on the upper West Side and, according to reports of the time, he achieved his goal admirably.

The Ansonia was built in 1904 and designed in the beaux-arts style by the firm of Graves & Duboy. Its unique and ornate towers, ornaments, and balconies make it an outstanding feature in the neighborhood landscape.

A number of famous musicians have lived in the building throughout the years, including Enrico Caruso, Igor Stravinsky, Arturo Toscanini, Giulio Gatti-Casazza, Mischa Elman, Yehudi Menuhin, Lily Pons, and Ezio Pinza, to name only a few. (This atmosphere may well have influenced non-musical celebrity residents. Babe Ruth was listed among the more notable tenants and was reported to have taken up the saxophone during his stay there.) Stories continue to circulate by the hundreds about eccentric residents—musical and otherwise—contributing to the illustrious history of the building.

Musicians and performers still live and rehearse here. They relish the building's musical heritage and camaraderie—not to mention the three-foot-thick walls which offer a welcome layer of soundproofing (so rare in more modern structures).

The Ansonia was given landmark status in 1972 and is certainly worth strolling by just to see its architecture, beautifully evoking a more elegant age. Old photos of the building and its history are usually on display in the lobby.

GERSHWIN PLAQUE
33 Riverside Drive at West 75th Street

The famous duo wrote several hit musicals here

George Gershwin, along with his brother, lyricist Ira Gershwin, lived at this address between the years of 1929 and 1933. George's 17th-floor penthouse evidently matched his taste for luxurious living. A beautiful view, fine furnishings, and tasteful art objects offered the perfect setting for his lavish gatherings—and were visible examples of the success he had achieved. (Ira occupied an adjoining penthouse.)

It was here that Ethel Merman—then Ethel Agnes Zimmerman—auditioned and won her coveted part in *Girl Crazy*. (Gershwin predicted her future stardom but warned her never to take singing lessons.)

The building is now part of the West End Collegiate Historic District, as designated by the New York Preservation Foundation. A plaque by the main entrance on West 75th Street commemorates both Gershwins as well as the shows that they created together during their years here as residents—*Girl Crazy*, *Of Thee I Sing*, and *Let 'Em Eat Cake*. The plaque was presented by the Historic Landmarks Preservation Center.

> Miles Davis lived at 312 West 77th Street. During his time here, this famous jazz trumpeter recorded several outstanding record albums.

RACHMANINOFF PLAQUES
505 West End Avenue (at West 84th Street)

Former residence of the world-renowned Russian pianist and composer

Sergei Rachmaninoff (1873-1943) is one of the few individuals who has been granted the distinction of two commemorative plaques on the same building. The famous Russian composer and pianist lived here during the last 17 years of his life.

Always in demand on the concert circuit, Rachmaninoff developed his career as a piano virtuoso later than most and somewhat out of the pointed economic necessity resulting from his relocation to America. He also conducted approximately 1,000 concerts on these shores. Still, this busy composer found the time to create a wide range of innovative orchestral and solo works. While a resident in this building, he composed the beloved "Rhapsody on a Theme by Paganini" as well as his Third Symphony and the "Symphonic Dances."

The first bronze plaque was dedicated in 1993 to commemorate the 50th anniversary of the composer's death, the 100th of his professional debut, and the 120th of his birth. It was jointly presented by admirers, corporate institutions, and the city. It is to the left of the main building entrance, somewhat above eye level.

The second plaque, placed by the Historic Landmarks Preservation Center in 1996, is to the right of the main entrance.

MANNES COLLEGE OF MUSIC
150 West 85th Street
212-580-0210

An intimate conservatory with an eclectic array of studies

This small conservatory was organized in 1916 by the husband and wife violin-piano team of David Mannes and Clara Damrosch (whose portraits are on display in the building). This duo performed extensive sonata literature for these instruments and introduced it to many parts of the country. David Mannes was once the concertmaster in the New York Symphony Society, under the leadership of Walter Damrosch.

After spending many years in the East 70s, the school moved to its current location and, subsequently, became a division of the New School. Its faculty represents an impressive array of internationally acclaimed artists with many unique musical specialties.

A variety of bachelor's and master's degree programs are available in classical studies as well as in jazz and contemporary music. The school is also proud of its offerings in historical performance and its in-residence chamber groups. A preparatory division for children, ages 4 to 18, and an adult extension area provide a wide selection of classes, as well.

The main concert hall, seating 300, and an intimate recital hall for an audience of 70 are the centers for both public and private concerts. In addition, Mannes has exceptionally fine recording facilities on the premises.

■ UPPER WEST SIDE/THE NINETIES AND ABOVE

SYMPHONY SPACE
2537 Broadway at West 95th Street
212-864-5400

"Wall to Wall" music and more

This unusual performance center has had a varied background. It was once the location of the Astor Market, the Crystal Palace Skating Rink, and the Symphony Theater. After falling on hard times, it became a shabby, and eventually empty, movie house. Allan Miller and Isaiah Sheffer turned it into a community arts center with a combination of enthusiasm, local support, and a Ford Foundation grant.

Although it is the site of a variety of performance genres, Symphony Space is quite well known for its musical presentations. The most famous of these are the "Wall to Wall" marathons, offering a diverse and intense—often day-long—series of concerts of the music of composers ranging from Bach to Cage. Many local organizations perform here, too, including The New York Gilbert & Sullivan Players as well as groups from the nearby Mannes College of Music. Performance/conversations with contemporary composers as well as frequent birthday celebrations in honor of celebrity composers help to round out the fare.

Symphony Space also sponsors several educational outreach programs that integrate the arts into the curriculum of city public schools.

THE WHITEHALL
Broadway and West 100th Street

George Gershwin's sanctuary for peace, quiet, and composition

In order to escape the constant noise and commotion in the busy Gershwin family home, George took a suite at the hotel originally located at this site.

It was here in 1925 that he completed his "Concerto in F," a work premiered at Carnegie Hall during the same year. He also finished the score to *Tip-Toes,* including such memorable songs as "That Certain Feeling" and "Sweet and Low-Down."

The Whitehall was built during a boom in hotel construction in the early 1920s.

GERSHWIN HOUSE
316 West 103rd Street (near Riverside Drive)

The first luxurious residence of this famous family

The entire Gershwin family moved into this house in 1925. It was definitely a move up in the world for them—a beautiful five-story edifice with a self-service elevator. The proceeds from *Lady, Be Good, Rhapsody in Blue,* and various songs went toward its purchase. Soon, even Ira and his wife occupied rooms in the house.

Despite its spacious quarters, there was still too much commotion for George to gain the solitude that he needed to compose. Therefore, he rented rooms at the Whitehall hotel for times when he required privacy.

Subsequently, George and Ira moved to luxurious penthouse suites on 75th Street and Riverside Drive—a further move upward on the social scale.

DUKE ELLINGTON BOULEVARD
West 106th Street from Riverside Drive to Central Park West

A street named in honor of a legendary jazz innovator

Composer, arranger, pianist, and bandleader, Edward Kennedy (Duke) Ellington (1899-1974) was known for his groundbreaking contributions to the jazz world. Long considered an innovator, Ellington shared the spotlight with Louis Armstrong in jazz circles in the late 1920s and early 1930s.

Labeled a sophisticated stylist, he recorded many of his works such as "Mood Indigo," "Echoes of Harlem," "I Got It Bad," "Sophisticated Lady," "Solitude," and "Hot and Bothered," among others. His 1927 recording of *Black and Tan Fantasy* is still viewed as a classic in its field. Many of his recordings featured the "jungle" style, one of the many hallmark creations of Ellington and his group.

Ellington's band regularly performed at the Kentucky Club, the Cotton Club, the Zanzibar, the Apollo Theater, and others. So great was their popularity that they even appeared in the film *Check and Double Check* in 1930. Many band members achieved recognition in their own right: Billy Strayhorn, Johnny Hodges, and Mercer Ellington (Duke's son).

Ellington also composed longer works for the concert stage such as his "Black, Brown, and Beige" of 1943. Premieres of his works were presented at Carnegie Hall. Noted for his many achievements, his 70th birthday celebration took place at the White House.

A longtime resident and New York enthusiast, Ellington lived at several city addresses, most notably 333 Riverside Drive (near West 106th Street) in a residence owned by his sister.

West 106th Street, previously associated with members of the jazz world, was renamed for its entire length in Ellington's honor in October 1977.

See also "Duke Ellington Statue"—Fifth Avenue at 110th Street.

THE NICHOLAS ROERICH MUSEUM
319 West 107th Street
212-864-7752

A musical series and some artwork relating to music are featured here

---

Nicholas Roerich (1874-1947) was an artist who believed that cultural development and emphasis was one of the critical components of peace. His efforts toward this end were significant.

In his early years, he became acquainted with the works of such composers as Mussorgsky, Rimsky-Korsakov, Stravinsky, Arensky, Wagner, Prokofiev, and others. This led to his creation of designs for sets and costumes for opera and dance productions for a range of groups from Diaghilev to the Chicago Opera. His paintings also reflect many musical influences.

Roerich founded the Institute of United Arts in New York in 1921, where Deems Taylor taught classes in theory and composition. This was one of many projects that he undertook to sponsor the arts.

This museum, established in 1949, displays many of Roerich's works—including some that are related to the musical world. There is also an extensive concert series in the auditorium of the building that presents young performers in solo and chamber recitals.

VICTOR HERBERT PLAQUE
321 West 108th Street

An ASCAP founder and operetta composer whose song hits included "In Old New York"

Victor Herbert (1859-1924) was a well-known figure on the New York musical scene for decades. Originally a cellist, he was also a conductor of varied experience, having served as leader of groups such as the Pittsburgh Symphony as well as the famous Twenty-Second Regiment Band (succeeding P.S. Gilmore).

As a composer, he wrote symphonic and band works, cello concertos, and instrumental solos, as well as "serious" choral and vocal pieces. However, his real fame was derived from the wonderful operettas that he created, with their beautiful melodies and lush orchestrations. These productions were all the rage in New York and included such familiar fare as *The Red Mill, The Fortune Teller, Eileen,* and *Babes in Toyland.* Songs from many of these shows are still heard today and include such favorites as "Kiss Me Again," "Thine Alone," "Ah, Sweet Mystery of Life," "In Old New York," and "Italian Street Song."

A firm supporter of copyright laws, he was also one of the founding fathers of the American Society of Composers, Authors and Publishers (ASCAP), which still operates today to protect the creative works of its members.

Victor Herbert lived in this dwelling from 1904 until his death in 1924. During this time he wrote his popular operettas *Naughty Marietta* and *Sweethearts.*

This plaque was presented by the Historic Landmarks Preservation Center.

THE BLOOMINGDALE HOUSE OF MUSIC
323 West 108th Street
212-663-6021

A well-established community music school with fine programs and concerts

---

Founded in 1971, this community music school has a number of unique programs. Its after-school and Saturday program provides instruction by highly qualified faculty on any of 25 different instruments, ranging from piano to African drums. There is also a class to introduce babies to music.

Classes in the Orff system, in conjunction with the city's public schools, as well as MAP, a project that prepares teenagers for entrance into musical programs at colleges and conservatories, are two particularly successful offerings.

Free concerts are also presented by faculty, students, and guest artists.

UPTOWN MANHATTAN

■ MORNINGSIDE HEIGHTS AND COLUMBIA UNIVERSITY AREAS

GERSHWIN SITE
501 West 110th Street (at Amsterdam Avenue)

Where Rhapsody in Blue *was completed*

The entire Gershwin family lived here prior to George's great success which financed more opulent quarters in a townhouse on West 103rd Street.

It was here that Gershwin composed his immortal *Rhapsody in Blue* (1924) on an aging upright piano. This famous piece was premiered by Paul Whiteman's Orchestra at Aeolian Hall. Gershwin was the soloist.

WEST END
2909-11 Broadway (near West 113th Street)
212-662-8830

A former center for poetry and jazz

A former hangout for writers of the "beat" generation in the fifties, this establishment, formerly known as the West End Café, offered poetry readings, discussions, and a meeting place for various literary figures. Jack Kerouac was just one of the familiar names known to frequent this locale.

Jazz was featured here, too—performances, jam sessions, and the like. The Countsmen, a group of sidemen from Count Basie's band, were organized by alto sax player Earl Warren and were among the many groups to perform here frequently. The Columbia University radio station broadcast many of these jazz shows from this site.

The West End still features jazz on occasion. It also sponsors a number of different types of musical and other performance events in an atmosphere that is somewhat reminiscent of the old days.

CATHEDRAL OF ST. JOHN THE DIVINE
Amsterdam Avenue at West 112th Street
212-662-2133

Eclectic musical programs can be enjoyed in this Gothic beauty

Built on the site of a nineteenth-century orphan asylum, this is one of the best-known "works-in-progress" anywhere. Episcopal Bishop Henry Codman Potter negotiated the purchase of the site and was the motivating force behind the building of the edifice. Begun in 1892 by Heins & La Farge, the cathedral—considered the largest in the world—is still inching toward completion.

The architecture is eclectic and the atmosphere fascinating. At least 150 stained glass windows adorn the building, and the eight imposing granite columns in the sanctuary weigh an impressive 130 tons each. Multiple chapel settings and an unusual assortment of art treasures, many quite exotic, are also to be found here.

Just as the edifice itself is grand, so are its musical appointments. There are five organs within its boundaries, the largest of which is the four-manual great organ built by E.M. Skinner in 1911 and enhanced by Aeolian-Skinner in 1954. The state trumpets—organ pipes comprising 61 resounding reeds and decorated with festive banners—are truly a work of art in every sense.

This inspirational setting has been a favorite of musicians and groups from Bernstein to Ellington to Kitaro to the Early Music Foundation. The New York Philharmonic has appeared here as well as numerous other top orchestras. Massive choir concerts, a fine organ series, and solo recitals are also among the musical presentations offered. Music of every type imaginable is performed at the cathedral—classical, liturgical, jazz, experimental, new age, and more. Special events are also popular here—from Paul Winter's winter solstice celebration to the Halloween silent movie festival with organ accompaniment.

COLUMBIA UNIVERSITY MUSICAL SITES & COLLECTIONS

Broadway and West 116th Street (main entrance)
212-854-1754

A treasure trove of concert spaces, scholarly collections, art, and history—all with musical themes

Music Division/Collections

This prestigious university, originally founded in 1754 as King's College, awards a range of bachelor's, master's, and doctoral degrees with concentrations in various scholarly areas of music.

The music library is of special note here, offering thousands of special recordings, rare microfilms, a collection of first-edition operas, and eighteenth- and nineteenth-century materials. Companion libraries on the campus contain autograph scores as well as various collections and manuscripts of Hector Berlioz, Anton Seidl, Edward MacDowell, and Bela Bartok. A number of rare liturgical manuscripts, American sheet music, and folk materials are also here.

Edward MacDowell was the first professor of music at Columbia University. Many of his manuscripts are now maintained in the music library collections.
Biggs Photography

The music department was officially formed in 1896—made possible through a series of endowments. Edward MacDowell was chosen as the first professor of music. Thereafter, many notables joined its ranks, ranging from Bela Bartok to Douglas Moore.

Kathryn Bache Miller Theater

Guests, faculty, and students offer regular on-campus performances at this popular spot. Opened in 1988, this 700-seat hall is a part of the University's School of the Arts. Its pivotal philosophy is to foster cultural enrichment not only within the confines of the school, but also within the neighborhood and the city as a whole. It lives up to this aim with its rich assortment of chamber, solo, ensemble, orchestral, and performance art presentations.

A number of smaller performance venues are also scattered throughout the campus.

St. Paul's Chapel

Designed by Howells & Stokes and constructed between 1904 and 1907, this Italianate Renaissance structure was a gift of the Stokes family. It houses a magnificent Aeolian-Skinner organ where guest musicians perform in regular concert series.

The Great God Pan
(west of Low Library)

The Greek mythological figure Pan is represented here in a relaxed pose, reclining on a rock and playing the panpipes. According to the legend of the water nymph Syrinx, this most ancient of instruments is said to be Pan's very own invention.

Completed in 1899, this was evidently the largest bronze figure ever cast in one piece in the United States in its time. The sculptor George Grey Barnard was originally commissioned to create this work for the courtyard of the Dakota apartment building, but due to a complicated series of events, this plan did not work out.

Pan led an eventful life, traveling to the Paris Exposition of 1900 where he received quite a bit of attention while on exhibit there. Later, he came home and was offered to the City of New York. When this plan also fell awry, the Alfred Corning Clark family, owners of this intriguing creation, donated Pan to Columbia University.

Half goat and half man, Pan's mischievous face is framed by goat ears and lots of curls. He is a favorite of Columbia students.

MANHATTAN SCHOOL OF MUSIC

120 Claremont Avenue (entrance on West 122nd Street near Broadway)
212-749-2802

A prestigious conservatory with a unique musical and social history

This famed conservatory was created in 1917 by Janet D. Schenck, a local philanthropist. Originally called the Neighborhood Music School, it occupied several addresses in the East 100s and was dedicated to providing musical instruction to city youth—particularly to the children of immigrants. Mrs. Schenck served as director of the school until 1956 and guided its growth into a widely recognized educational and cultural institution. She was succeeded by John Brownlee, who was responsible for a $9.5 million enhancement program that further broadened the school's horizons.

The school moved to its present location at 120 Claremont Avenue after the Juilliard School of Music left in 1969 and relocated to its new home in Lincoln Center. George Schick was named president at that time.

MSM now possesses an international reputation as a fine musical conservatory. It grants undergraduate and graduate degrees in a variety of musical disciplines and has an active preparatory division for younger students, in keeping with the spirit of its founder. Its faculty includes many world-renowned performers.

The school boasts an auditorium that seats 1000 as well as several smaller recital halls which have both acoustical and architectural appeal. The current president, Marta Istomin, offers a variety of professional-caliber concerts and operas as well as orchestral and jazz programs made available to the public with extremely reasonable ticket prices.

The MSM building first housed the Institute of Musical Art founded by Frank Damrosch and James Loeb in 1905, which became the Juilliard School of Music in 1946. The structure was completed in 1910 with later additions in 1931. When attending a concert, the visitor can see beautiful windows at the top of the main staircase which still display the insignia of the original Institute of Musical Art. Nearby, in the charming foyer and parlor areas just outside the intimate Hubbard Recital Hall, are several antique instruments as well as a plaque dedicated to founder Janet Schenck.

A photo gallery is located in the hallway on the main floor, adjacent to Borden Auditorium, the school's tastefully refurbished main concert hall. It contains exhibits commemorating special events, school and guest performers, and memorable concerts that trace the institution's history. Additional plaques, including one recognizing the achievements of John Brownlee, are in the lobby outside of Borden Auditorium.

A statue of Dvorak is displayed in the main lobby. A model of the original in Stuyvesant Square Park, it was presented in honor of former school president George Schick by the Czechoslovakian Society of Arts and Sciences in America. (A favorite of the students, Dvorak can often be seen sporting a jaunty cap or festive seasonal decoration!)

STATUE OF DANIEL BUTTERFIELD
Sakura Park—northwest corner of West 122nd Street
(between Claremont Avenue and Riverside Drive)

Composer of "Taps"

Although Daniel Butterfield (1831-1901) was known for his career in the military and, later, in various business enterprises, he made an interesting—and indeed famous—contribution to the world of music.

In 1862, while commanding a brigade in the Army of the Potomac, he evidently became dissatisfied with the bugle call played before "lights out." As a result, he composed a new tune, ultimately known as "Taps." The derivation of the title remains a mystery.

"Taps" first appeared in print in the 1874 edition of *Infantry Tactics* and has gone on to fame, particularly for its use at the close of a military or state funeral.

This bronze statue was created by John Gutzon de la Mothe Borglum, best known for his work at Mt. Rushmore. The granite pedestal was by Ludlow & Peabody. It was placed at its present location in 1918 through funds from the estate of Butterfield's wife, Julia, after a good deal of controversy over the accuracy of Butterfield's likeness.

RIVERSIDE CHURCH & CARILLON

490 Riverside Drive (between West 120th and 122nd Streets)
212-870-6700

Diverse concerts and a spectacular carillon are among the musical treats to be enjoyed in this world-famous place of worship

This is one of the most famous churches in the world. Complementing the beauty of its vast interior is the beauty of the many musical programs offered here. Classical, chamber, jazz, folk, ethnic, and contemporary musical events are held here year-round. The performers range from international names to community professionals and students. The massive Aeolian-Skinner organ can be heard in a special concert series, too. (You may also spy a musical motif or two in stained glass or other decoration while attending one of these events.)

The church is justly proud of its enormous carillon with a complex mechanism—a gift of the late John D. Rockefeller, Jr. in memory of his mother, Laura Spelman Rockefeller, for whom it is named. Seventy-four bells, ranging in weight from 10 pounds to 20 tons, play before services and on a variety of special occasions. Although there is an official carillonneur for the church who plays special service music and recitals, the carillon automatically plays a motif from Wagner's *Parsifal* each day.

Visitors can tour both the church and the memorial tower where the carillon is located and from which a panoramic view of the city and its environs can be enjoyed.

■HARLEM

AFRICAN-AMERICAN WAX MUSEUM
316 West 115th Street
212-678-7818

Musical greats are included in this unique collection

Harlem has honored its legends in songs, statues, plaques, murals, and a variety of other ways. This is one of the more unusual—a small, privately owned museum in which life-sized wax figures as well as wire and wood sculptures by artist Raven Chanticleer are on display.

Many individuals are represented, and musical greats are not forgotten. One can see likenesses such as Duke Ellington and Josephine Baker, both Harlem musical celebrities who once performed at the Cotton Club.

Tours are by appointment only.

MINTON'S
208-210 West 118th Street

The site of the "bebop" revolution

This building has lived an illustrious life within the neighborhood. It began in 1895 as the dining room of the Cecil Hotel. However, in 1938, it was converted to a jazz club (with a beautiful mosaic in the foyer bearing its name) by the saxophonist Henry Minton. This brought it lasting fame. A number of jazz greats performed here, including Thelonious Monk, Charlie Parker, and Dizzy Gillespie. An open atmosphere prevailed where performers could sit in and play.

It was here that the bebop revolution of the 1940s was said to have been born. One version has it that Fats Waller came up with the term "bop" at Minton's. Others say that it came from the title of a Dizzy Gillespie tune. Whatever the true derivation, the style thrived at Minton's and was long associated with this location, even after it closed in 1956.

The building is now a local senior residential housing facility. However, there is a movement within the community to revive this once-illustrious spot to its former glory as a jazz club.

Plans are underway to honor the jazz musicians who once performed at Minton's Playhouse, as well as other figures of the Harlem Renaissance. Two mosaic panels by Vincent Smith are slated for installation at the 116th Street subway station (number 2 and 3 lines), courtesy of the MTA Arts for Transit program.

MTA ARTS FOR TRANSIT— "FLYING HOME"
125th Street and Lenox Avenue Subway Station (downtown platform)

Murals with musical tributes

Dozens of well-known musical figures are associated with Harlem's rich heritage. Faith Ringgold, acclaimed artist and writer, honors them equally with other area notables from the worlds of sports, art, politics, literature, and religion. Currently a professor at the University of California, Ms. Ringgold has been the recipient of a variety of awards, including the Coretta Scott King Award for Best Illustrated

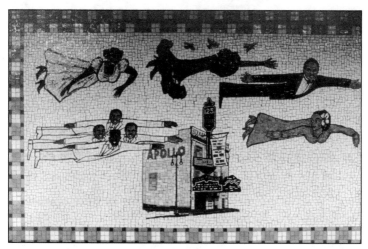

These fine musicians, depicted on the mural "Flying Home," were long associated with their performances at the Apollo Theater. They include Dinah Washington, Florence Mills, Ralph Cooper, Billie Holiday, and the Ink Spots. *An original artwork owned by MTA New York City Transit and commissioned by the Metropolitan Transportation Authority/Arts for Transit*

Children's Book and the Caldecott Medal. Her beautiful 1996 murals at this station in the heart of Harlem are a wonderful tribute to all and depict each of these figures floating above the sites with which they were associated.

The work is entitled "Flying Home," the title of a Lionel Hampton song. The mural itself was replicated with a striking assortment of thousands of Italian glass tesserae by Miotto Mosaics. On the downtown platform, one can see Dinah Washington, Florence Mills, Ralph Cooper, Billie Holiday, and The Ink Spots all floating above the Apollo Theater where they once performed. Marian Anderson and Paul Robeson are depicted over the Harlem Opera House, and the Cotton Club is the focal point for Josephine Baker, Duke Ellington, and Bessie Smith.

The spirit of these performers, loved so well by the artist, provides inspiration and a connection to the neighborhood's history for thousands of travelers at this busy locale.

Josephine Baker, Duke Ellington, and Bessie Smith, as depicted on the mural "Flying Home," were among the famous performers at the Cotton Club. *An original artwork owned by MTA New York City Transit and commissioned by the Metropolitan Transportation Authority/Arts for Transit*

APOLLO THEATER
253 West 125th Street
212-749-5838

This stage has seen hundreds of musical greats

This building began its life in 1913 as Hurting & Seaman's New Theater for burlesque and vaudeville. By the 1930s, however, it came into its own as the Apollo, a pivotal showcase for black entertainers. It was purchased by Sid Cohen in 1934, who launched a revue called "Jazz à la Carte." The following year, the first Amateur Night was held, a tradition that has long been associated with the Apollo.

Until the 1960s, hundreds of famous performers appeared on its stage, including Bessie Smith, Billie Holiday, Duke Ellington, Louis Armstrong, Ray Charles, Aretha Franklin, Ella Fitzgerald, Lionel Hampton, Count Basie, Sammy Davis, Jr., and the Supremes.

After closing in 1975 and undergoing extensive renovation in the 1980s, the Apollo reopened, adding many special shows. It also achieved National Landmark status.

The stage is still open to all at special times, and the tradition of Wednesday Amateur Night lives on. An enthusiastic audience registers its critique of performances quite openly—also a time-honored tradition.

The trunk from the "tree of hope" is backstage at the Apollo. Jazz performers used to touch it for good luck in the old days outside of Connie's, a few blocks away. Now it gives inspiration to hopeful performers here.

A gallery of photos and memorabilia tracing this institution's history provides another treat for the visitor.

SCOTT JOPLIN HOME & PLAQUE
163 West 131st Street

Home of one of ragtime's best

Scott Joplin (1868-1917), one of the great composers and innovators in the era of ragtime, was known for his "Maple Leaf Rag," the smash hit published in 1899, and other catchy instrumental tunes. He also composed a ragtime opera,

Treemonisha, which, unfortunately, did not achieve the fame of his other works. Its lukewarm reception caused him much heartache. Ironically, Joplin's popularity soared in the 1970s, long after his death, when a score of his songs was adapted for the soundtrack of the movie *The Sting*.

This is one of several addresses in New York that are associated with Joplin. The plaque was installed in 1996 in his honor by the Historic Landmarks Preservation Center.

MTA ARTS FOR TRANSIT— "HARLEM TIMELINE"

135th Street and Lenox Avenue Subway Station
(uptown and downtown platforms)

Musical figures are included in an artistic rendering of Harlem's history

Various images of Harlem life are depicted in Willie Birch's "cultural signatures." Birch was the recipient of fellowships from the National Endowment for the Arts and the Guggenheim Memorial Foundation. Various aspects of Harlem's life and cultural heritage are reflected in these striking murals, which were fabricated by Miotto Mosaics. The energy and vast diversity of the community are richly evoked.

Since music has always been a large part of Harlem's life, it is only natural that an array of famous figures is to be found here. In each of four vignettes, musicians play an important part.

On the uptown platform, John Coltrane and Paul Robeson are shown in "Black Manhattan." The "Village of Harlem" depicts Thelonious Monk and Billie Holiday.

This portion of the mural "Harlem Timeline" depicts musicians John Coltrane and Paul Robeson. *An original artwork owned by MTA New York City Transit and commissioned by the Metropolitan Transportation Authority/Arts for Transit*

On the downtown side, "What's in My Hand?" features Charlie Parker, and "Black Bird" includes Louis Armstrong, Florence Mills, and Duke Ellington.

These musicians are an integral part of the mood evoked by each vignette.

SCHOMBURG CENTER FOR RESEARCH IN BLACK CULTURE
515 Malcolm X Boulevard (103 West 135th Street)
212-491-2200

Varied musical holdings are a part of this splendid research center

A branch of the New York Public Library, this landmark building was designed by the renowned firm of McKim, Mead & White and completed between the years of 1903 and 1905. It was said to have been inspired by the design of a palazzo in Verona, Italy.

In the 1920s, librarian Ernestine Rose began collecting books pertaining to black culture. In 1926, the library purchased the holdings of Arthur Schomburg—bibliophile, researcher, African historian, and ardent participant in the Harlem Renaissance. Subsequently, the institution became one of the foremost resources for research on black culture. Thousands of books, papers, memorabilia, and exhibits, many relating to music, all contribute to this remarkable collection. Many original Duke Ellington scores are a part of the holdings here as are a substantial selection of musical recordings.

Special exhibits, cultural and musical events, and superb research facilities make this an artistic and intellectual gem.

The Abyssinian Baptist Church (132 West 138th Street / 212-862-7474) is one of the oldest African-American congregations in the U.S. Adam Clayton Powell, Jr. and his father were among its most famous ministers. The church's music program is exceptional with a gospel choir that is one of the best, and a superb five-manual, 67-rank organ. Special performances have been held here by the New York Philharmonic as well as such famed soloists as Leontyne Price.

FLORENCE MILLS HOME
220 West 135th Street

Onetime residence of a popular entertainer

This versatile singer, dancer, and entertainer was a well-known figure in Harlem and elsewhere. She appeared on Broadway as well as at the Apollo and various other New York venues and toured extensively in Europe. Her performances in such productions as *Shuffle Along*, *Plantation Revue*, and *Dixie to Broadway* received rave reviews.

She lived in this home from approximately 1910 until her sudden death in 1927. Florence Mills was so beloved that it was said that almost 10,000 people paid their respects prior to her funeral. She was buried at Woodlawn Cemetery in the Bronx, where scores of musical and theatrical notables are interred.

A Walk of Fame has been installed on West 135th Street between Seventh and Eighth Avenues (Adam Clayton Powell, Jr. Boulevard and Frederick Douglass Boulevard). Twenty bronze sidewalk plaques, designed by Ogundipe Fayoumi and Otto Neal, line the street. Many musicians who once performed in Harlem are among those honored: Billie Holiday, Ella Fitzgerald, Charlie Parker, Dizzy Gillespie, and Tito Puente. More illustrious names should follow. Plans for a jazz museum are also being discussed for the future.

FAMED MUSICAL RESIDENTS OF STRIVER'S ROW
West 138th and 139th Streets
(between Adam Clayton Powell, Jr. and Frederick Douglass Boulevards)

Lovely streets with equally lovely houses once occupied by some musical greats

This fine grouping of urban row houses was created during the 1890s and became a favorite locale of successful entertainers after World War I. These elegant dwellings were home to several beloved musicians.

Will Marion Cook Home
221 West 138th Street

A classically trained violinist who once studied composition with Dvorak at the National Conservatory of Music, Will Marion Cook (1869-1944) later turned to conducting and composing for the musical theatre and other popular forms. He wrote scores for such all-black musicals as *Clorindy, or the Origin of the Cakewalk* (1898), *In Dahomey* (1902), *In Bandanna Land* (1908), and others. Many of these shows were headlined by the famous team of Williams & Walker. Cook also composed an opera, *St. Louis 'ooman*.

This house, built in 1891, was occupied by Cook from 1918 until his death in 1944.

Eubie Blake Home
236 West 138th Street

Pianist and composer Eubie Blake (1883-1983) delighted audiences with his renditions of songs in the catchy ragtime style.

Early in his career, he wrote many songs for the theater with his partner, Noble Sissle. The two were responsible for the hit show *Shuffle Along*, which enjoyed a long run on Broadway. His own instrumental compositions included "Charleston Rag" and "Tickle the Ivories."

A composer who was influenced by a number of diverse styles, he was continually motivated to learn more about composition and music throughout his life—even studying composition at New York University in his fifties.

Blake's popularity soared in later life with the renewed interest in ragtime. He made many recordings, toured extensively, and was the recipient of a wide variety of awards and honors. His life was the basis for the 1978 Broadway show *Eubie*.

W.C. Handy Home
232 West 139th Street

W.C. Handy (1873-1958) was often referred to as "the father of the blues" because of his efforts to bring this sound to the notice of general audiences. A successful trumpeter, he was an experienced member of many types of bands, including ragtime groups.

Best known for his composition "St. Louis Blues," he wrote a number of popular songs, made numerous recordings, and opened a publishing firm in New York. Handy's work was made famous by a number of blues singers, including Alberta Hunter, and he consistently encouraged and sponsored black entertainers in their careers, producing many large concerts to showcase major talents.

See also "W.C. Handy Place" in the Midtown section.

Fletcher Henderson Home
228 West 139th Street

A jazz pianist at the outset and onetime staff member of Pace-Handy Music (co-owned by W.C. Handy) as well as the famous Black Swan recording company, Fletcher Henderson (1897-1952) ultimately became a bandleader. Henderson's talent for discovering and hiring great musicians was legendary. While leading his dance band at New York's famous Roseland Ballroom, he not only attracted fame for the hall, but he also brought in Louis Armstrong, who helped to spread the new jazz style to other band members and beyond through performances and recordings.

Henderson was also noted as a fine band arranger, with such hits to his credit as "King Porter Stomp," and eventually worked for Benny Goodman as a staff arranger. Later on, he led his own swing band and was especially remembered for helping to form the big band sound.

■ HARLEM'S HAMILTON TERRACE DISTRICT AND POINTS NORTH

HARLEM SCHOOL OF THE ARTS & THEATER
645 St. Nicholas Avenue (at West 141st Street)
212-926-4100

A highly acclaimed community arts education center

Quality instrumental, vocal, dance, drama, and art instruction is offered here to more than one thousand students. Some former pupils have gone on to professional careers in the arts.

Soprano Betty Allen has further enhanced the school's offerings during her tenure as president. There are ensembles, Suzuki training, and outreach programs.

From its beginnings in the 1960s as a piano studio led by Dorothy Maynor, the school continued to grow in scope and in size. It is now housed in a large building with studios, concert spaces, classrooms, and offices and is renowned not only within the community, but also within the city at large.

The school also maintains a theater, seating 200, which is used for concerts and special programs.

AARON DAVIS HALL
at City College
Convent Avenue at West 135th Street
212-650-7148

A concert complex serving the college, the community, and the city

This renovated concert space is the home of Opera Ebony, the Boys Choir of Harlem, the City Opera National Company, and the Dance Theater of Harlem. Many programs focusing on African-American music and culture are presented here. Now a part of the campus of the City College of New York, the hall is on the site of the former Lewisohn Stadium where many beautiful concert series were also presented in days gone by.

Several theaters are a part of the complex, most notably the Marian Anderson Theater with a seating capacity of 750. Two smaller spaces are also available for intimate recitals and performances.

MARY LOU WILLIAMS HOME
63 Hamilton Terrace

Residence of a famous jazz pianist/composer

Mary Lou Williams (1910-1981) was a jazz pianist and composer known for her distinctive arrangements. Her contributions to swing, bop, and jazz placed her at the forefront of the musical scene for several decades. Her work included arranging swing band scores for such luminaries as Benny Goodman and Earl Hines as well as performing extensive solo and combo engagements in a variety of New York clubs—the latter amply exhibiting her unique style with its particularly interesting bass patterns.

She also composed many larger sacred works. Among the most popular of these was "Mary Lou's Mass," written in 1970 and eventually choreographed by Alvin Ailey.

This was the building where she lived in the 1940s. Her guests included many jazz figures such as Charlie Parker and Thelonious Monk.

JOHNNY HARTMAN PLAZA
Amsterdam Avenue (between West 143rd and 144th Streets)

A tribute to a modern jazz vocalist

A renowned jazz, pop, and country singer, Johnny Hartman (1923-1983) performed with such greats as Dizzy Gillespie, John Coltrane, and Earl Hines. He appeared at Carnegie Hall, Town Hall, and Avery Fisher Hall as well as at numerous top clubs around the country.

Hartman had a real love of modern jazz, and he recorded a number of albums with this distinctive sound. He received a Grammy nomination for the album *Once in Every Life*. His beautiful baritone vocals were also featured on movie soundtracks, most notably for *The Bridges of Madison County*.

This neighborhood triangle park was dedicated in Hartman's memory at a ceremony attended by such notables as Congressman Charles Rangel and singer Margaret Whiting.

PAUL ROBESON HOME & PLAQUE
16 Jumel Terrace

Former home of the singer who was known for his film role in Showboat

A versatile musician and actor, Paul Robeson (1899-1976) possessed a rich bass/baritone singing voice. His first concert was held in 1925, and his nationwide tour the following year was widely acclaimed. Robeson's overseas performances in concerts and in shows, particularly in England, were also quite successful. He was noted for the moving spirituals that he included on his programs.

Robeson's portrayal of "Joe" along with his rendition of "Ol' Man River"—both in the 1928 London production of *Showboat* and in the 1936 movie version—brought him additional fame. His career also included serious dramatic roles in such plays as *All God's Chillun Got Wings* and *Emperor Jones*.

This plaque, installed in 1996 by the Historic Landmarks Preservation Center, marks the place where Robeson lived from 1963 to 1966.

If you are in the mood for something in a medieval setting, visit the Cloisters in Washington Heights (Fort Tryon Park at 192nd Street / 212-923-3700) for one of its many concerts of early music.

The Bronx

At one time, New York was the center of the American piano manufacturing industry. Many of these companies, run by German immigrants during the mid-1800s, set up shop in the Mott Haven area of the Bronx. East 132nd Street between Lincoln and Alexander Avenues contained three piano factories—Krakauer, Estey, and Kroeger. The original buildings for these firms remain, but their tenants are long gone.

HOSTOS CENTER FOR THE ARTS & CULTURE
Hostos Community College
450 Grand Concourse at 149th Street
718-518-4455

An exciting new music and arts center

This new arts center, opened in October 1994, serves as a focal point for the college and has also brought a vibrant spark to its South Bronx neighborhood. The college itself, the first bilingual school within the City University, opened its doors in 1970 and was named in memory of Eugenio Maria de Hostos, a nineteenth-century Puerto Rican patriot, orator, writer, and educator. The arts program originated in 1982 in the school's gymnasium, and its concept of multicultural artistic outreach continued to grow, culminating in the development of the center.

The inaugural season saw concerts by a variety of groups representing Mexican, Venezuelan, Andean, and other cultures. Classical, jazz, traditional, and experimental works were performed. In keeping with its mission, the arts center continues to specialize in Latin American music and related events.

The structure itself, designed by Gwathmey, Siegel & Associates, consists of a large theater/concert hall, seating 907, and a smaller repertory theater that can accommodate 367. Highly sophisticated lighting and counterweight systems enhance its professional atmosphere and effectiveness. Museum-grade galleries, dance studios, and costume and set-design shops also complement the facilities.

This vital center provides the college, the local community, and the city with an eclectic array of multicultural events that have brought a new artistic life to this neighborhood.

PREGONES THEATER
700 Grand Concourse
718-585-1202

A theater where music is one of the stars

Since 1979, the Pregones Theater has offered its unique blend of dramatic/musical productions to the Bronx community.

Its performance space was once located in the historic St. Ann's Church and is currently housed in a 50-seat theater in a redesigned office space. The group performs a variety of intriguing fare for adults and children. Presentations stress themes integral to Latino and Afro-Caribbean cultures and include dramas into which music, poetry, and dance are creatively interwoven—often with music acting as a focal center of the work. (Music was once referred to by a reviewer as a character unto itself in one of the Pregones' productions.)

Workshops in music and the arts are also offered to the community, and the troupe tours regularly and occasionally performs at nearby Hostos Center for the Arts.

HALL OF FAME FOR GREAT AMERICANS
Bronx Community College
University Avenue and 180th Street
718-289-5100

A majestic site honoring great Americans, including some musical figures

---

Once a part of New York University and now on the campus of Bronx Community College, this beautiful semicircular vaulted colonnade with classical columns was designed by McKim, Mead & White and dedicated in 1901. Both tablets and bronze busts pay tribute to great Americans from many fields, among them several musicians.

The musical figures include an interesting collection of individuals, representing different facets of the art. Stephen Foster (born in 1826) was well known for his minstrel songs, including "Oh! Susanna." He lived in New York for a time, where his publisher—Firth, Pond & Co.—was based. Foster wrote a number of works for Christy's Minstrels, a group whose fame was secure on the local entertainment scene. He died in New York in 1864. The first musician nominated to the Hall of Fame, Foster's bust was installed in 1940.

Edward MacDowell (1860-1908), best known for his piano and orchestral compositions, was a city resident for many years. He served as Columbia University's first professor of music and participated in a variety of local musical activities (e.g., conducting the Mendelssohn Glee Club). He was honored by the Hall of Fame with a bust installed in 1960.

John Philip Sousa (1854-1932) was renowned as a musician, band director, composer, and founding member of ASCAP. Affectionately referred to as the "March King," Sousa was immortalized through such works as "The Washington Post" and "The Stars and Stripes Forever." A commemorative bust of the composer was placed in the Hall of Fame in 1973.

Listed on the National Register of Historic Places, it is open for all to enjoy.

John Philip Sousa is one of three musician/composers honored in the Hall of Fame for Great Americans. *Biggs Photography*

THE BELMONT MUSICAL CONNECTION
Belmont Avenue in the 180s

An area with a rich heritage in both ethnic culture and rock music

---

This area is known as the Little Italy of the Bronx, and it contains a number of musical connections.

Tunes such as the 1959 hit "Teenager in Love" brought fame to the '50s rock group Dion and the Belmonts. They grew up here, and the influence of their neighborhood locale is plain to see. They created many of their arrangements and honed their particular style at the corner of 187th Street and Belmont Avenue. The New York City Music Trail honors this site as the "Doo-Wop Corner."

Nearby, at 610 East 186th Street, is the Belmont Library/Enrico Fermi Cultural Center. A branch of the New York Public Library, the building doubles as a center for the preservation of its local ethnic culture. Along these lines, its 100-seat hall provides many concerts for the enjoyment of neighborhood residents.

A FORDHAM LEGEND
Fordham University
Rose Hill Campus
441 East Fordham Road

The music of the bells lives on

The bell at Fordham has always been a familiar sound in the neighborhood—even back in the nineteenth century. Edgar Allan Poe, once an area resident, is said to have been captured by the haunting musical sound and was subsequently inspired to write his poem "The Bells" in 1849.

In the more optimistic portions of this poem, Poe describes the harmony, melody, and "molten-golden notes" emitting from what has come to be known as "Old Edgar." Thus did literature immortalize a musical feature of this Bronx locale— a legend commemorated on a plaque to the left of the entrance to the university's chapel, the 1845 structure where Old Edgar resides.

The bell still tolls, and other music permeates the campus, too, in the form of the Bronx Arts Ensemble, the resident group at Fordham. They present orchestral, chamber, and children's concerts here and at a variety of other local sites. Perhaps Poe would have been even further inspired.

The Bronx Arts Ensemble (c/o Golf House, Van Cortlandt Park / 718-601-7399) was founded in 1972 and has been a resident group at Fordham University since 1979. Composed of a variety of orchestral instruments, it presents performances for small ensembles or full symphony. Repertoire is varied and has included premieres of new works by such composers as Morton Gould, Roberto Sierra, and Meyer Kupferman as well as traditional compositions. The Ensemble has appeared at every major Bronx historic landmark as well as at Carnegie Hall and Alice Tully Hall. Its outdoor summer concerts in Van Cortlandt Park and at Fordham are favorites. The group sponsors competitions, provides outreach to schools and community institutions, and has successfully recorded a wide variety of works.

The New York Botanical Garden (200th Street & Southern Boulevard / 718-817-8700) hosts concerts in exceptionally beautiful surroundings. The Bronx Arts Ensemble has performed here along with other local and guest groups.

LEHMAN CENTER FOR THE PERFORMING ARTS
LEHMAN COLLEGE (CUNY)
250 Bedford Park Boulevard West
718-960-8833

A flexible cultural center for both local groups and guest performers

---

This innovative arts center is on the 37-acre campus of a branch of the City University. After several years of delays, the $50 million complex opened in the fall of 1980 with a gala concert featuring Zubin Mehta and the New York Philharmonic.

Designed by David Todd and Jan Pokorny, the center
accommodates a variety of events that contribute greatly to
the cultural life of the college, the surrounding community,
and the metropolitan area at large. The major concert hall seats
more than 2300 and is an impressive asymmetrical space that
is three stories high. Its stage has seen performers ranging
from Ella Fitzgerald to Pinchas Zuckerman to the Boston
Symphony Orchestra. A 500-seat space, the Lovinger Theater,
offers musical productions, chamber concerts, and recitals.
The complex also boasts two smaller halls, several dance studios, art galleries, and a library.

The Bronx Symphony Orchestra, composed of members
with a wide blend of musical backgrounds, calls this center
home and presents a fine concert series each season. The
Bronx Opera is another organization that has performed here
for many years.

The Bronx Opera Company (718-365-4209) was created in
1967 and has strong roots in this borough, performing frequently at Lehman College (its previous home) and at other
Bronx locales. Now based at John Jay College's theater in
Manhattan, it presents regular productions, with full orchestra,
of standard operatic repertoire (such as *The Barber of Seville*
and *Die Fledermaus*) and more rarely heard works (such as
Moore's *Ballad of Baby Doe* and Auber's *Fra Diavolo*).
Community concerts and comprehensive programs for schools
and libraries are among the other activities of this company.
Members include approximately 120 soloists, chorus, orchestra,
and production staff. Talented singers gain a wealth of experience here. The Bronx Chamber Orchestra is also associated with
the company and performs on its own in addition to its work
with the opera.

WOODLAWN CEMETERY
Webster Avenue and East 233rd Street
718-920-0500

Many famous musical "residents" are here

This is one of the most famous resting places in the world. Its list of celebrity residents reads like a "who's who." Tours are available by arrangement, and the visitor can see fine examples of funereal architecture, including replicas of renowned European monuments.

A multi-faceted group of musical figures is entombed here. A partial list includes: George M. Cohan (songwriter known for "Give My Regards to Broadway" and other hits); Miles Davis (jazz legend); Duke Ellington (beloved musician/bandleader/composer who appeared at the renowned Cotton Club); W.C. Handy (sometimes called "the father of the blues"); Irving Berlin (legendary Tin Pan Alley songwriter); Victor Herbert (foremost operetta composer); Augustus Juilliard (who provided the original funding for the famous musical conservatory); Oscar Hammerstein II (lyricist who collaborated with Richard Rodgers); Chauncey Olcott (composer of "My Wild Irish Rose"); Frank Damrosch (founder of the Institute for Musical Art); David Mannes (founder of the Mannes School of Music); Fritz Kreisler (violinist and composer); Josef Stransky (conductor of the New York Philharmonic from 1911 to 1923); Charles K. Harris (early Tin Pan Alley figure and composer of "After the Ball"); King Oliver (leader of the famous Creole Jazz Band); and a host of others.

Woodlawn is justifiably proud of its concerts, which have included July 4th spectaculars honoring some of its residents such as George M. Cohan. Members of the Bronx Arts Ensemble, a local professional group, perform here often. Concerts are held on the parklike grounds outside or in the chapel (during inclement weather).

WAVE HILL
675 West 252nd Street (enter on West 249th Street)
718-549-2055

Toscanini once lived here

This picturesque Riverdale locale has a famous past as well as present pertaining to music. The beautiful stone home was built in 1843 and included such prestigious residents as jurist William Lewis Morris, publisher William Henry Appleton, the family of a young Teddy Roosevelt (during several summers), and Mark Twain, to name a few.

However, the musical world will remember Wave Hill as the onetime residence of the flamboyant Arturo Toscanini, former conductor of both the New York Philharmonic and the NBC Symphony Orchestra. He lived here from 1942 to 1945 during his NBC and recording years.

Today, this gorgeous mansion, set on 28 acres of property with gardens and woodlands, offers series of classical and chamber music, along with jazz concerts each season. In addition, recordings of Toscanini's orchestra are often played for specific occasions. Here, one can enjoy beautiful music, and also roam some of the same halls as the famous maestro.

Way off at the eastern end of the Bronx, tucked away on City Island in a fishing village-type locale, is Le Refuge Inn (620 City Island Avenue / 718-885-2478). The City Island Chamber Ensemble presents fine performances at this charming inn each Sunday with post-concert receptions, as well.

STATUE OF ELLA FITZGERALD
Trolley Barn Plaza (next to Yonkers train station)
Main Avenue near Riverdale Avenue
Yonkers

A beloved singer is immortalized here

Just slightly north of the New York City boundary is a musical site that should not be missed.

Ella Fitzgerald was a Yonkers resident from 1919 to 1932. This beloved vocalist was known for her unique jazz sound and distinctive stylings. She was a frequent performer in New York, appearing with a long list of other jazz greats including Duke Ellington, Count Basie, and Oscar Peterson. A Grammy Award winner, she was acclaimed for her series of recordings paying tribute to great American popular songwriters.

This bronze, life-sized statue was unveiled in October 1996. It was created by Yonkers resident Vinnie Bagwell.

Brooklyn

BARGEMUSIC
Fulton Ferry Landing (near the Brooklyn Bridge)
718-624-4061

A unique floating concert space

This was once a barge used by the Erie Lackawanna Railroad to transport coffee, but it has now been renovated into a unique concert hall, moored near the Brooklyn Bridge. The structure is 102 feet long and seats 125 guests. It has lovely views and equally lovely music.

Olga Bloom created this unusual concert space. A professional violinist with experience performing in numerous venues—chamber music, symphonies, recordings—Ms. Bloom was one of the first women to perform in the traditionally male territory of Broadway pit orchestras.

Her initial concept of Bargemusic raised a few eyebrows in the beginning, but it has evolved into one of the most popular musical series in the city. Its exquisite chamber music concerts, presented twice weekly throughout the year, usually play to full capacity audiences. Performers include a diverse selection of top-quality musicians ranging from young prize winners to established professionals. The reviews have been consistently glowing.

In addition to the series sponsored by Ms. Bloom, the space may be rented for special events.

Grand Prospect Hall (263 Prospect Avenue / 718-788-0777) was built in 1901 and started its life as a German opera house. Its Victorian decor and spacious interior have been restored to their former splendor. Now it is used as a center for special catered events.

ARTS AT ST. ANN'S

Church of St. Ann and the Holy Trinity
157 Montague Street
718-858-2424

An eclectic music and arts program in a historic Brooklyn setting

---

This Gothic Revival church was built in the 1840s and has approximately 7,000 feet of stained glass windows, equaling the splendor of many European cathedrals. A restoration program is returning this edifice to its original glory.

A performance series, created in 1980, features musical works of many styles—rock, jazz, experimental, Broadway, chamber, classical, and more. Theater and poetry events, some integrated with special music, are also presented. The church and its surrounding neighborhood make this a lovely setting in which to enjoy these programs.

Once a popular vaudeville and concert venue, the magnificent Brooklyn Paramount Theater was taken over by Long Island University (385 Flatbush Avenue). Although little of its former life can be seen, one vestige of the old days remains—its famous Wurlitzer theater organ. The New York Theater Organ Society sponsors concerts here, keeping this musical tradition alive (concert information at website: http://www.nytos.org). Eddie Layton, organist at Yankee Stadium, is among the performers who have been featured. The organ is also played at college basketball games!

The Majestic Theater at 651 Fulton Street is a historic site that was renovated by the Brooklyn Academy of Music. This more than 80-year-old theater and movie house had been empty for years. After a massive renovation, it is now happily back in action, presenting a variety of musical concerts as well as other performance events.

BROOKLYN ACADEMY OF MUSIC
30 Lafayette Avenue
718-636-4100

A historic performing arts center

The Brooklyn Academy of Music was formed in 1859 and is considered to be the oldest performing arts center in continuous existence in the country. It began offering performances to the public in 1861 and was housed in a building on Montague Street. The Philharmonic Society of Music was responsible for the opening of the Academy. The original building burned down in 1903, and the institution then reopened in its present location. Many historic performers have appeared here, including the famous tenor Enrico Caruso.

There are several performance halls, the largest of which is the Opera House, seating more than 2,000. There is also a 1,000-seat playhouse and a smaller hall, the Leperq Space. The complex contains rehearsal spaces, offices, and additional facilities.

Cultural events at BAM range from the traditional to the avant-garde. Opera, concerts, theater, children's events, and dance productions are among its many featured offerings. A variety of international groups perform here, and BAM is also the home of the Brooklyn Philharmonic.

The Next Wave Festival has been one of the Academy's more popular contemporary series throughout the years. Blending many types of performing arts genres, particularly those of an experimental nature, both new and established performers appear in this series. The work of Philip Glass and others has been featured.

The Brooklyn Philharmonic Orchestra was founded in 1954 and quickly established a reputation for its premieres of new works and its unique programming. Concerts have included everything from Bach marathons to jazz presentations. The Orchestra has worked in conjunction with other groups to present thematic concerts relating to international culture and American musical traditions. Conductors have included Lukas Foss, Dennis Russell Davies, and Robert Spano (the current director). Other projects have included recordings, appearances on National Public Radio, educational outreach, multi-media presentations on specific topics, and award-winning publications about music. The Brooklyn Philharmonic is the resident orchestra at the Brooklyn Academy of Music. (For ticket information, call 212-307-4100.)

GREEN-WOOD CEMETERY
25th Street and Fourth Avenue
718-469-5277 (tours)

A burial place for many musical notables

Equally a park and a resting place, this beautiful 478-acre tract of land received its charter for incorporation in 1838. Recognizing the expanding need for appropriate burial sites, Henry E. Pierrepont, son of a gin distiller and prosperous landowner, led the group who founded Green-Wood. Pierrepont, ever the enthusiast for his project, visited other rural cemeteries both here and abroad to gather ideas for design. It was Mount Auburn, near Cambridge, Massachusetts, however, that was to be his final inspiration.

Under the able direction of David Bates Douglas, the landscape was developed into a network of paths, lakes, and drives which led through rolling hills. It was said to be the inspiration for Central Park and Prospect Park. Because of its unparalleled beauty, it was often called the "Garden City of the Dead."

Overlooking the Gowanus Bay, Green-Wood encompasses the highest point in Brooklyn. It was here that the first shots were fired in the Battle of Long Island during the American

Revolution. Green-Wood soon became dotted with ornate tombstones and mausoleums, noted for their exquisite (if not unusual) sculptural designs. A popular place for carriage rides and strolls, the prevailing sentimental spirit of the Victorian era was reflected in this setting (as it was in the music of the time).

Today, visitors can take a tour of the still well-maintained grounds and admire the resting places of its many notable "residents," who include politicians, war heroes, actors, criminals, and inventors.

A number of musical figures are at rest here, too—both famous and not so famous. The tomb of the Steinway family—manufacturers of the world-renowned line of pianos—is among the more notable. (Henry Engelhard Steinway must have believed in togetherness, since his mausoleum contained space for up to 138 family members.)

One very touching musical monument commemorates Clarence McKenzie. A sculpture of the 12-year-old Clarence, playing his drum, sits atop his tombstone. He was the first soldier from Brooklyn to die in the Civil War—an innocent little drummer boy.

Edwin Christy of the early Christy Minstrels, popular in nineteenth-century New York and elsewhere, resides here. So does Billy West, another minstrel performer. West, depicted here with his banjo, also generously provided gravesites for other members of his troupe. Thomas Dartmouth Rice, often called the father of the American minstrel form, is also buried here.

Percy Gaunt is on the list at Green-Wood. He wrote the song entitled "The Bowery," which alludes to the infamous goings-on in the heyday of this center of gaudy entertainment.

William Niblo, owner of the famed Niblo's Garden, is entombed in a spectacular mausoleum guarded by an impressive stone lion. Niblo's grand entertainment palace was a fixture in New York for years, providing music, food, theater, and various amusements.

Piano virtuoso, composer, and headliner in scandal, Louis Moreau Gottschalk (1829-1869) is another of Green-Wood's musical group. Famed composer and New York Philharmonic conductor Leonard Bernstein and his wife Felicia are also at rest here—but with more modest markers.

Other famous musical figures here include bandleaders Harvey Dodworth and Claudio Grafulla, Thomas Hastings (composer of "Rock of Ages"), and Roy Smeck (the "Wizard of Strings").

Musically, historically, and visually, Green-Wood provides a unique experience for visitors.

BROOKLYN CONSERVATORY OF MUSIC
58 Seventh Avenue
718-622-3300

A historic school of music in a historic mansion

This fine institution, established by Edward Adolph Whitelaw, has just passed its hundredth anniversary. It has the distinction of being one of the oldest and largest of its type in the nation.

The Brooklyn Conservatory of Music is housed in this historic Victorian mansion. *Courtesy of Brooklyn Conservatory of Music*

The school has had quarters here since 1944, when it purchased this fine 1881 Victorian mansion. The house was originally owned by the Brasher family, who were in the oil cloth manufacturing business. Its lovely detail and historic atmosphere make it the perfect setting for the musical activities that now resonate within.

A true community school of the arts, it offers all types of classes and instruction from classical to jazz to ethnic traditional music. Students range in age from 18 months old to 90! There are approximately 1500 students at this location and the Queens branch.

Frequent concerts are presented, including student recitals, faculty events, and guest artist appearances. Some recent popular programs have included "Jazz at the Conservatory" and a Charlie Parker festival.

The Brooklyn Museum (200 Eastern Parkway / 718-638-5000) offers a grouping of concerts in the galleries—often focusing upon the theme of an exhibition. Past performances have included classical guitar, voice, and the St. Luke's Chamber Ensemble. Jazz concerts have also been presented in warm weather in the outdoor sculpture garden.

BROOKLYN BOTANIC GARDEN

1000 Washington Avenue
718-622-4433

Music and musical tributes in a lush setting

Enjoy the beautiful landscape and flowers, and check out the commemorative "Celebrity Path" that honors Brooklynites—musicians and performers among them. These plaques, set into the pathways, pay tribute to such musical figures as George Gershwin, Carole King, Beverly Sills, Lainie Kazan, and Lena Horne, the singer who appeared on Broadway in *Jamaica* and in her own Tony Award–winning one-woman show.

There is also an auditorium on the premises that is the site of concerts and other events. It has presented programs of music ranging from jazz to harp to spirituals.

PROSPECT PARK MUSICAL SITES

Flatbush Avenue & Prospect Park West (at Grand Army Plaza)
718-965-8999

A beautiful park, designed by Olmsted & Vaux, with many musical sites

This lovely 526-acre rustic setting, designed in 1866 with lovely trees, arbors, lakes, and winding paths, is a perfect place for outdoor concerts—a regular occurrence in the park's early days as well as now. Several older structures designed for summer concerts in the past, such as the Music Stand, were demolished or put to alternative uses. However, outdoor music is now performed at the Bandshell at Prospect Park West and Ninth Street as well as near the shores of Prospect Lake, among other locales.

The Concert Grove, designed in the 1870s, also pays tribute to some great composers whose music has entered the standard classical repertory. Linger on one of the nearby benches and admire the natural setting and the musical sculptures.

> Long Meadow is a beautiful open area with a countrylike atmosphere. The Metropolitan Opera and the New York Philharmonic Orchestra perform here in the summertime.

Bust of Beethoven

Singing societies were quite popular in New York, particularly among the German immigrant population. In addition to their meetings and rehearsals, they sponsored a variety of concerts, festivals, competitions, and social events.

This bust of Beethoven was received by the United Singers as a prize won in a singing contest at Madison Square Garden. The group graciously donated it to the City of Brooklyn to be placed in Prospect Park for all to enjoy.

Formal unveiling ceremonies were held on October 20, 1894. There was a lavish parade, several speeches, and performances of Beethoven's "The Heavens Are Telling," "Am Ammersee" (the prize song), and the "Star-Spangled Banner."

The Park Commissioner and the Mayor of Brooklyn were among the many dignitaries in attendance.

Bust of Mozart

Again, a coveted prize was won by the United Singers of Brooklyn—this time at the eighteenth national "Saengerfest" held in Philadelphia. And, once more, the singing societies donated their prize to the City of Brooklyn for installation in Prospect Park on October 23, 1897.

The various societies comprising the United Singers held a great parade, and many speeches were made in honor of the unveiling.

Performances of Mozart's "Blessing of the Song," Kreutzer's "Der Tag des Herrn," Buck's "Robin Adair" (the prize song), and the "Star-Spangled Banner" were offered by the United Singers.

An inscription, citing the occasion of the gift, can be found on the sculpture.

Bust of Karl Maria von Weber

This sculpture, created by Chester Beach, was won by the United Singers of Brooklyn at a Saengerfest in Madison Square Garden. The group, in turn, donated it to the city in 1909. At a ceremony attended by 1,000 spectators, the statue was formally presented by Adam Fehmel, president of the society, and it was accepted by the Park Commissioner.

A number of speeches were made on this festive occasion. Carl Lentz, the director of the northeast Saengerbund, commented that Brooklyn was famous for its singers and parks as well as for its beautiful women.

Two hundred members of the society sang "This is the Day of the Lord" and the "Star-Spangled Banner," among other selections. The statue was then unveiled by Maxine Neiderstein, daughter of the County Clerk of Queens.

Bust of Edvard Grieg

The Norwegian Societies of Brooklyn donated this statue to the city in 1914. At a formal ceremony, the Fourteenth Regiment Band, directed by Frank Martin, performed along with the United Scandinavian Singing Societies of Brooklyn, led by Ole Windingstad. They performed repertoire by the famous Norwegian composer.

Speeches were made in honor of Grieg, and the statue was accepted by the Park Commissioner of Brooklyn. This life-sized bust was created by Sigvald Asbjorsen.

This bust of composer Edvard Grieg is located in the Concert Grove area in Prospect Park. It was donated by the United Scandinavian Singing Societies of Brooklyn in 1914. *Simon Benepe/New York City Parks Photo Archive*

The Concert Grove also contains a statue of Thomas Moore from 1879 by John G. Draddy. Although Moore was best known as a poet, he was also a composer and a pianist.

Famous 1950s graduates from Erasmus Hall High (911 Flatbush Avenue / 718-856-3571) include singers Barbra Streisand and Lainie Kazan. Their photographs are among those displayed in the alumni hall of fame at the school's museum. The museum building housed the original school (until the early twentieth century) and dates to 1786. It also contains many marvelous exhibits and period rooms that provide a look at educational traditions from another era.

BROOKLYN CENTER FOR THE PERFORMING ARTS & BROOKLYN COLLEGE CONSERVATORY OF MUSIC

2900 Bedford Avenue
718-951-4500

A branch of the City University that is bursting with musical activity

This well-respected division of the City University of New York was founded in 1930 and is especially noted for its music department and related activities.

Special musical areas include the Institute for Studies in American Music, a special research center focusing upon the study of all styles of American music. Its lectures, concerts, newsletter, and monograph series are all well known. It houses extensive materials for researchers and sponsors scholars and various projects.

Another special musical area is the Center for Computer Music. Its equipment and technological resources are said to be among the best in the country.

The Brooklyn College Conservatory of Music offers bachelor's and master's degrees in a variety of musical disciplines. Fine faculty members include many renowned professional musicians, such as Itzhak Perlman. The school has excellent facilities, an extensive collection of instruments, and a cluster of rehearsal and practice studios. The Salter W. Gerboth Music Library is a helpful resource for students with its collection of scores, collected works, recordings, and American music. The Conservatory of Music is also the home of an active pre-college division.

Several attractive concert halls are a part of the Center for the Performing Arts. The George Gershwin Theater, named after the composer who was born in Brooklyn, seats 500. It is noted for its excellent acoustics. The 2500-seat Walt Whitman Hall and the intimate Sam Levenson Recital Hall (168 seats) accommodate a wide variety of performances from full-scale productions to chamber groups. Performances include student and faculty recitals, traditional ethnic presentations, and guest artist events as well as orchestral and popular concerts. In the past, the college has featured such guest performers as Vladimir Horowitz and John Raitt.

Many programs for schools within the community are also offered.

CHARLES IVES STATUE

Bear's Community Garden
Southwest corner of Flatbush & Pacific Avenues

An interesting memorial to the modern American composer whose works include such New York themes as "Central Park in the Dark"

Acknowledged as one of the leading innovators in composition during the first half of the twentieth century, Charles Ives (1874-1954) produced a large body of work for orchestra, band, chamber group, keyboard, chorus, and solo voice.

Originally trained by his father—who held the distinction of being the youngest bandmaster in the Union Army—he was exposed to a variety of rigorous musical exercises and learned many complex vocal and instrumental techniques. Ives not only gained a great deal of musical knowledge from his father, but he also idolized him throughout his life. It was through his father's influence, no doubt, that Ives was able to develop the polystructures of tonality, rhythms, and textures for which he was famous.

Ives lived in New York during a portion of his life, and several of his compositions pay tribute to the city (e.g., "Central Park in the Dark" from *Two Contemplations for Small Orchestra* and "Romanzo di Central Park" for voice).

This innovative wooden sculpture of Charles Ives and his father is a beautiful tribute by Scott Pfaffman. It is located near the Brooklyn Academy of Music and is not far from Brooklyn

College's Conservatory of Music, which serves as the home of the Institute for Studies in American Music.

In 1963, ASCAP commemorated George Gershwin's birthplace on Snedicker Avenue in East New York with a plaque. The composer's family only lived here for a short time before relocating to Manhattan.

CONEY ISLAND, BRIGHTON BEACH, MANHATTAN BEACH

From glitzy amusement parks to elegant resorts, these beach communities were once filled with the sounds of summertime fun and music

In the late nineteenth and early twentieth century, these beaches were the site of a great variety of leisure activities and musical entertainment.

Coney Island is still remembered as one of the world's most famous amusement areas. From the mid-1800s through the 1940s, visitors enjoyed bathing on the vast stretch of beach, going on one of the many thrill rides, marveling at the side shows, and attending the various glitzy and popular entertainments such as revues and concerts that were offered in restaurants and out-of-doors. Many famous performers worked here in the busy seasons. Jimmy Durante was a rag pianist here, and evidently Eddie Cantor, Al Jolson, and Irving Berlin all worked at Coney Island at one time or another in their youth.

Coney Island USA (1208 Surf Avenue / 718-372-5159) is a museum that seeks to preserve the memorabilia as well as the spirit and traditions of the old amusement park culture. Its new exhibits will contain historical information and artifacts. Musical presentations are also offered, including burlesque and vaudeville shows that were once so popular here.

Brighton Beach and Manhattan Beach were once the setting for many outdoor concerts. Considered to be a fairly elegant resort area, many hotels were constructed here in the latter part of the 1800s. It then became popular to hold outdoor entertainment in the summertime for guests at these establishments. Band music was a favorite, and Patrick Gilmore, Victor Herbert, and John Philip Sousa all led their groups in concert here. ("The Manhattan Beach March" was written in honor of this locale.)

Years later, dance bands took over with entertainment provided by Artie Shaw, Benny Goodman, Les Brown, and other groups, much to the delight of outdoor audiences.

The hotels are gone, and the old bands are but an echo. However, visitors can walk on the beach and enjoy the setting where beautiful music once reigned. Also, occasional concerts are still held on the boardwalks, reminiscent of days gone by.

Queens

STEINWAY FACTORY

One Steinway Place (between 38th Street and 19th Avenue)
Astoria

The last and most famous piano manufacturer in New York City

This factory creates what has been called one of the greatest
pianos in the world. It is also the last piano manufacturer in
New York—once the premier city within the industry.

Steinway's first factory in the United States was located at 85
Varick Street in Manhattan during 1853, and then at 82-88
Walker Street from 1854 until the major move to Park Avenue
in 1860. The Park Avenue site was located between East 52nd
and 53rd Streets. (The family lived in a cluster of houses at
121-125 East 52nd Street.)

In 1870, William Steinway bought land in the Astoria area for
a new factory and village and began work on his project. The
family maintained the Park Avenue factory until the Astoria
facility was fully completed and ready for operation in 1910.

The Steinways were among the first piano manufacturers to
use power-driven machinery. Many pieces of this machinery
were useful during World War II in helping to produce airplane parts for the war effort.

Despite modern equipment, skilled craftsmen still complete
many processes painstakingly by hand—just as in the early
years of the firm's existence. A piano is the sum total of many
thousands of parts, and the Steinway system is a careful blend
of man and machine—the final result being its world-
renowned masterpiece.

STEINWAY MANSION

18-33 41st Street
Astoria

An endangered Steinway landmark

This villa in the Italian country style was built in the mid-1850s for Benjamin Pike, a manufacturer of scientific instruments.

William Steinway, of the Steinway Piano empire, occupied this 27-room mansion with its spectacular view of the East River. Many gala social events have taken place within its walls. It was also near the piano factory and the remarkable workers' village that Steinway built for his employees.

Now a private residence, the mansion is considered to be an endangered historic site.

What is now La Guardia Airport was once North Beach Amusement Park, built by William Steinway and opened in 1886. The rides, concerts and entertainment, water amusements, and refreshments were an instant success with the eager public.

This was once the mansion of William Steinway, head of the famous piano empire. *Courtesy of the Queens Historical Society*

SITE OF STEINWAY WORKERS' HOUSING
South Side of 20th Avenue (between Steinway and 42nd Streets)
41st Street (between 20th and 21st Avenues)
Astoria

A charming architectural reminder of the once-thriving Steinway Village

William Steinway certainly saw after the welfare of his employees. In 1872, he began the construction of Steinway Village, a 400-acre area which supplied rental housing, parks, a post office, a library, subsidized teaching of music at school, and other amenities for workers at the nearby factory.

Steinway was evidently quite civic-minded. He was a motivating force behind several banks, a streetcar line, a ferry, and other community services. Although the workers' community is all but gone, the Steinway influence is still much in evidence in Astoria, including a street and a subway stop bearing the name of this illustrious family.

These lovely Victorian brick row houses, once inhabited by the Steinway workforce, still remain. The original streets were named after Steinway family members, and there are several stone nameplates on corner houses attesting to this fact. "Albert," "Theodore," and "Winthrop" can be seen while strolling in the vicinity.

The Steinway Reformed Church is an interesting 1890 Gothic Revival building at 41-01 Ditmars Boulevard (between 45th & 46th Streets). The Steinways generously donated funds to help build the edifice, and William Steinway also contributed a lovely pipe organ in 1891 (later replaced). As a result, the church changed its name in honor of its benefactor.

BOHEMIAN PARK & HALL

29-19 24th Avenue (northeast corner of 29th Street)
Astoria
718-274-4925

Reminder of a vanished musical past where ethnic musical traditions once thrived

Beer gardens and beer halls were quite popular in New York from the 1850s into the twentieth century. Here, visitors could not only partake of this most popular of beverages along with a hearty sampling of food, but they could also enjoy a variety of musical entertainment, including an assortment of bands and singers. (The audience could actively participate in the singing and dancing, too.) Ethnic musical traditions were preserved at these establishments.

This is said to be the last remaining beer hall and garden in the city. Built in 1910, it is now run by the Bohemian Citizens' Benevolent Society of Astoria, and still sponsors old-fashioned, traditional outdoor beer fests and musical events for the neighborhood and for specific ethnic organizations. In 1997, this was the site of a tribute to Antonin Dvorak and to Czech culture—with music, lectures, and food—in celebration of the installation of the composer's statue in Stuyvesant Square Park in Manhattan.

Although the American Museum of the Moving Image (36-01 35th Avenue, Astoria / 718-784-0077) focuses on visual presentations, the visitor can learn much about the accompanying musical elements of the cinematic form from special exhibits and resources. The adjacent Kaufman Astoria Studios houses Master Sound Astoria—said to be the largest recording institution on the East Coast.

SITE OF SOHMER PIANO COMPANY FACTORY
31-01 Vernon Boulevard (southeast corner of 31st Avenue)
Astoria

A ghost from the golden age of piano manufacturing

This building was constructed in 1886 by the Sohmer Piano Company, a firm which was created by Hugo Sohmer in 1872. Sohmer was a German immigrant, and his product was once on the forefront of the New York piano scene, renowned for its fine craftsmanship—a story amazingly similar to that of Steinway.

It seemed like more than coincidence that Sohmer's factory was located so close to that of Steinway. These firms were considered to be top competitors in the golden age of the piano during the latter part of the nineteenth century. As business improved, more floors were added to the top of this once impressive establishment.

However, despite years of respect within the industry and a prosperous sales record, the firm did not ultimately have the same longevity in New York as its neighboring competitor.

> Socrates Sculpture Park (Broadway and Vernon Boulevard, Long Island City) often displays artistic works that contain elements of music and sound.

LA GUARDIA & WAGNER ARCHIVES
at La Guardia Community College
31-10 Thomson Avenue ("E" Building)
Long Island City
718-482-5065

Repository for the Steinway papers and archival resources

Piano connoisseurs will appreciate the vast wealth of material pertaining to the Steinway family and business that is maintained here. The famous piano firm turned over their papers and memorabilia to this archival facility. There are 20 different series of research subjects, each dealing with a different facet of the Steinway story. Included are materials pertaining to corporate history, information on company-sponsored concerts and performing artists, family diaries and correspondence, production and employee records, and details about the firm's centennial, among other categories. A rare 1858 piano is also a part of the collection. Researchers may call for an appointment to use this facility.

In addition, the building displays an open exhibit about Steinway, containing 11 panels of pictures and information that trace the history of this illustrious firm from 1850 to 1950.

The archive also maintains materials on local history as well as the papers of several major city political figures, including Fiorello La Guardia.

GRAVESITE OF SCOTT JOPLIN

St. Michael's Cemetery
72-02 Astoria Boulevard
East Elmhurst
718-278-3240

Final resting place of a famed ragtime composer

Scott Joplin (1868-1917), composer of the famous "Maple Leaf Rag," was a key figure in the instrumental ragtime craze around the turn of the century.

Long associated with New York City, his publishing firm on 29th Street was near the heart of Tin Pan Alley, and he and his wife once ran a small boarding house on West 47th Street. Joplin also lived in what is now a historically designated residence on West 131st Street in Harlem.

In 1917, Joplin died in Ward's Island Hospital and was buried in this Queens cemetery in an unmarked grave. His music enjoyed a strong revival in the 1970s, particularly as heard in the catchy score to *The Sting*, a popular film starring Paul Newman and Robert Redford. He was honored with this bronze grave plaque in 1974, the same year that his rag "The Entertainer," featured in the film, topped the song charts. The plaque is inscribed: "Scott Joplin, American Composer."

LOUIS ARMSTRONG MURAL
Louis Armstrong Middle School
32-02 Junction Boulevard
Jackson Heights

A touching tribute to a world-famous Queens resident

This 1981 mural was created as a tribute to longtime Queens resident and jazz musician Louis Armstrong. It decorates the facade of the building, which was also renamed in his honor.

Designed by Lucinda Luvaas, a former teacher at the school, who also acted as team director for the project, the mural was painted by students. It was sponsored under the auspices of the City Arts Workshop.

Louis Armstrong is buried in Flushing Cemetery at 46th Avenue and 162nd Street, not far from Queens College where his papers and much of his memorabilia are housed in the special research archives.

LOUIS ARMSTRONG HOUSE
34-56 107th Street (between 34th and 37th Avenues)
Corona
718-478-8274

A wonderful museum and historic site honoring the great jazz trumpeter

---

Louis Armstrong (1901-1971) was a longtime Queens resident as well as a popular entertainer on the jazz scene in Harlem and elsewhere. "Satchmo" was noted for his jazz trumpet solos, groundbreaking improvisational approaches, unique style of scat singing, famous recordings, and engaging personality on stage, screen, and television.

This house, built in 1910 by Thomas Daly and altered over the years, was Armstrong's residence along with his wife Lucille from 1943 until his death in 1971. Armstrong was evidently quite popular in the neighborhood and would occasionally entertain local residents with his trumpet music from the front stoop. He also presented an annual concert for children in the garden.

The house was declared a National Historic Landmark in 1977 and a New York City Landmark in 1983. Already a small museum with music, instruments, tapes, recordings, and many personal effects, the house is undergoing renovations sponsored by Queens College. Plans are underway to enhance the collections and to provide local educational programs—a fitting tribute to this great man as well as to the jazz scene that he loved so much.

> Nearby, in the courtyard of the Louis Armstrong Cultural Facility (at Northern Boulevard and 107th Street) is an abstract sculpture of steel and cast iron entitled "Little Dances" by Howard McCalebb. Both sculpture and community center are in honor of Armstrong.

FLUSHING TOWN HALL
137-35 Northern Boulevard
Flushing
718-463-7700

A historic building that is seeing new life as a musical and cultural center

This magnificent architectural gem of the Romanesque Revival style, with its unique round-arched door and window design, was built during the Civil War by a local carpenter. Having served as a town hall, library, political center, police station, and—according to one unsubstantiated legend—a local showcase for Jenny Lind, it was in severe danger of demolition in recent years. Through the efforts of the Flushing Council on Culture & the Arts as well as local politicians and citizens, the building is now enjoying its renaissance (not to mention its landmark status) as an arts center.

Concerts of jazz and chamber music, with many name performers, happily co-exist side by side on the hall's schedule of performances. The building contains a beautifully paneled Jazz Café with an intriguing photo exhibit of past performers.

Its weekly jazz series is especially popular. An art gallery, several cultural organizations, and rehearsal rooms occupy other space in this remarkable historical treasure.

THE AARON COPLAND SCHOOL OF MUSIC AT QUEENS COLLEGE (CITY UNIVERSITY OF NEW YORK)
65-30 Kissena Boulevard
Flushing
718-997-5000

A well-respected center of education, research, and performance

Although the music division of this school was formed in 1937, it was renamed in honor of the famed American composer, Aaron Copland, in 1981 on the occasion of his eightieth birthday.

A variety of bachelor's and master's programs are offered, and the school boasts of exceptional research, recording, performance, and practice facilities. A preparatory division for pre-college students is another highly successful endeavor. The new Music Library contains special collections, scores, books, and sound recordings, as well as the Karol Rathaus Archives—a collection of music manuscripts, lecture transcripts, and related materials from the Polish composer and former college faculty member.

Queens College houses a number of performing groups, specializing in repertoire ranging from baroque to jazz to ethnic ensembles. Diverse master classes are sponsored by the school and conducted by guest artists. The college's children's concerts are also a fixture on its cultural calendar.

Several concert halls are located on the campus, including the famed Colden Center Auditorium, which seats more than 2100. The adjacent Goldstein Theater, with a seating capacity of 476, is attractive for smaller performances. The new LeFrak Concert Hall, seating 489, offers a wonderful venue for recitals and professional recording. It also houses a fine tracker-action organ.

Queens College is the site of the Louis Armstrong Archives. Here, the papers, manuscripts, tapes, and related materials from "Satchmo" are maintained, catalogued, and preserved for use by scholars as well as the general public. This archival division also mounts several annual exhibitions related to the life and work of this great jazz musician, and it provides related slide/tape presentations to schools and special interest groups.

Queens College is sponsoring the restoration of Armstrong's house in nearby Corona which will serve as a museum and educational center in his honor.

The Queens Symphony Orchestra (718-786-8880) is known well beyond the local area for the high quality of its performances, excellent community outreach programs, and its internationally famous guest soloists. The group performs at a variety of concert spaces within the borough, and many programs are planned in conjunction with specific events—from those held at local colleges, to the Tennis Center, to local parks, and beyond. It is especially known for its outreach to different ethnic groups, its exceptional youth gospel choir, and its competition for young instrumentalists.

QUEENSBOROUGH COMMUNITY COLLEGE
56th Avenue and Springfield Boulevard
Bayside
718-631-6311

The setting for many fine musical performances

A well-respected local college, this institution sponsors a fine professional performing arts series.

The college theater is used not only for student and faculty performances, but it is also host to many outside concert groups for special events and musical series. Musical stars including Anna Maria Alberghetti and John Raitt have appeared here as well as the Harry James Orchestra, local opera companies, and multicultural musical groups. The Queensborough Orchestra also performs here on a frequent basis.

CLAUDIO ARRAU HOME
202 Shore Road
Douglaston

The acclaimed concert pianist once lived here

This plaque, installed by the Historic Landmarks Preservation Center, honors concert pianist Claudio Arrau (1903-1991), who was a well-respected resident of this quiet Queens community.

A native of Chile, Arrau settled in the U.S. in 1941 with his family. During his distinguished career, he presented concerts in the United States, South America, Europe, and Asia over the course of many decades. (At the age of 80, he still had a schedule of approximately 90 annual concerts!)

Although Arrau specialized in the compositions of Beethoven as well as of Chopin, Schumann, and other Romantic composers, he completed the extraordinary feat of presenting all of Bach's keyboard works in a series of concerts held in Berlin, just before the outbreak of World War II.

Arrau was the recipient of a variety of international awards, and he made scores of recordings that are considered to be lasting treasures. He was also noted for his teaching activities and for his superior work on the Urtext edition of Beethoven sonatas published by Peters.

SEUFFERT BANDSHELL
Woodhaven and Forest Park Boulevards
Woodhaven
718-235-0815

Summer music in a pastoral setting

Forest Park was created in 1895 with the purchase of its first piece of land. The famous landscape architect Frederick Law Olmsted was requested to survey the park as well as to design its drive, and he had nothing but praise for the natural wonders of the site. The park officially became a part of Queens in 1898, the same year that the borough joined the city of New York. Its boundaries touch five Queens communities: Forest Hills, Richmond Hill, Glendale, Woodhaven, and Kew Gardens.

The bandshell was opened in 1920 and named in honor of George Seuffert, who conducted many popular Sunday band concerts in this park. His group had a permanent place on the Queens cultural calendar for many years.

Recently renovated, the bandshell is the site of many other varieties of classical and popular concerts each season. Visitors can enjoy all of this music in the park's 538-acre pastoral oasis, which also contains a classic early 1900s carousel. "Oak Ridge," the remodeled clubhouse, is located on the park grounds and provides quarters for the Queens Council on the Arts.

Number 159-13 85th Street in Howard Beach (south of Forest Park) was the home of folk singer/composer Woody Guthrie from 1955 to 1967. He sang of the hardships of the poor and the working class and was well known for his song "This Land Is Your Land."

The Triangle Hofbrau (Jamaica Avenue and 117th Street, Richmond Hill) was said to have been a favorite haunt of song-writer Ernest R. Ball, who composed "When Irish Eyes Are Smiling" as well as the music to "Will You Love Me in December As You Do in May?" (with lyrics by former mayor James J. Walker).

BLACK AMERICAN HERITAGE FOUNDATION MUSIC HISTORY ARCHIVE AT YORK COLLEGE

94-20 Guy R. Brewer Boulevard
Jamaica
718-262-2644

A fascinating collection of musical research materials and memorabilia

---

Many famous black composers and musicians, particularly in the field of jazz, were residents of southeastern Queens. The area is rich in music—both in past history and in current performance.

York College has sought to preserve and share this heritage, providing a center for further artistic research and education. A variety of material connected to the African-American musical world is housed in this archive. Papers, manuscripts, instruments, artifacts, and recordings associated with such names as Duke Ellington, Count Basie, Fats Waller, and Billie Holiday are maintained here, tracing a rich tradition for the visitor and researcher to study and enjoy.

The Jamaica Center for Arts and Learning (161-04 Jamaica Avenue / 718-658-7400) is housed in an 1898 building, once the county office for the Register of Titles and Deeds. Now it is a community school for the arts and a performance center specializing in fine concerts and performances of diverse ethnic cultural works. An active outreach program is a favorite within the community.

FATS WALLER HOME & PLAQUE

173-19 Sayres Avenue
Jamaica

Former home of a jazz great

Thomas Wright Waller (1904-1943) was a multi-talented jazz musician who performed as a pianist, singer, organist, composer, and bandleader.

Greatly influenced by the famous James P. Johnson, he was known for his piano renditions arranged in the flamboyant Harlem stride style. Among the more famous of these were recorded performances of his own works, including "Handful of Keys" and "Smashing Thirds."

As a popular composer, he was best known for such tunes as "Honeysuckle Rose," "Black and Blue," and "Ain't Misbehavin'." These titles have become an integral part of the standard jazz/pop repertoire over the years. Ever versatile, Waller composed works for several Broadway shows including *Keep Shufflin'* (1928), appeared at Carnegie Hall, regularly performed on radio programs, and even became famous for his humorous demeanor in live performance.

Waller was one of many famous musicians who resided in this general vicinity in Queens. This plaque, marking his former home, was installed in Waller's honor by the Historic Landmarks Preservation Center in 1996.

A number of famous black musicians and entertainers made their homes in the St. Albans section from the 1940s on. A large mural, bursting with musical activity, is located under the tracks at the local branch of the Long Island Rail Road station— paying tribute to these illustrious figures who include Ella Fitzgerald, Lena Horne, Fats Waller, Brook Benton, Billie Holiday, and others. Count Basie once lived nearby at 174-27 Adelaide Lane in the Addisleigh Park area. His house is a local landmark, as well.

Staten Island

MANDOLIN BROTHERS, LTD.
629 Forest Avenue
718-981-3226

An internationally known leader in the world of fretted instruments

---

A well-known institution not only on Staten Island, but also nationwide and beyond, Mandolin Brothers bills itself as the "world's most comfortable and complete showroom of guitars, banjos, and mandolins." That it is.

Founded in 1971, the store's name was chosen to elevate the status of the mandolin which had taken a back seat to its relatives in the world of fretted creations. Set in a low-keyed neighborhood of family-owned businesses, the building contains five showrooms chock-full of rare and historic as well as new fretted instruments—all of which are definitely in the world-class category.

Proprietor Stan Jay has been able to boast of a stock that ranges from a guitar owned by John Lennon, to an 1895 Gibson handmade mandolin, to an unusual 1958 Gibson Flying V guitar, to brand-new C.F. Martin models. The store has supplied instruments to such performers as Tom Chapin, Randy Travis, Paul Simon, Joni Mitchell, and many more. George Harrison has even been a customer!

For the connoisseur, a detailed catalog and *Vintage News* updates are to die for—with pictures and descriptions of hundreds of instruments. A visit is heaven!

Recommended far and wide by such famed establishments as the Gibson Guitar Corporation of Nashville, this shop is, in the words of *The Boston Globe*, "one of the best in the world."

Mandolin Brothers is world-famous for its fretted instruments.
Stan Jay/Mandolin Brothers

This Gretsch 1957 White Penguin electric guitar, from the Mandolin Brothers collection, is among the rarest of its kind in the world.
Stan Jay/Mandolin Brothers

SNUG HARBOR CULTURAL CENTER
1000 Richmond Terrace
718-448-2500

A community for all of the arts in a beautiful and historic setting

This wonderful complex houses a number of fascinating sites, including several superb destinations for music lovers.

Snug Harbor began its life in 1801 as a result of the contributions of philanthropist Robert Richard Randall. Originally called Sailors' Snug Harbor, it served as a retirement community for seamen, the first of its kind in the United States. A sprawling 83-acre landscape, its 28 historic buildings were beautifully designed in Greek Revival, Italianate, beaux-arts, and other attractive styles.

After its purchase by the City of New York, it was officially opened in 1976 as a cultural center and listed in the National Register of Historic Places. Now, many institutions reside within its boundaries. They include the Staten Island Children's Museum, the Newhouse Center for Contemporary Arts, the Staten Island Institute of Arts and Sciences, and the Staten Island Botanical Gardens, to name just a few. More than 70 smaller arts groups and individuals also call this their home and utilize the center's many professional work spaces.

Music facilities constitute an eclectic mix of indoor halls and outdoor landscapes. Concerts are presented in the 850-seat Music Hall, originally built in 1892 for use as a vaudeville house. It is listed as second only to Carnegie Hall in the category of oldest music hall within the city. The smaller Veterans Memorial Hall accommodates 200 and is appropriate for smaller recitals and performances. Rehearsal space may also be rented within the music complex. Outdoors, South Meadow features summer programs for audiences of upward of 5000.

Concerts of all types are presented at these facilities—classical, jazz, folk, and chamber music. A number of well-known groups have appeared here, including the Preservation Hall Jazz Band. Local performing and resident organizations give concerts regularly each season at Snug Harbor. Many outreach programs are available on the premises to bring school children closer to music and the performing arts. The entire complex services music, art, theater, and the general humanities.

An international artists-in-residence program has also been recently instituted here.

The Staten Island Conservatory is located at Snug Harbor. It provides a full program of musical studies for students of all ages—instrumental instruction, music history, theory, and related subjects—according to European tradition. Student and faculty concerts are given at the concert halls on the grounds of the complex. The school also operates an orchestral summer camp and provides visiting music education programs for public schools.

Visitors will enjoy not only the musical portion of their stay, but also the setting with its lovely gardens and stunning views of New York Harbor.

The Staten Island Chamber Music Players (718-356-2094) presents a regular series of concerts at Veterans Memorial Hall with selections ranging from Mozart, Haydn, and Monteverdi to Hindemith, Grainger, and Joplin. In existence since 1974, the group performs chamber music as well as jazz, string, brass, and woodwind repertoire in various combinations, not only at Snug Harbor, but also at Richmondtown Restoration, the College of Staten Island, Wagner College, outdoor sites, schools, civic centers, and WQXR radio.

WAGNER COLLEGE
631 Howard Avenue
718-390-3259

The home of an exciting musical theater series and more

This college sits atop Grymes Hill on 105 acres of attractive landscape. Here, in its Main Hall Theater, housed in a landmark building, the school presents a fine series of musicals with a high reputation on the Island and beyond.

Deemed one of the best musical theater departments in the country, its productions have included such shows as *Crazy for You, West Side Story, Pippin, Guys & Dolls, Damn Yankees*, and *The Robber Bridegroom*, to name just a few—all with outstanding reviews. A highly professional faculty provides intense training for young hopefuls, many of whom have gone on to Broadway and other leading performance venues.

Also, Wagner's music department offers a varied range of courses and musical instruction leading toward a bachelor's degree and is especially proud of its many performing organizations. Its choirs, opera workshop, chamber groups, band, and guitar and lute ensemble have appeared on campus, at local churches and schools, and at major performance centers within the city and beyond.

COLLEGE OF STATEN ISLAND
CENTER FOR THE ARTS
2800 Victory Boulevard
718-982-2000

A new and versatile performing arts complex, serving both college and community

This beautiful new facility, on the 204-acre Willowbrook campus of the college, provides varied artistic offerings to the community.

The center houses several attractive performance spaces, including a modern and spacious concert auditorium. Smaller halls suitable for recitals, chamber music, and lectures are also a part of the complex. A lovely atrium is often used for post-concert receptions.

Both the music and art departments call this complex home with lecture halls, galleries, and studios in frequent use by students and faculty. Undergraduate degrees are offered in music, with a selection of courses and seminars in various disciplines.

Fine orchestral, recital, and chamber music series are presented at the center, and are available to the public, as are performances by guest opera companies. Many local and college music groups perform here regularly. Children's programs, ethnic music presentations, and a full range of theater and dance are also on the cultural calendar.

The professional Staten Island Symphony (718-390-3426) performs in a regular series at the College of Staten Island. Formed in 1980 by Robert Kogan, the group has appeared in concert with Tony Bennett at Snug Harbor, at holiday arts festivals at Lincoln Center, and in numerous other venues. Its educational outreach and young artist programs are well known. Concerts have included traditional orchestral repertoire, modern compositions, and new works by such composers as Beth Anderson, Shaun Davey, and Galt Macdermot.

HISTORIC RICHMONDTOWN

441 Clarke Avenue
718-351-1611

A restored village with some musical treats

This village dates back to 1690, and the current restoration traces Staten Island life from the seventeenth century on. Visitors can enjoy period furnishings, craft and trade demonstrations, and other historic delights to be found in the approximately 30 buildings of varying ages set upon a scenic 100 acres of landscape.

A tavern from the 1820s offers weekly folk music programs with refreshments served by staff in period costume. Here one can enjoy a historic setting for unique musical entertainment.

Local performing groups present occasional concerts here, particularly in conjunction with special or seasonal events.

Musical researchers might also be interested in the library at Richmondtown. It contains a small cache of holdings pertaining to Staten Island's past. Included are papers and files from the former Staten Island Quartet Club as well as a miscellaneous collection of sheet music.

The Richmond Choral Society (c/o Snug Harbor Cultural Center, 1000 Richmond Terrace, Staten Island, NY 10301) was founded in 1950 by Dr. Anders Emile. The group fosters the study and enjoyment of choral works. It performs everything from masses by Haydn and Mozart to works by Copland and P.D.Q. Bach, has appeared at every major performance space on Staten Island, and has joined with other groups to sing at Alice Tully Hall and other leading concert centers. The society provides scholarships for young singers, outreach to community and educational institutions, and special music seminars.

BIBLIOGRAPHY

Allen, Oliver E. *New York, New York: A History of the World's Most Exhilarating and Challenging City.* New York: Atheneum, 1990.

Ammer, Christine. *Unsung: A History of Women in American Music.* Westport, CT: Greenwood Press, 1980.

"Balloon Carried Aloft Veil of Verdi's Statue." *The New York Times,* October 13, 1906, p. 7.

"Band Shell Dedicated." *The New York Times,* September 30, 1923, p. 6.

Batterberry, Michael and Ariane. *On the Town in New York: From 1776 to the Present.* New York: Charles Scribner's Sons, 1973.

Biondi, Joann, and James Haskins. *Hippocrene U.S.A. Guide to Black New York.* New York: Hippocrene Books, 1994.

Blau, Eleanor. "Lehman College Opens New Cultural Complex." *The New York Times,* September 26, 1980, Section III, p. 4.

Brierly, J. Ernest. *The Streets of Old New York.* New York: Hastings House Publishers, 1953.

Browning, Judith H. *New York City: Yesterday & Today.* Stamford, CT: Corsair Publications, 1990.

"Burns Statue Unveiled." *The New York Times,* October 3, 1880, p. 10.

Chase, Gilbert. *America's Music: From the Pilgrims to the Present.* New York: McGraw-Hill, 1955.

"Coming Opera War." *The New York Times,* July 11, 1883, p. 4.

"Concerts for Young People." *The New York Times,* December 23, 1883, p. 6.

"Dedication of the Verdi Monument." *The New York Times,* October 21, 1906, pictorial section, p. 1.

Delaney, Edmund T. *New York's Turtle Bay Old & New.* Barre, MA: Barre Publishers, 1965.

Dolkart, Andrew S. *Guide to New York City Landmarks.* Washington, DC: The Preservation Press—National Trust for Historic Preservation, 1992.

Dolkart, Andrew S., and Gretchen S. Sorin. *Touring Historic Harlem: Four Walks in Northern Manhattan.* New York: New York Landmarks Conservancy, 1997.

Dolkart, Andrew S. *Touring the Upper East Side: Walks in Five Historic Districts.* New York: New York Landmarks Conservancy, 1995.

Dox, Thurston. "George Frederick Bristow and the New York Public Schools." *American Music,* Volume 9, Number 4, Winter 1991, pp. 339-352.

"Dream Comes True for Mrs. Richard Tucker." *The New York Times*, April 21, 1980, p. B9.

Dunshee, Kenneth Holcomb. *As You Pass By*. New York: Hastings House Publishers, 1952.

Ellis, Edward Robb. *The Epic of New York City*. New York: Old Town Books, 1966.

Encyclopedia of New York City. Edited by Kenneth T. Jackson. New Haven, CT: Yale University Press and The New-York Historical Society, 1995.

Ewen, David. *All the Years of American Popular Music*. Englewood Cliffs, NJ: Prentice Hall, 1977.

Fine, Larry. *The Piano Book*. Boston: Brookside Press, 1990.

Fuller, Samuel. *New York in the 1930s*. Paris: Hazan Pocket Archives, 1997.

Gayle, Margot, and Michele Cohen. *The Art Commission and the Municipal Art Society Guide to Manhattan's Outdoor Sculpture*. New York: Prentice Hall, 1988.

Goldstone, Harmon H., and Martha Dalrymple. *History Preserved: A Guide to New York City Landmarks and Historic Districts*. New York: Simon and Schuster, 1974.

"Group Marks 100th Year." *The New York Times*, February 2, 1947, p. 47.

Guinness Encyclopedia of Popular Music. Edited by Colin Larkin. London: Guinness Publishing, 1995.

Hamm, Charles. *Yesterdays: Popular Song in America*. New York: W.W. Norton, 1983.

Harrison, Marina, and Lucy D. Rosenfeld. *Artwalks in New York*. New York: Michael Kesend Publishing, 1994.

Hellman, Peter. "Where History is at Rest." *The New York Times*, September 6, 1996, pp. C1, C20.

Henahan, Donal. "Richard Tucker, the Met Tenor, is Dead." *The New York Times*, January 9, 1975, pp. 1, 29.

Henderson, Mary C. *The City and the Theatre: New York Playhouses from Bowling Green to Times Square*. Clifton, NJ: James T. White, 1973.

Hernandez, Raymond. "How New Chief is Putting Park Back on Map." *The New York Times*, November 28, 1993, Section XIII, p. 9.

"Hogs and Opera Boxes." *The New York Times*, November 28, 1883, p. 4.

Homberger, Eric (with Alice Hudson, Cartographic Consultant). *The Historical Atlas of New York City: A Visual Celebration of Nearly 400 Years of New York City's History*. New York: Henry Holt, 1994.

Hone & Strong Diaries of Old Manhattan. Edited by Louis Auchincloss. New York: Abbeville Press, 1989.

Howard, John Tasker. *The Music of George Washington's Time.* Washington, DC: United States George Washington Bicentennial Commission, 1931.

Howard, John Tasker. *Our American Music: Three Hundred Years of It.* New York: Thomas Y. Crowell, 1954.

Howe, Marvine. "Rita Ford, 92, Dies; Owned Shop Serving Fans of Music Boxes." *The New York Times,* July 27, 1993, p. 24.

International Cyclopedia of Music and Musicians. Edited by Oscar Thompson. New York: Dodd, Mead, 1939.

Israelowitz, Oscar. *Oscar Israelowitz's Lower East Side Tourbook.* Brooklyn, NY: Israelowitz Publishing, 1996.

Jasen, David A. *Tin Pan Alley: The Composers, the Songs, the Performers and Their Times.* New York: Donald I. Fine, 1988.

Johnson, Kirk. "Black Workers Bear Big Burden as Jobs in Government Dwindle." *The New York Times,* February 2, 1997, pp. 1, 36-37.

Kaye, Joseph. *Victor Herbert: The Biography of America's Greatest Composer of Romantic Music.* New York: G. Howard Watt, 1931.

Kleiman, Dena. "New Lehman College Arts Center Underscores Change in an 'Oasis,'" *The New York Times,* September 26, 1981, p. 25.

Lawrence, Vera Brodsky. *Music for Patriots, Politicians, and Presidents: Harmonies and Discords of the First Hundred Years.* New York: Macmillan, 1975.

Lawrence, Vera Brodsky. *Strong on Music: The New York Music Scene in the Days of George Templeton Strong, 1836-1875. Volume I: Resonances, 1836-1850.* New York: Oxford University Press, 1988.

Lawrence, Vera Brodsky. *Strong on Music: The New York Music Scene in the Days of George Templeton Strong, 1836-1875. Volume II: Reverberations, 1850-1856.* Chicago: University of Chicago Press, 1995.

Lieberman, Richard K. *Steinway & Sons.* New Haven, CT: Yale University Press, 1995.

"Liederkranz Banquet." *The New York Times,* January 10, 1897, p. 6.

Lockwood, Charles. *Manhattan Moves Uptown: An Illustrated History.* New York: Barnes & Noble, 1976, 1995.

Loesser, Arthur. *Men, Women and Pianos: A Social History.* New York: Dover Publications, 1954, 1982, 1990.

Lowens, Irving. *Music and Musicians in Early America.* New York: W.W. Norton, 1964.

Lyman, Susan Elizabeth. "The Search for the Missing King." Clippings files under "New York City Monuments," Library of the Municipal Reference and Research Center, The City of New York Department of Records & Information Services.

"Maennerchor's Fest-Commers." *The New York Times*, July 23, 1884, p. 3.

Martin, Ralph. *Lincoln Center for the Performing Arts*. Englewood Cliffs, NJ: Prentice Hall, 1971.

"Mayor Dedicates Bird Bath in Park." *The New York Times*, May 29, 1937, p. 21.

"Mayor Speaking at Unveiling of Victor Herbert Bust." *The New York Times*, November 30, 1927, p. 3.

McDarrah, Fred W. and Gloria. *Museums in New York*. New York: St. Martin's Press, 1990.

Monaghan, Frank, and Marvin Lowenthal. *This Was New York: The Nation's Capital in 1789*. Garden City, NY: Doubleday, Doran, 1943.

Morris, Lloyd. *Incredible New York: High Life and Low Life from 1850 to 1950*. Syracuse, NY: Syracuse University Press, 1951, 1996.

Moscow, Henry. *The Street Book: An Encyclopedia of Manhattan's Street Names and Their Origins*. New York: Fordham University Press, 1978.

"Mozart Bust Unveiled." *The New York Times*, October 24, 1897, p. 23.

"New Broadway Memorial to Irving Berlin." *Notes from the Songwriters Showcase*, Volume 3, Number 1, January 1995, pp. 1, 6.

New Grove Dictionary of Music. Edited by H. Wiley Hitchcock and Stanley Sadie. New York: Grove's Dictionaries of Music, 1986.

New York: A Collection from Harper's Magazine. New York: Gallery Books, 1991.

New York City Museum Guide. Edited by Candace Ward. New York: Dover Publications, 1995.

NYC Culture Catalog: A Guide to New York City's Museums, Theaters, Zoos, Libraries, Botanical Gardens, Concert Halls and Historic Houses. New York: Harry N. Abrams and the Alliance for the Arts, 1994.

Oringer, Judith. *Passion for the Piano*. Los Angeles: Jeremy P. Tarcher, 1983.

Pareles, John. "At Hostos, a New World of Culture." *The New York Times*, October 14, 1994, Section C, pp. 1, 32-33.

Raddin, George G., Jr. "The Music of New York City, 1797-1801." *The New-York Historical Society Quarterly*, Volume XXXVIII, Number 4, October 1954, pp. 478-499.

Redway, Virginia Larkin. "A New York Concert in 1736." *The Musical Quarterly*, Volume XXII, Number 2, April 1936, pp. 170-177.

Reed, Henry Hope, and Sophia Duckworth. *Central Park: A History and a Guide*. New York: Clarkson N. Potter, 1967.

Reynolds, Donald Martin. *Monuments and Masterpieces: Histories and Views of Public Sculpture in New York City*. New York: Macmillan, 1988.

Roell, Craig H. *The Piano in America, 1890-1940*. Chapel Hill, NC: The University of North Carolina Press, 1989.

Rosenblum, Ira. *The New York Book of Music*. New York: City & Company, 1995.

Schwartz, Charles. *Gershwin: His Life & Music*. New York: DaCapo Press, 1973.

Seyfried, Vincent F., and William Asadorian. *Old Queens, N.Y. in Early Photographs*. New York: Dover Publications, 1991.

Shaver, Peter D. *The National Register of Historic Places in New York State*. New York: Rizzoli, 1993.

Shepard, Richard F. (photographs by Carin Drechsler-Marx). *Broadway: From the Battery to the Bronx*. New York: Harry N. Abrams, 1988.

Singleton, Esther. *Social New York Under the Georges, 1714-1776*. New York: D. Appleton, 1902.

Sonneck, O.G. *Early Concert-Life in America (1731-1800)*. Leipzig: Breitkopf & Hartel, 1907.

"Stars Unveil Statues of Women of Stage." *The New York Times*, October 21, 1929, p. 30.

"Statue of Cohan Gazes on Broadway." *The New York Times*, September 12, 1959, p. 12.

Steinway, Theodore E. *People and Pianos: A Century of Service to Music*. New York: Steinway & Sons, 1961.

Still, Bayrd. *Mirror for Gotham: New York as Seen by Contemporaries from Dutch Days to the Present*. New York: Fordham University Press, 1994.

"Sturdy German Citizens." *The New York Times*, July 22, 1884, pp. 8, 12.

"Their Prize for Brooklyn." *The New York Times*, October 21, 1894, p. 12.

"Tribute from Women." *The New York Times*, March 5, 1896, p. 8.

"Tribute to Youmans is Unveiled Near Park." *The New York Times*, September 29, 1970, p. 37.

"Unveiling Moore's Bust." *The New York Times*, May 29, 1880, p. 8.

Vogel, Frederick G. "Green-Wood: Brooklyn's 'Garden City of the Dead'" (pamphlet reproduced from a four-part article in *American Cemetery Magazine*, January–April 1985).

Wilder, Alec. *American Popular Song: The Great Innovators, 1900–1950.* New York: Oxford University Press, 1972.

Willensky, Elliot, and Norval White. *AIA Guide to New York City* (3rd ed.). New York: Harcourt Brace Jovanovich, 1988.

Wolfe, Gerard R. *New York: A Guide to the Metropolis.* New York: McGraw-Hill, 1994.

Wolfman, Ira. "A Building is Reborn." *New York Daily News,* September 3, 1989, p. 1.

Woll, Allen. *Black Musical Theatre: From Coontown to Dreamgirls.* New York: DaCapo Press, 1989.

WPA Guide to New York City: The Federal Writers' Project Guide to 1930s New York. New York: Pantheon Books, 1939, 1982.

Wright, Carol von Pressentin. *Blue Guide: Museums and Galleries of New York.* New York: W.W. Norton, 1997.

Wurman, Richard Saul. *Access NYC.* New York: Access Press, 1996.

SPECIAL RESOURCES

The City of New York Department of Records & Information Services. Municipal Reference and Research Center. New York City clippings files.

INDEX